THE GIRL WHO CLIMBED EVEREST

Sue Williams is the author of a number of bestselling books, including *Father Bob: The Larrikin Priest*; *Women of the Outback*; *No Time for Fear* – the story of shark attack survivor Paul de Gelder; and *Mean Streets, Kind Heart: The Father Chris Riley Story*. Her other books include *Welcome to the Outback* and *And Then the Darkness*, about the disappearance of the British backpacker Peter Falconio, which was shortlisted for the prestigious international Gold Dagger Award. Also an award-winning journalist, Sue was born in England, and worked in print and television in the UK and New Zealand before settling in Australia, writing for many of Australia's leading newspapers and magazines, and for TV.

suewilliams.com.au

THE GIRL WHO CLIMBED EVEREST

THE INSPIRATIONAL STORY OF ALYSSA AZAR AUSTRALIA'S YOUNGEST ADVENTURER

SUE WILLIAMS

MICHAEL JOSEPH
an imprint of
PENGUIN BOOKS

MICHAEL JOSEPH

UK | USA | Canada | Ireland | Australia
India | New Zealand | South Africa | China

Penguin Books is part of the Penguin Random House group of companies whose addresses can be found at global.penguinrandomhouse.com.

First published by Penguin Random House Australia Pty Ltd, 2016

10 9 8 7 6 5 4 3 2 1

Text copyright © Alyssa Azar, Glenn Azar and Sue Williams, 2016

The moral right of the author has been asserted.

All rights reserved. Without limiting the rights under copyright reserved above, no part of this publication may be reproduced, stored in or introduced into a retrieval system, or transmitted, in any form or by any means (electronic, mechanical, photocopying, recording or otherwise), without the prior written permission of both the copyright owner and the above publisher of this book.

Cover design by Laura Thomas & Louisa Maggio © Penguin Random House Australia Pty Ltd
Text design by Samantha Jayaweera © Penguin Random House Australia Pty Ltd
Cover photographs: Amanda Neilson of Neilson House Photography (Alyssa Azar), Alex Treadway/Getty Images (Everest), Gillmar/Shutterstock (sky)
Colour separation by Splitting Image Colour Studio, Clayton, Victoria
Printed and bound in Australia by Griffin Press, an accredited ISO AS/NZS 14001 Environmental Management Systems printer.

National Library of Australia Cataloguing-in-Publication data is available

ISBN 9780143799573

penguin.com.au

*To Dad, for your unwavering belief and support,
to Mum, for your example of strength, and to Brooklyn,
Christian and Samantha*

ALYSSA AZAR

It matters not how strait the Gate,
How charged with punishment the scroll.
I am the Master of my Fate,
I am the Captain of my Soul.

— INVICTUS, WILLIAM ERNEST HENLEY

Then there are the people who call others lucky:
'She's lucky, he's lucky, they're lucky, I'm so unlucky.'
I believe people generally create their
own luck – it's called hard work.

— WARRIOR TRAINING, KEITH FENNELL

CONTENTS

PART ONE A HEAD FOR HEIGHTS 1

1. Dad, Have You Ever Climbed Everest? 3
2. The Push for Kokoda 6
3. On the Track 16
4. A Taste for Danger 23
5. Looking for the Next Adventure 35

PART TWO THE CALL OF THE SKY GODDESS 47

6. Everest, the Rugged Giant 49
7. Love at First Sight 57
8. Everest's First Dynasty: Edmund and Peter Hillary 67
9. The First Trials 71
10. Everest's First Australians: Tim Macartney-Snape 79
11. Dare to Dream 84
12. Everest's World Record-holder: Dave Hahn 92

PART THREE THE ROAD TO MOUNT EVEREST 97

13. Climbing Kilimanjaro 99
14. Everest's First Australian Woman: Brigitte Muir 109
15. Setting the Goal 112
16. Everest's Youngest Australian: Rex Pemberton 127
17. Climbing in Ice and Snow 131
18. Everest's Hero: Dan Mazur 144
19. Pushing Your Body to the Limits 150
20. Everest's Most Unusual Champion: Bo Parfet 164

PART FOUR THE FINAL COUNTDOWN   167

21. Icefall on Manaslu   169
22. Everest's Best of the Best: Andrew Lock   188
23. Aconcagua: The Last Practice Climb   193
24. Everest's First Australians: Greg Mortimer   210
25. Ready to Risk Everything   214
26. Everest at Last   224
27. In the Event of My Death   234
28. The Deadliest Year   243
29. Touch and Go   251
30. Cyclone Alert   259
31. Triumph and Tragedy   269

Acknowledgements   275

PART ONE

A Head for Heights

CHAPTER 1

Dad, Have You Ever Climbed Everest?

It happens just three days into one of the world's most gruelling treks.

Eight-year-old Alyssa Azar is almost halfway along the rugged Kokoda Track in the remote wilds of Papua New Guinea, and she knows that when she completes it – *if* she completes it – she'll have the world record as the youngest person ever to do so. But suddenly, she stops dead. The mud beneath her walking boots oozes up over her ankle gaiters as she sinks into the quagmire and lifts first one foot, then the other, to try to free them, but makes no attempt to continue.

The local porters look at her curiously. Over the past week they've learnt to expect the unexpected from this tiny little white girl, with her gap-toothed grin and mop of blonde hair tied into a rough ponytail. When she'd first been introduced to them as the youngest member of a new expedition along the historic trail, they'd shaken their heads in disapproval. She was far too young, and much too small, to embark on such an arduous challenge.

But she's already taken them by surprise many times, striding along the track through dense rainforest, heaving herself up giant steps hewn into the mountains that most fully grown adults have trouble with, scrambling up the steep sides of valleys and trotting down the other side. A couple of times, as they reach for her arms to try to guide her across a raging river crossing, or help her along a particularly precarious mountain ridge, she politely but firmly asks them to leave her be. She already has dark bruises on both elbows where the guides, terrified of losing such fragile cargo, grabbed her so hard she winced. She wants to do this with as little help as possible.

Alyssa seems to be coping well. In every village they pass through she causes a sensation. Little children hide behind their mothers as they regard her shyly; it's the first time they've ever seen a girl their own age who doesn't share the same dark skin. Then, as she smiles back at them, they grow in courage, running over to touch her face and hair to check that she isn't some kind of doll. Alyssa laughs and plays with them while the other trekkers in the party rest.

But now, in the middle of the track, she has stopped and the guides stand back to see what's going on. She looks over to her dad, Glenn, who is quickly catching her up. 'What's up?' he asks casually as he draws level, trying to keep any note of alarm out of his voice.

If she's hurt herself, or suddenly decided she doesn't want to go on, he doesn't know what they'll do. The only way back to civilisation is either to return the 40 km they've already slogged along, or continue onwards through the 56 km of mountainous country ahead of them. In his mind he's already hauling her onto his shoulders and carrying her on the marathon that lies in wait. But she doesn't look as if she's injured, exhausted or ready to give up. He's expected tears before now, either because the trek is much harder than she imagined, or because the conditions are so tough, with the oppressively steamy heat during the day and mind-numbing cold at night. But Alyssa has shown no signs at all of not being able to cope.

'Dad?' she asks softly.

He moves closer to her. 'Yes, mate?'

'Dad,' she repeats, 'I was just wondering . . . Have you ever climbed Everest?'

Glenn looks at his daughter with astonishment. He has no idea she's even heard of Everest, let alone been thinking about it as they've all been struggling up this part of the track.

He shakes his head. 'No,' he says. 'No, I haven't.'

Alyssa beams. 'Oh, okay,' she replies. He has no idea why she looks so pleased. 'I just wondered . . .'

And then she pulls her boots out of some of the thickest, stickiest mud on the planet and stomps off, leaving her dad, motionless, behind. As he watches the tiny figure disappear through the thick leaves and branches of the overhanging forest, he feels, as well as his usual pride, a vague sense of foreboding.

CHAPTER 2

The Push for Kokoda

The idea of walking the Kokoda Track was totally Alyssa Azar's, and hers alone.

When she first mentioned it to her parents at the age of just six, they were horrified at the thought and dismissed it out of hand. 'No,' Glenn told her firmly. 'You're far too young. It's tough for people even three times, four times, your age.' Her mum, Therese, was even more aghast. 'She first asked if she could go when she was six years old!' she says. 'That really concerned me. She was always so small for her age, but she was always so determined too. We tried to persuade her for a long time that it wasn't a good idea.'

Alyssa, however, wouldn't budge. Born in 1996 in Townsville, Queensland, the second of four children, and then moving with the family to Toowoomba in the state's south-east, she was always a kid who seemed to know her own mind. She idolised her dad, an army medic and fitness trainer who worked out at the gym regularly and, in his time off from work, loved nothing more than bushwalking around the surrounding countryside. Every Sunday Alyssa would beg to come with him, and the tall, well-built man striding out with his tiny five-year-old daughter scampering along at his heels became a familiar sight to locals.

'I liked the outdoors,' says Alyssa. 'I liked the different tracks, some of the hills. Just being out there and discovering the places was all part of the fun for me, especially when you're so little and everything else seems so big. It was always a great adventure.' The walks were usually about three hours and gradually they grew longer and harder, eventually becoming four or five hours. 'I just loved tagging along, being out there, walking, being with my dad and having adventures.'

Despite her diminutive stature, she loved climbing trees and although she always made it to the top, sometimes she wasn't quite so capable of getting down again.

'When we lived in Townsville,' says Glenn, 'she'd climb a tree and couldn't get down and you'd have to get her down. Then when we moved to Toowoomba, it was exactly the same.'

Therese, an army mechanic and later a registered nurse, also became a regular rescuer. 'Even when she'd just learnt to walk, a little toddler in nappies, I'd hear her calling me from the garden and I'd go out to find her in a small tree,' she says. 'I had to get her out, then she'd just get right back up. I worried all the time she'd have an accident. Other people were rescuing cats from trees. For us, it was always Alyssa.'

Everyone noticed how much the little girl enjoyed heights. Glenn's older sister, Tanya Azar, has a vivid memory of Alyssa as a tiny three-year-old on a trampoline. 'She was jumping as high as she could go, with a Dorothy Dinosaur tail on,' she says. 'She was giggling and smiling. She was always racing around, hyperactive. She obviously so loved getting as high as she could.'

From an early age, Alyssa simply loved heights. She scrambled to the highest point she could manage to have a view of her garden, her house, her neighbourhood . . . never worrying about how she'd manage to get down again. Toowoomba is Australia's largest inland regional city, 130 km west of Brisbane and at an altitude of 700 metres, on the edge of the Great Dividing Range escarpment and the dramatic Lockyer Valley. It proved the perfect place for Alyssa to grow up.

At six, Alyssa climbed her first local mountain, Tabletop. Just a few kilometres east of the city, it's a flat-topped mound with an 11.5 km hike to the top, also 700 metres above sea level. 'It's not huge, but it's a good climb,' says Alyssa. 'The first time Dad let me go up with him, I remember being really excited. We always did a lot of walking together but this was different. There are some large steps over the part known as the camel's hump, and then there are a lot of boulders and loose gravel, so at some points you really have to scramble over the rocks.

'I loved those bits. There's one section right before you hit the top that was just scrambling and pretty steep, and for me that was the best part. Then when we reached the top, there were great views over the valley and I felt a real sense of achievement. I felt on top of the world!'

From that point on, Tabletop Mountain became a favourite destination for Alyssa and Glenn, and they regularly walked and climbed the circuit with the family's little black rescue Staffordshire bull terrier, Kimba. With her short legs, the dog wasn't keen on the scrambling, and Glenn or Alyssa often carried her part of the way. Alyssa's older sister, Brooklyn, accompanied them once too, but decided early on in the walk that it wasn't her idea of fun.

But for Alyssa, doing something physical out in the fresh air, surrounded by nature and enjoying a companionable silence with her dad, became her favourite way of passing the time. People they met along the way, however, didn't always understand. One group watching the tiny girl skip her way down from Tabletop, sucking on the tube leading from the CamelBak water pack on her back, asked whether she was actually on oxygen. Another woman snarled at Glenn that making his daughter walk in such tough country was tantamount to child abuse.

When Alyssa did settle down with a book, it was always about dramatic adventures. She liked a good Tashi story, a series of fabulous tales involving a character dispatching monsters, dragons and anything else that ever threatened him or the world at large.

She much preferred sport, though, any sport, and excelled at gymnastics, tennis, soccer, cross-country, boxing – whatever was going. Glenn trained people in boxing and keeping fit, and ran boot camps, as well as working out himself, and while Brooklyn showed not the slightest interest in sport, Alyssa hung around the gym every moment she could, copying the way she saw adults and older kids train.

When she was five years old, her grandmother Carmel Clark, Glenn's mum, came to stay, and was woken by a noise in the backyard, just before daybreak. 'I looked out and the sun wasn't even up, but there was this little girl running from one side of the backyard to the other, with a stopwatch in her hand,' she says. 'She went back and forth, back and forth. She seemed to be timing herself and she'd look at her watch at the end of every lap. You could tell when she presumably beat her last time. She raise her fist in the air, and yell, "Yeah! I've done it!"'

Alyssa developed into an active kid, who was quiet and thoughtful and didn't talk a lot, but who put everything into whatever she happened to be keen on at the time. She also had a strong streak of stubbornness, something that would later serve her well.

'I think the love of trekking came from her dad, and the ability to do such a solitary activity,' says Therese. 'But if I'm being totally honest, I think she has the stubbornness from me.

'Personality-wise, she was always quite reserved, but just into everything. She'd walk in with one of my Tupperware containers, open the lid and, without any warning at all, out would jump a big blue-tongue lizard. She was always outside, and she was up for everything. When she started school, she'd get into school sports and all her teachers would pull me aside and say she really had a knack for gymnastics or ballet or soccer . . . Practically everything she did, she was good at. They all said, physically, she put everything she had into whatever she was doing, which was what made her so good at everything she tried. That was obvious from a very early age.'

At her primary school, The Glennie, she quickly became known as a daring kid, afraid of nothing. 'She was a natural leader,' says Hannah Mason, who was in Alyssa's gang of four besties. 'She was the head of our group and we always followed her lead. She was always up to something, doing interesting things that were fun. Having adventures seemed to be part of her nature even when she was very young.

'She didn't have a wide group of friends; she mostly stuck to the three of us, and she wasn't loud or anything. But when she decided she wanted to do something, she was always incredibly focused on what it was she wanted to do, and what she needed to do to get there. She was never afraid to take the lead and certainly had a lot more confidence than I did. Sometimes I'd feel a little bit inferior to her as she was so impressive and driven. She'd get excited by plans and dreams, and they were always much bigger and better than anyone else's.'

Alyssa was just pretty much absorbed in her own world, unaware of how others felt, and was intent on getting physical whenever she could. 'I liked the idea of becoming an athlete,' she says. 'I tried all the traditional sports and loved them all.' Her determination showed through constantly. As a tiny five-year-old, she caused consternation at her first school carnival after a 60-metre race by complaining to officials about another runner veering into her lane.

Regular activities were just never enough, however. When Glenn was asked if he'd like to lead an expedition along the Kokoda Track, Alyssa, then aged six, asked him all about it, and begged her parents to be allowed to take part. They would have none of it.

Glenn devised a rigorous training regime for the participants in the months before they were due to leave, and Alyssa came along and watched them go through their paces. Sometimes she'd join in at the side, pretending she was one of them. And she never stopped asking if she could accompany the group.

'The first time I met Alyssa was when I was asked to take the people planning on going to Kokoda on some walks deep in the bush,' says Andrew Mills, a neighbour of the family and an experienced local bushwalker. 'They'd been doing a lot of circuits around the streets of Toowoomba, but wanted to see how they'd fare in the bush. Glenn was leading that expedition, so I got to know him through walking his walkers, and that's when I first met his daughter too. She always wanted to join in.'

Before the group left for PNG, Alyssa grilled her dad on every step of the expedition, working out where they'd be and when, what hurdles they'd have to face, and how they'd surmount them. After their departure, and throughout their absence, she drew maps and told her mum, her friends and anyone else who'd listen what stage they'd be up to and what they'd be doing next.

When Glenn returned, she listened spellbound to his stories of the places he'd seen and the people he'd spoken to along the way. She asked about every detail of the trek, memorising the names of each of the stages, the villages and the historic battle sites, poring over the souvenirs he brought back and treasuring each one. And when he set off on the next Kokoda expedition, after again refusing all her pleas to be allowed to come along, she hugged him hard and told him to remember plenty of stories for his return.

'I loved to hear about all the different people who'd go on his expeditions,' Alyssa says. 'He'd tell me both the good stories and the bad, probably to try to turn me off ever wanting to go! He'd talk about the people who don't prepare properly and obviously pay the price over there and regret it, as well as the people who do really well. I guess that's where my mentality started to come from. I always told myself I wanted to train really hard because I'd heard of people who didn't and didn't achieve what they wanted to, and regretted it big time.'

By the time Alyssa celebrated her seventh birthday, she'd grown wilier about arguing her corner. Glenn loved inspirational quotes and would pin his favourites up around the house to keep himself motivated. One day when he told Alyssa that she was just too small to go to Kokoda, her jaw firmed and her head went up. 'Dad, you're always telling me we're not too small to do *anything*,' she countered. 'How can you now say different to me about this?'

Glenn laughed; it was a fair call. So when he returned from his next Kokoda trip, and she started asking again if she could come on another he had planned, he was finally more conciliatory. 'Okay, Alyssa,' he told her, 'I'll take you next year under one condition: I'm going to set you a training program and even when I'm away, even in the middle of winter, you've got to go out walking. If it's raining or it's 4°, that doesn't matter. If you miss even one training session out of a minimum of three every week, I'm not going to take you because it says to me that you don't really want to do it. When I'm away, I'll arrange for a friend to take you. But miss one, and it's over.'

His daughter grinned back at him, nodding enthusiastically. She had absolutely no idea that he'd set the bar deliberately high, thinking there was no way she'd be able to reach it. 'I'll be honest,' says Glenn. 'I did that because I was certain she'd miss at least one training session. I thought she'd do it for a month and then after that she'd have had enough of it and drop out. I had no idea how determined she really was . . .'

For at least three days every week, and usually more, Alyssa went out walking to complete her training regimen. In a year, she never missed a single day. By the time twelve months was over, Glenn was forced to admit defeat. Therese was appalled; Alyssa was ecstatic.

The expedition company Glenn ran the trips for had one setting out soon after this, so he organised a separate side trek for himself, Alyssa, Andrew Mills and Mills' then girlfriend, Sandy Paterson, as he was worried his daughter wouldn't be able to keep up with all the adults. The four would camp with the others but walk by themselves, just in case. Therese wasn't keen, and didn't want to encourage her daughter at all, but on the other hand, she tried to be supportive, knowing how determined Alyssa was. 'She eventually came to terms with it,' Alyssa says. 'But she wasn't thrilled about it.'

Alyssa shared the news about her upcoming trek with her mates at school and they took it in their stride. Nothing surprised them about Alyssa. They knew she went off walking all the time and had privately marvelled at her determination. 'We knew how much she was training for that trek and I think a few of us thought she was crazy for putting so much effort into it,' says Hannah Mason. 'We were all about seven or eight, and at that age you don't usually have any motivation for anything other than having fun with your friends. None of us would have been prepared to put anything like that amount of time into anything and miss out on the fun stuff, like the Saturday cartoons.'

Glenn and Therese had brought Alyssa up with the philosophy of giving back to the community where possible, and they talked to Alyssa about trying to raise funds with her trek for a suitable charity. She was enthusiastic and the three came up with the idea of nominating the Toowoomba Hospital children's appeal. That instantly created more publicity for her quest, too, and support came from some unexpected quarters. Four-time world light welterweight champion Kostya Tszyu even visited Toowoomba for a fundraising dinner for the hospital organised by Glenn, and spoke at the function, showing clips of various fights throughout his career, holding a Q&A session and then presiding over a silent memorabilia auction.

The local newspaper heard an eight-year-old girl was about to take part in one of the toughest endurance tests known to humankind, and ran a couple of stories. Others followed. A news crew from the TV station turned up at her school and interviewed her. 'I remember watching her with everyone else through the classroom windows with the TV camera on her,' says Mason. 'We all thought what she was doing was incredibly exciting, although we never quite understood what exactly it was she was doing!

'We talked about it, but none of us appreciated what a huge challenge it was. We had a class photo with Alyssa, and we all held up a banner saying, "Good Luck, Alyssa!" I think a few people were a bit jealous of her as she was going to be doing something so exciting, and she was getting all this attention, and the rest of us were still stuck at school. But she never boasted. She was just always excited about what was coming, and so focused on making it happen.'

The stories in the media about an eight-year-old going off to do Kokoda and, in addition, raising funds for the local hospital caused a sensation in the community. Her mum's workmates bailed her up: surely she wasn't really prepared to countenance her daughter doing such a thing? 'I would just cringe,' Therese says. 'Of course I was proud of her and wanted to support her, but people were saying, Are you *sure* that's something an eight-year-old should be doing? But they didn't know her.

'We put a lot of support in place and if she wanted to change her mind she could, and there was medical help there too. But a lot of people said negative things at the time.'

Glenn was having a hard time too. A few people accused him of trying to live through his daughter. He reacted angrily: by now he'd completed ten Kokoda treks of his own, so where was the personal satisfaction for him in dragging Alyssa along? The Toowoomba newspaper ran a poll on its opinion page, asking readers if they felt he was being irresponsible in taking his young daughter to Kokoda. 'I watched that paper for a week, but no one wrote in to say yes,' Glenn says. 'I thought that was pretty cool.

'But I knew that if something happened to her, that would be the worst thing ever, and that would be tough to live with. I would live with it forever, and part of me would always think, Did I do the right thing or not?'

In the meantime, he did everything he could think of to ensure Alyssa's safety. He put in extra days as a precaution, running the expedition over sixteen days rather than the normal eight or nine. He tried to work out what he could do if she wanted to drop out. His contingency planning included being prepared to carry Alyssa if she didn't want to continue or injured herself, and his mates carrying her to safety if anything happened to him. He was sure he'd thought of everything.

In the event, it turned out he hadn't.

CHAPTER 3

On the Track

The little group sets out in August 2005 on their flight to Papua New Guinea, ready to tackle the world-renowned Kokoda Track.

Eight-year-old Alyssa Azar is excited, but nervous. As the plane touches down in the capital, Port Moresby, she stares out of the window, her heart thumping. On the ground, there's a flurry of activity; inside the plane there's a noticeable frisson. Among the Australian passengers there are oil workers, copper- and gold-mining personnel and aid workers, as well as the band of Kokoda trekkers.

Not many others choose to visit the place that's been ranked number 139 on the 140-long list of the world's least liveable cities, only just nudging out Dhaka in Bangladesh. For most, it's merely a stopping-off point to anywhere else.

Alyssa, her dad, Andrew Mills and Sandy Paterson stay in a hotel within a security compound in Port Moresby – absolutely necessary in a city well known for its violent crime, carjacking and muggings – as they prepare to head out to the start of the Kokoda Track. The night before they're due to leave, a man of about sixty from another trekking group approaches Glenn and Alyssa in the hotel foyer.

'Hey, mate!' he says to Glenn, in a tone of voice that doesn't sound at all friendly. 'This girl . . .' he gestures at Alyssa, 'I've heard you're taking her to Kokoda.'

Glenn nods. He's not sure what's coming.

'Well,' the man snarls. 'You're joking if you think she'll make it!'

Glenn smiles genially back at him and ushers Alyssa back to their room, hoping she didn't hear or, if she did, that she didn't understand. But as soon as the door's closed, she looks up at him.

'Why do people think I can't make it?' she asks, baffled.

He realises then, for the first time, that the possibility she might fail hasn't even crossed her mind.

He tells her that in life you often find people judge you and put their limitations onto you. That man might be nervous about making the trek himself, and feeling anxious that he mightn't make it. In those circumstances, he would obviously feel pretty threatened by the sight of an eight-year-old girl who's about to try it too. Glenn tells her not to take any notice of it, or to use it as a motivation to succeed. She seems to really take that to heart.

The Kokoda Track has certainly never been for the faint-hearted. A single path running 96 km across brutally challenging terrain, it climbs up and down the Owen Stanley Range, through thick jungle, across raging rivers and up and down steep steps. Its highest point is 2190 metres, as it passes by the peak of Mount Bellamy. The track is usually submerged in mud from days of torrential rainfall, and the days tend to be hot and humid, around a constant 30° C in August and September, with thunderstorms, drizzle and rain. By contrast, the nights can be bitterly cold.

At every stage, it evokes memories of the series of brutal World War II battles fought between the young, inexperienced, hopelessly outnumbered Australian soldiers and the Japanese troops who were trying to secure Port Moresby to isolate Australia from the US and use it as a base for a possible incursion into Australia. More than

600 Australians lost their lives on the track during some of the bloodiest clashes of the Pacific War, and the battle sites are remarkably well preserved, with weapon pits and relics from each side still remaining. It's easy along the route to imagine the intense hardship both sides faced in such horrendously hostile terrain.

As the group fly out of Port Moresby over the series of emerald-green thicketed ridges to Kokoda and the start of the track, following the direction of the original battle in 1942, their mood is sombre. On landing thirty minutes later, they wander over to the War Museum and look at the hospital and memorial sites. And then, finally, they begin their march.

Alyssa has learnt all about the history of Kokoda beforehand, so actually being there and seeing where all those things happened makes it very special for her. It is touching to hear those stories again, and see where the soldiers had to walk. It feels amazing to be there, treading in their footsteps.

But she's very nervous. She knows the first day is the toughest, because your body has to get straight into the rhythm of getting used to it. That first day will also be very hot.

It doesn't help either that, at Kokoda Village at the start, all the local kids come out to see Alyssa and take her to a field and insist on playing soccer with her for over an hour. By the time she begins walking again, and hits the next village, she's wilting. Glenn starts to worry he's made a bad decision in letting her come along, and asks her if she'd prefer to return to Kokoda Village and fly home from there.

'If you want to turn back, we can,' he says. 'You don't have to go through with this.'

Alyssa looks up at him. 'I'm not going back,' she declares. 'As if that's going to happen!' And then she storms off up the path.

But she is finding it difficult. The sun is beating down and she has to trek all day long. 'Oh my God!' she thinks somewhere in the back of her mind. 'I've got eight to nine days of this to go!' But she is determined to keep pushing through it, and after a few days she gets used to that rhythm of trekking all day, camping at night, getting up in the morning, then doing it all again. And after that she never looks back.

There are twenty people on the main expedition and a few of those look askance at Alyssa when they first notice her. Glenn holds back with her and his two mates, however, to avoid getting in their way. He's not sure how fast she'll be able to walk and is eager not to delay anyone or put them off their own trek, so for that reason has scheduled extra days to do the trip. He also wants to monitor Alyssa closely and see how well she's holding up in the conditions. It's difficult, though, to keep quiet the fact that there's an eight-year-old western girl attempting the Kokoda Track. The news she's there is spreading quickly all the way up the track, through all the villages and among the other trekkers on the mountain.

Alyssa is off in her own little world and doesn't really realise she's anything special. She doesn't think that she is different to anyone else doing the track because in order to do it, her dad has treated her exactly the same as everyone else. He's told her she isn't special, that if this is something she wants to do she'll have to have the same standards as any twenty- or thirty-year-old had, as it is the same goal they are trying to achieve. So in the beginning she has the mentality that she is one of them.

The first reaction to strike her is the behaviour of the villagers along the way. Many have never seen a little white kid before, and are plainly fascinated. Many stand and stare, open-mouthed, then gather their courage to approach her. As she stands patiently smiling before them, they touch her blonde hair and her face in wonderment. She thinks it's a little freaky until she gets used to it. A lot of the little kids are scared of Alyssa. Walking out of one village, she turns around and there is a whole group of them staring at her. She waves and they all wave back.

The day she first tries out a few words of the local creole language, Tok Pisin, derived from the phrase 'talk pidgin', the screams of local surprise – then laughter – can be heard kilometres down the track. Clearly, they find the sight of a little white Australian girl attempting to speak in their tongue so bizarre, it is absolutely hilarious.

On the second day, Alyssa and Glenn visit the Isurava Memorial, a significant battle site that was only uncovered five years ago. Next is the walk along the high ridge into Eora Creek. Glenn keeps an eye on his daughter, but she still seems to be managing well. She takes him completely by surprise with her question about Everest, but he soon dismisses that from his mind. He knows her biggest test will be on the fourth day: the climb to the top of Mount Bellamy. She'll have to focus all her energy on that

Alyssa is not sure how she'll fare either. Physically, it's the worst part of the trip. It's around the middle of the track and it's the highest point. There are some steps to assist trekkers, but they're big for an eight-year-old. The porters have carved her a stick with her name on it, and she uses that to help get herself up. Alyssa makes it, and she enjoys it, and the view from the top is incredible. She doesn't realise it at the time, but it's the start of her love of climbing mountains. That first summit becomes the moment that changes her life forever. Standing at the highest point, gazing out at the view and feeling on top of the world, she knows this won't be the last mountain she wants to summit. It's going to be simply the first, hopefully of many.

Another highlight is meeting a 'Fuzzy Wuzzy Angel' – one of the PNG locals who escorted and helped injured Aussie soldiers down the track – in Naduri Village. Again, she causes a sensation, with people as keen to have their photograph taken with her as she is to have hers taken with them. It provides some light relief as the going becomes harder still, with mosquitoes, dirt trails stubbed with tree roots, branches giving way to mud, and river crossings with narrow wooden walkways that look frighteningly delicate. But still she seems totally unperturbed by the difficulties.

Glenn says he's accounted for all eventualities – except the one where she'd do so well. The hardest single thing for her, he thinks, is that the adults would sit down for half an hour to have a break, and five or ten minutes into that break she'd be doing cartwheels and saying, Are we going yet? What have we stopped for? Kids recover so quickly. It's easy to keep her entertained in the villages with the other kids, but the boredom would set in at any time they stopped. Alyssa can't really tell the time so Glenn would string it out. She'd ask, How long have we got to go? And he'd tell her ten minutes, five minutes . . . and they'd sit for twenty minutes and then get going.

Andrew and Sandra walk ahead and Glenn and Alyssa walk behind, at a little distance. Mills notices what a close bond father and daughter have. At one point he also notices that Alyssa is a little teary. Glenn tells them she's missing her mum. It's something Alyssa today doesn't remember.

Later in the day, she's regained her composure and sidles up to Glenn and gives him a big smile.

'Dad, what do you think our next challenge will be?' she asks him.

He sighs. Suddenly this doesn't seem like it will be the first and last. He puts a hand on her shoulder.

'Alyssa, how about we just get through this one?' he says. 'Then we'll think about it . . .'

For the real killer of this trip, he knows, is yet to come: the Nine False Peaks of the Maguli Range – nine hills that each beckon as though they're the crest, until they're climbed and another one appears just beyond.

But again, Alyssa rises apparently effortlessly to the challenge, and she and Glenn finally make it to the end of the track, Owers Corner, on the eighth day – eight days ahead of what he's allowed for. Alyssa walks through the memorial arch, shakes hands with the porters, takes some photos and poses for a few more. She has a huge feeling of achievement, and is so proud and relieved to have made it.

She phones her mum on the satellite phone. Therese is extremely pleased to hear from her, and glad too that she's had a good time. She's interested to hear that Alyssa has done better than some of the adults. Some kids, Therese thinks, seem to have that element of toughness. Adults tend to talk themselves out of things sometimes, whereas some kids just go ahead and do them.

Glenn is amazed at how well she has done. The steps were big for adults, let alone little kids, but she managed. Uphill she was good and then she just flew downhill. He carried a lot of her gear but jokingly wonders whether it was a mistake, as she was faster than he was.

Now with that great adventure out of her system, Glenn and Therese hope that Alyssa will settle down back at home, and concentrate on her schooling. But they couldn't be more wrong. Instead, it's the start of something much, much bigger.

CHAPTER 4

A Taste for Danger

Alyssa Azar's dad, Glenn, embarked on an adventurous life early, too. For him, however, it wasn't necessarily his choice. A difficult childhood with a father he sees as having bullied him all his young life led to him running away from home at the age of fifteen and living in a broken-down old Kombi van, parked in a mate's family's backyard.

It was 1988 and Glenn was in distance education at the time, having been kicked out of all the schools in Melton on the western outskirts of Melbourne – and one of them twice. He was the archetypal angry young man: furious with his dad, quick to lash out in arguments with his peers, and pretty damn full of rage about life in general.

'I remember getting into a lot of physical altercations with my father, who was obviously much bigger and stronger than me,' says Glenn. 'But I didn't have a very good personality for backing down. My two sisters, one younger and one older, both now go to counselling and say it's largely because of the stuff they saw happening to me.

'If anyone said anything to me that wasn't acceptable in my world, there was no discussion; it was on – right then and there. It didn't matter if they were older or bigger, I'd take them on. I wasn't a big kid, but it didn't matter to me if I lost. It was more anger with my dad that was the big issue. I look back and see my dad as an unhappy man, always with a chip on his shoulder. But I don't worry too much about it now. I think of it as having made me who I am today, and I'm a lot tougher because of it.'

Glenn's father, Richard, had been adopted at the age of three by his grandparents after his own parents split, leaving him also a troubled child. Glenn's older sister, Tanya, believes it was a start in life he never managed to come to terms with. 'He perceived himself as not wanted by his parents,' she says. 'As a result, he had a lot of issues. I can understand that, but it doesn't mean I excuse my father, or forgive him.

'A lot of awful behaviour came from that. When he came home, you never knew what mood he'd be in. I still can't look at Glenn today without seeing him as a small, quivering boy, with a 6 foot 4 man breathing down his neck. My parents never got on and, because I was the eldest child, I was like the caretaker of the family. I always tried to protect Glenn, but he was very intelligent and sensitive and there was a lot of pain my father put him through as a boy. Every now and again, he would nick off and disappear and take solace in other people and other people's families.'

These days, Richard looks back and sees himself as a tough disciplinarian, trying to bring up his only son in the one way he knew how: just as he himself was brought up by his strict grandparents, George and Eva Azar. George was Australian-born, with Egyptian and Lebanese heritage, the eldest of twelve children brought up on a cane farm in Gordonvale, a southern suburb of Cairns. He went on to run hotels, become a small business entrepreneur and keep racehorses. His daughter, Phyllis, married Australian-born Irishman

Jack, who turned out a chronic alcoholic. The couple had Richard but gave him away to Phyllis's parents to raise.

'My grandfather was a tough man who defended his whole family,' says Richard. 'Probably as a result, I was a real disciplinarian-type father, too, more so than many people today. Our culture has changed a lot. Many wouldn't agree with the way I brought up my children. But Glenn was a very sensitive child growing up, and had a lot of problems with my discipline, I could see that. He had a big element of mischievousness, and he was a challenger. You would buy him a new pair of jeans and he'd then go and climb a tree and rip the knee out.'

Occasionally, Glenn would go to stay with Richard's father, Jack, and to this day he remembers the sound in the middle of the night of his grandfather drinking from the flask of wine he kept by his bed, the metal knocking on his teeth as his hand shook. As an adult, Glenn has rarely touched alcohol.

Richard had been in the Royal Australian Air Force and met his wife Carmel at the RAAF base in East Sale, in Victoria's Gippsland region. Soon after, he transferred to the army, to the Royal Corps of Australian Electrical and Mechanical Engineers, and was there for many years while the couple had the three children. Glenn was born as the middle child in 1972 in Sale. Six months later they moved to North Melbourne, then to Toowoomba in Queensland, then to Oakey, 40 km further west, and finally back to Victoria, to Melton. Carmel stayed home to care for the children, and to take in foster kids.

Glenn turned out to be bright and good at school, but always seemed to be in trouble. 'His father said to me that we spent more time at the school than he did!' says Carmel. The teachers interpreted it as boredom and urged them to find him more interests. They took him to karate classes, and he turned out – not perhaps surprisingly – to have a natural aptitude for fighting, becoming a brown belt. It began a long love affair with karate, kickboxing and boxing, and the gym.

But he hated some of the things that happened in their home, from the army-type room inspections to the tasks they were set with punishments if they failed, from his dad's challenges to wrestle him to the putting up of posters over the holes in the lounge room walls that were often a consequence.

Throughout his youth, Glenn remembers, the children urged their mum to leave their dad. 'But she wouldn't,' he says now. 'She only eventually left him when she found someone else.'

Carmel now says perhaps she was wrong not to have heeded their advice. The couple eventually split in 2000, and divorced in 2002. They've both since remarried. 'Their father was a good man, but he was very strict,' she says. 'He used to say having a strict upbringing hadn't hurt him, and he thought he should bring up his boy tough. But Glenn was a different boy, in a different time, to what Rick was.

'They used to clash a lot and go toe-to-toe. Rick tends to be, *You do as I say*, but if Glenn didn't think it was right, he wouldn't go along with it. He was bullied by his dad. That was Rick's idea of making Glenn a man. In hindsight, I should have left earlier, but I thought that the kids needed a father. I should have got out, but hindsight is a wonderful thing.'

Today, none of the three children have much contact with their father. 'We don't see a lot of each other,' says Richard. 'But Glenn is a good man and I'm proud of him and what he's achieved.'

While living in the Kombi made Glenn feel like the coolest kid on the planet for a while, very soon he grew bored with his life. In between the distance studies, which were fast going nowhere, he was working as a kitchen hand and cook for a catering company, but decided he needed to take drastic steps if he wasn't going to end up there forever more. He turned eighteen in July 1990, and a month later Iraqi troops invaded Kuwait, a move that ultimately sparked the Gulf War. It was the call to action Glenn had been waiting for. Always having enjoyed karate classes and boxing as a kid, he thought he might as well continue fighting and get paid for it. He decided to join the army.

'I guess I was just looking for something, and thought it might be good to get over to fight in the Middle East, as an eighteen-year-old does,' he says. 'The 8th/9th Battalion, Royal Australian Regiment, was an infantry battalion based in Brisbane that was recruiting, and I thought it would be pretty cool to get a guaranteed job there. To be honest, I think the main reason I joined, though, was because my dad said I wouldn't hack it. But the war ended long before I finished recruit training. I remember being disappointed about that. It's not till years later you realise how crazy that is.'

Glenn started out in infantry, being immediately nicknamed 'Razor' since, when people mispronounced his name, they could make it rhyme with Azar, but then transferred to the medical corps. It hadn't really been his decision. During a bayonet assault course, he broke his leg badly in two places, which everyone knew would rule him out of heavy physical activities for a lengthy period. As a result, he was given the choice of two jobs in the medical corps: in admin or as a medic. He chose the latter.

Not being able to move around freely concentrated his mind wonderfully when it came to studying the medical course, something he quickly found he enjoyed. As soon as he was well enough, he also did a physical training instructor's course to give himself more of an edge, and dropped martial arts to concentrate more on boxing. Then he took the infantry commander's course, and was sent on his first overseas tour – to Bougainville in the North Solomon Islands as part of the peace-monitoring team following decades of strife with PNG.

The wilful destruction of all the infrastructure and the resultant poverty and desperation came as a shock to Glenn. One night, a man stumbled into the medical centre after having been stabbed in the chest. It turned out he'd rowed a boat five hours with a deflated lung to get there. 'We were all a bit blown away by it,' says Glenn. 'But when you think about it, he had no choice. The only other option he had was to lie down and feel sorry for himself and die. I guess he thought he might as well die on the way, trying.'

Another day, a woman close to full-term pregnancy hobbled in. Something had fallen on her foot and broken it, and she'd walked over 30 km on her heel to reach help. But even when people were much closer to medical aid, it could still prove traumatic. Supplies of all medicines were very limited, and frequently the only post-operation pain relief was a simple Panadol. It all proved one hell of an eye-opener, and Glenn determined to try to help people in every way he could.

'A couple of days a week I volunteered at a local high school, teaching PE with others from the army,' he says. 'You had kids there who might have been sixteen to twenty years old but still in Grade 4, because through the twenty years of conflict there'd been very little schooling. The school ended up with about 500 kids – most of whom were really adults – and they worked in a split shift, so they would come to school from 7 a.m. till 1 p.m. and then from 2pm up until 5 p.m. or 6 p.m. So we ran sports sessions in the middle of the day and we had hundreds of kids turning up.'

Having had a difficult childhood himself, helping kids was close to Glenn's heart. When he was posted back to Townsville, he and three mates, two from the army and one from the police force, got together and decided to hold an event to raise money for SIDS and Kids. They planned a 1500-km bicycle ride from Townsville to Brisbane, but when a group of schoolchildren completed a ride in the opposite direction – and markedly more uphill than the one the adults were planning – they switched it to a run instead, billing it as

1400 km in fourteen days by the team they christened 'Combined Forces for SIDS'.

The army provided support vehicles and a backup crew, and the logistics were all figured out by another soldier mate, Kyle Williams. 'I wasn't a runner at all and it was bloody hard,' says Glenn. 'It was so hot! Every day the heat of the road would burn our shoes, and you could feel it on your feet. In the end, we started getting up at midnight so we could run at night instead. You only really had to run during the day when you were coming into a town and wanted to rattle some collecting cans.' They ended up raising $20 000, and Glenn determined to raise money for kids' charities whenever he could.

After such an ambitious slog, army bosses said he and his two colleagues could have a two-week break. A week later, however, he received a phone call: he was being dispatched to East Timor on an urgent mission.

There, Glenn led an evacuation team of six ambulances with crews spread around the country to support different elements during the Australian-led international peacekeeping effort of 1999, following the explosion of Indonesian-backed violence after the vote for independence. Originally he was supposed to be there for just thirty days, but gradually, as the full extent of the fighting and horrific genocide slowly became apparent, the period was extended to four months.

Glenn arrived on a beach landing at Suai in south-western East Timor and, surrounded by infantry units, helped take over the area, supporting the locals' rebuild and providing medical care at a level they hadn't seen before. 'That experience definitely changed me,' he says. 'One of the jobs I had over there was going out to locate bodies, and make notes for the war tribunal that was going to happen later. So locals would tell us what happened and where, and we'd go and find the remains. It was terrible. One of the villagers told us about two guys whose hands were tied behind their backs and told to run down a trail. They were given a five-minute head start, and then soldiers chased after them and hacked them down with machetes. Seeing so many bodies, and pulling them out of dams and everywhere, changes your view on life a little bit.

'After that, I found myself a lot more emotional – and I still do – watching certain things on TV. I don't like seeing kids harmed, even in make-believe drama. It was bad having to deal with the deaths and slayings of so many kids over there, and that was just the circle of life to so many people at that time. It was all so tragic.'

The army proved a watershed in Glenn's life in other ways, too. 'I don't think I really felt love in our family, growing up; it felt a bit like everyone was out for themselves,' he says. 'But what the army taught me was that there was a support network of other people out there, and that you could also work as a team and help other people, not just yourself. So I learnt to become more of a team player as opposed to just being a survivalist, or someone who thought solely about themself.'

He'd also met someone who would change him, too. While working as a medic at Oakey, Glenn had treated another soldier who'd injured her back and, was working with the physio to get her up and running. The soldier's name was Therese Finch and she was, unusually for that time, a vehicle mechanic in the army. A Sydneysider, she'd had a problematic family life too; her parents had split up and she no longer had contact with them. Glenn and Therese got together, and found their relationship worked well for them. After a while, they had their first daughter, Brooklyn, then married and Therese fell pregnant again with Alyssa.

At that point, disaster struck: Therese was posted up to Townsville and the army refused to post Glenn up there too until the end of that year. 'The army used to have a saying: "If we wanted you to have a family, we'd issue you with one!"' says Glenn. 'I didn't get posted up there straight away, so I discharged myself, intending to get back in later, which was a big risk. The army said they might not accept me back when I was ready, but I chanced it, and went up to be with Therese, Brooklyn and the new baby.'

While there, he took a cleaning job to keep the money coming in, but soon went back to the army and asked to be allowed back in. They didn't hesitate. They were short of medics, and he rejoined within two weeks.

This time, it was Therese's turn to quit the army, and the family moved back down to Toowoomba, the site for all the army's aviation medicine, in 1999. Therese took a nursing course via distance education through James Cook University in Townsville. 'I used to work with medical people and saw what they were doing, and thought it was really worthwhile, so I wanted to try it too,' she says.

With a young family and hopes for more children, Glenn resolved to start taking more control of his own life, rather than just waiting to see where the army posted him. While the army was about obeying orders, it also offered young men like him a lot of opportunities if they were determined enough to seize them. Having joined the army with an education only up to Year 9 before dropping out, he applied to take a nursing degree through the army at the same university as his wife, specialising in aviation medicine for helicopter medical evacuations.

He'd always enjoyed emergency work and being out in the field, but discovered he didn't much like sitting still studying at a desk. He was determined to stick it out, however. It didn't help either that, while he was enrolled at uni, he wasn't allowed to work for the army. Boredom quickly set in. It was then that he received a call from a friend of a friend, a lawyer who wanted to learn to box but didn't want to go to a boxing gym. Could Glenn teach him in his spare time?

Glenn tried it out, using the techniques he'd known from his own days of fighting, and the training techniques he'd learnt in the army. He quickly found he loved it. Very soon he was training the lawyer, as well as a growing number of other clients, every week. Within just a few weeks, he was running more than thirty training sessions a month, and struggling to cope with the rising demand for his services. To fit them all in, Glenn started his day at the gym at 4.30 a.m. and ended it at 9 p.m., with his uni work and spending time with his family squeezed in between.

Many of his clients were so buoyed by the improvements they were seeing in their fitness that they were keen to do more, and he started to take some of them out trekking over the weekends. Very soon, he had a close-knit, loyal bunch of clients who seemed ready to follow him to the ends of the earth. As his treks became more and more popular, so did the eagerness of his little band to walk further and further over ever rougher terrain to challenge themselves and their new levels of fitness. 'I had to find an adventure for them,' he says.

Throughout his military career, Glenn had always been fascinated by the story of Kokoda. He loved reading about the sacrifices and the heroism of his fellow soldiers on the godforsaken little track in the middle of nowhere, where the enduring myth of Japanese invincibility was smashed for the first time. Someday, he planned to walk the Kokoda Track to experience it first-hand. 'These guys wanted to do something else,' he says, 'so I suddenly thought Kokoda could be the answer.'

Eighteen people took part in the 2003 expedition to PNG, and every single one of them loved it. Glenn did, too. 'As we were doing it, it was going so well, I started thinking that I could imagine doing that for a living. It's very closely related to being in the army in some ways, and I knew that having medical training would always be a very handy thing in that kind of work. It was a completely accidental start to another kind of business . . .'

News soon spread about the adventure treks to Kokoda, and Glenn was asked to run another, and then another. Alyssa begged to be allowed to go along, but he wouldn't hear of it. In the meantime, to give the members of his upcoming expeditions a gym to train in, as well as his regular boxing and fitness clients, he subleased a dance studio at an hourly rate and named it Fighting Fit. When he arrived one day to find it locked up because the principal lessee hadn't paid the rent, it was only through the intervention of his very first client – the lawyer – that Glenn was able to retrieve all his gear, which was still inside. He then rented an old upstairs restaurant, did some minor renovations and used that for Fighting Fit from then on.

With both the gym and expedition business building, it was tough deciding whether to chance his arm with leaving the army and throwing himself fulltime into a new career, or to stay with a guaranteed income, especially as the family was growing. Glenn and Therese's son, Christian, was born in 2004, eight years after Alyssa. Almost immediately, however, they realised there was something different about the little boy. He was very slow to develop and, at eighteen months, he was still neither walking nor even crawling. They hoped it might merely be a sign that boys develop more slowly than girls, and agreed to have one more child in the hope that the company of a younger brother or sister would help him. Their third daughter, Samantha, was born on Glenn's thirty-fifth birthday in 2007, two years after Glenn eventually agreed to take Alyssa to Kokoda. At about the same time, Christian was finally diagnosed with autism and an intellectual impairment.

By then, Glenn had decided to quit the army to concentrate on his ventures full-time. He'd received four medals, for time served and for his work in East Timor and Bougainville, but still had to buy his way out to pay for the degree course he'd done. A new opportunity had presented itself, however: he'd been using another adventure business part-owned by an ex-soldier in Brisbane as the ground operator on his Kokoda trips and, when one of the other shareholders left, he was invited in as a partner. Therese was cautious but Glenn was keen and, on a handshake, he invested most of his savings in the company, and set to work organising more Kokoda treks and thinking about new and even more challenging expeditions he could mount.

He had no idea how much of a challenge the new company would end up presenting.

CHAPTER 5

Looking for the Next Adventure

On Alyssa Azar's return from Kokoda, she was taken completely by surprise by all the interest in her achievement. As the youngest kid ever to have completed the Kokoda Trek, she became something of a minor celebrity, featured in newspapers and magazines and called on to take part in interviews on TV and radio.

Therese and Glenn were left open-mouthed at the ease with which she seemed to handle all the demands, the questions and the cameras. Although she looked tiny next to all the journalists grilling her on what it was like, how it felt, what she planned to do next, everyone came away extraordinarily impressed with the composure of one who was still a little eight-year-old kid. David Koch, co-host of the *Sunrise* program on Channel 7, said she was an 'amazing' girl, and was so taken with her he even ended up going on the Kokoda Track later with Glenn's company.

What Alyssa lacked in size, she made up for in resolve. Immediately she started badgering Glenn about what their next adventure was going to be. 'I think both my parents thought I'd done Kokoda and that would be it!' she says. 'At that time, that was the only trekking-type adventure they were running through the company. But when I got back into school and into the usual rhythm, it didn't take long to get bored with it and I wanted to do something else.

'I felt lost without a goal to work towards. People who've done Kokoda often call it the Kokoda Blues. You do all that training, you get ready for it, you do it and then it's like, okay, what do I do next?'

In the past, Alyssa had seen some photos of Kilimanjaro, the highest mountain on the African continent, and the tallest free-standing mountain in the world, at 5895 metres above sea level. She read that climbing it was a demanding trek up through snow and ice, and gradually became entranced by the idea. She asked Glenn if it might be possible and he told her to check it out herself, hoping she might be put off by the task. Instead, she simply took it on as her next challenge, and spent the next few weeks poring over the accounts of others who had successfully climbed the dormant volcanic mountain close to the town of Moshi in north-eastern Tanzania, and the different routes to its summit. But then she chanced on one crushing fact: the Tanzanian national park authorities had ruled all climbers had to be over a minimum age of twelve.

'You needed a permit to do Kilimanjaro, and they wouldn't issue one to anyone under that age,' says Alyssa. 'I was very disappointed as I'd learnt so much about it and I was so keen to do it. I realised I'd have to put that back for another time, and I started to look up other trips and treks I could do instead. It was then that I discovered you could trek to Everest Base Camp.

'I gathered lots of info about that trek and gave it to Dad. I told him that was what I really wanted to do next. He said he'd look into it. I was so excited. I don't know when I'd seen my first picture of Everest, but somehow it had really captured my imagination. I loved the sight of all that snow and ice, especially as I'd never seen snow in my life. I used to wonder what it might feel like to climb a mountain like that, and how it would be to stand on the highest point on earth.'

Glenn was taken aback by how much research his young daughter had done on Everest Base Camp, and started studying everything she'd given him. It certainly looked an interesting trip, and it occurred to him that perhaps it would even offer an alternative trek for his training clients who'd already completed the Kokoda Track. He also looked into the effects of altitude sickness and strategies to prevent it, and explained what it was to Alyssa. He honestly had no way of telling how well – or badly – she might react to altitude. Some people seemed to be able to handle it much better than others, but no one knew why.

But there were three things Glenn did know. Firstly, he wouldn't be able to afford the trip until 2007, two years away. Secondly, this could well be a trip he could organise for his clients but the first time would just be an exploratory trip with Alyssa and a couple of friends to work out the logistics. And, thirdly, if she really, really wanted to do this, she would have to train even harder than she did for Kokoda.

* * *

Over the next two years, Alyssa trained as if her life depended on it. On weekdays she was in her dad's Fighting Fit gym by 5.30 a.m. before school, and by 5.30 p.m. after school, to do weights to build up her strength, and at least an hour of cardiovascular exercise to increase her fitness. Every Sunday she got up at 4 a.m., had a hurried breakfast and then went out for a four-hour trek with her dad or, if he was away, with Andrew Mills, the friend and neighbour who'd accompanied the pair to Kokoda. In winter, those before-dawn hours were bitterly cold, but all the better to simulate the temperatures they'd face on the way to Everest. Alyssa seemed indefatigable.

Like her dad, she was never much into team sports. 'Glenn

always said that he preferred to compete on his own, so he couldn't blame anyone else if he lost,' says his mum, Carmel Clark. 'He'd know it was his fault if he didn't do well. Alyssa is exactly the same. She likes individual sports where she can compete on her own, rather than being a team player. She says it would frustrate her when teammates dropped the ball or hadn't trained enough.'

Mills says he found Alyssa a real loner; a quiet, almost melancholy little soul. She could handle her own company for long periods and rarely opened up about herself or her feelings. 'It was as though she loved the danger of treks and mountains, and felt really alive when she was doing something so tough and possibly dangerous, and so exhilarating. I think back then she was starting on a never-ending quest to prove something to herself or other people.'

One of Alyssa's favourite training sessions was boxing, and she soon came onto the radar as one of Queensland's best young boxers. Although she was still small for her age, she was fit, she was light on her feet and she moved constantly around the ring. She also had fast fists, her technique honed by all the hours she'd spent practising. And, most importantly of all, she was absolutely determined to do the very best she could.

'It was purely for fitness at first that my dad was teaching me – because we had a gym we thought we might as well use it for training,' says Alyssa. 'But I really enjoyed it as well. Boxing at that age is more about speed and points than it is about knocking people out. I was quite light, but women tend to pick up the technique better because they don't have as much of an ego, I guess; they don't just want to punch everything, they watch the technique a bit more. It taught me mental toughness and self-discipline.'

It was still never a tame sport, however, even for little girls. Alyssa started out competing in a few local competitions, and was selected for the gym's official amateur boxing team, Fight Club, which travelled around the region fighting other teams. With her hair tied back in a ponytail, and dressed in a baggy blue singlet and silk boxing shorts with flames around the hem, she looked tiny in the ring. As soon as the bell sounded, however, she was always first to the centre spot. She was fearless, confident and ruthlessly efficient. She made a lot of her opponents look big and clumsy by comparison and usually took them completely by surprise.

'I went to one of the championship fights in the Lockyer Valley one night to see her,' says Mills. 'I was horrified at the ferocity of the fight between Alyssa and another young girl. They were just flogging each other in the head, going as hard as they could. There was such determination there, and courage. I thought a lot of those punches to the head would have really hurt.'

One night, when Alyssa was ten, the first age at which kids are allowed to fight to win on points – before that, they're confined to exhibition matches with no one declared the winner – she entered the ring and discovered her opponent was two years older, and 11 kg heavier.

Glenn, watching on from her corner, was appalled and asked her if she really wanted to go through with it. But there weren't a lot of girls of Alyssa's age and in her weight division fighting, and she dearly wanted the experience of testing herself against a bigger opponent in the ring. Kokoda, at the time, had seemed a huge challenge, and she'd come out of that well. Why not this? She turned to her dad and nodded that she was ready, her face disappearing into the huge padded boxing helmet she was wearing. 'Are you *sure*?' he asked again. She stepped towards the centre of the ring, her gloves already up.

'Alyssa's that kid who always, if she's decided to do something, just does it,' says Glenn. 'I see it as my role to prepare her physically and mentally for everything she wants to do. There are points where I've said she could quit but she always refuses. I'm not soft on her. That day was so hard for me, seeing her in the ring with a girl so much bigger and who looked as if she wanted to kill Alyssa.'

For Alyssa, the start of the first round was a shock. The other girl had been told to go easy on her much smaller opponent, but she came out swinging heavily from the start. Immediately, Alyssa realised she had no intention of holding back at all. She understood she was going to have to give back as good as she was getting if she'd stand any chance of lasting the three rounds.

'In that fight, I gave away a fair bit of weight, which is always pretty dangerous when you're fighting,' she says. 'It was a tough fight. The whole idea was that she'd go easy but she didn't. She got in the ring and tried to take my head off. I remember originally I was quite upset, it was a shock and it hurt getting hit a lot by someone who was much, much bigger than I was.'

'Alyssa was crying,' Glenn says, 'and I told her to stop fighting, but she wouldn't give in. So eventually, at the end of that first round, I said, Okay, if you want to continue, you've got to stop crying. That's a tough call for any parent. But at the end of the day, she has to learn how to make her own decisions. Her mental toughness constantly amazes me and I'll protect her as much as I can, but I won't stop her from doing something she really wants to do.'

Glenn then urged her to make more use of her better technique against her opponent. The other girl might have been taller and bigger and heavier, but Alyssa should try to use her adversary's strength and weight against her. 'I took that advice and after that, I wasn't getting hurt as much. While I lost the first round, I actually won the second and the judges said the third was a draw. It all ended up pretty even.

'In the end, it turned out to be a good life lesson. Even though the odds sometimes look as if they're stacked against you, you can still win through. You shouldn't be put off. You just have to buckle down and make the best possible use of what you have. Nearly always there's a way through. I learnt that anything worth doing doesn't come easy.

'I did love the toughness of being a fighter, being one of the boys. I can be intense internally and boxing is a good outlet for that. I think it also really helped to shape me mentally. I love that line from the movie *Fight Club*: "How much can you possibly know about yourself if you've never been in a fight?"'

That newfound confidence and resolve stood Alyssa in good stead in the ring from that point forward. A few months later, still at the age of ten, she fought in Gatton, between Toowoomba and Brisbane, for a national title, another moment she later looked back on as life-defining. She ended up winning the Australian Global Amateur Title for the under 32 kg division, and was featured in all the TV news reports of the event.

'I was pretty nervous in my title fight, but it was exciting too,' Alyssa says. 'It was against a girl I'd fought several times before, but I wasn't sure how I'd go. I think it was probably worse for Dad, having to watch. It was nerve-racking for him sometimes, being in my corner in fights.'

Alyssa won comfortably on points and was presented with her medal, which she still has today. 'It was a big day for me, and for my dad too,' she says. 'I was still very quiet so I was never overtly aggressive. I was never the kind of person to go around hitting anybody. But maybe I naturally had a bit of aggression on the inside.'

As a result of the win, and of the Facebook publicity Alyssa received, she was invited to carry Sam Soliman's belts into the ring for his World Boxing Association super-middleweight title fight against Anthony Mundine in Sydney. Soliman, however, didn't do quite as well. He lost in the ninth round.

And, like him, Alyssa totally failed to see the blow coming that threatened to fell her too.

* * *

While Alyssa never actively courted the press, people were naturally fascinated by this pint-sized girl who was so driven in every aspect of her life. Not only had she created a world record with her Kokoda trek, she was clearly punching well above her weight in boxing championships and was now talking about journeying through ice and snow – even though she'd never seen either before – to Everest Base Camp.

The TV cameras filmed her at school, at home and at the gym, and the local newspapers kept tabs on her to see what she'd be up to next. Alyssa was still mystified about their curiosity, but shrugged and took it in her stride.

There were some people, on the other hand, who didn't.

It started slowly, quietly, insidiously, on social media. There were posts on Facebook suggesting Alyssa was far too big for her boots, that she thought she was better than anyone else, that she didn't have any friends, and that no one liked her. Alyssa saw the jibes, and they shocked her. She tried to ignore them, but they became more and more spiteful. She was upset, but tried not to show it.

Her friends gathered round to support her and urge her to ignore them. They were proud of her achievements, and had taken delight in what she was doing. 'At school, when she was away on Kokoda, we used to trace her progress on a map and imagine where she'd be each day,' says her schoolmate Hannah Mason. 'For most of us it was great fun, and we kind of felt involved in her journey. Then when she came back, there were lots of interviews on TV and radio and newspapers, and we'd pore over them to see what she'd said.

'But I do think there were some who didn't like her getting so much attention. They felt jealous and tried to make up stories about her. It was so unfair because she never boasted about what she was doing, she was just totally absorbed by it, and worked incredibly hard. But some people can be very mean-minded.'

Alyssa was hurt by the criticism, but tried to ignore them. She didn't hit back, as the first rule of the gym had always been that you never used your skills on anyone outside. Instead, she sat tight and hoped they'd tire of it if she didn't react. The opposite happened; it became more and more vitriolic. With comments coming even from people she didn't know, or posters using false names, she retreated a little more into herself and stuck only with her immediate group of close friends. That incited the bullies to start claiming that she thought she was too good for the rest of her schoolmates.

She didn't know what to do, and became even more withdrawn. 'I think it was a bit that I was different, doing all this trekking and having adventures, and a bit about jealousy,' she says. 'It's hard for me to understand why, but bullying can be pretty common in school. This was mostly over the internet, rather than in person, which is sometimes even harder to deal with.

'I suppose everyone at that age is figuring out who they are and I had sort of made that decision and I knew exactly what I wanted to be doing. But obviously a lot of other people didn't like it, didn't like me and didn't like all the attention I was getting.'

In addition, Alyssa was starting to garner more attention from her teachers, concerned that her life was so different from those of their regular pupils. While other girls were asked up on the school stage during assembly to be congratulated when they did well at any hobbies, like ballet or horseriding, Alyssa's boxing triumph was ignored, perhaps because they didn't want to encourage such sports among girls. Alyssa, however, felt slighted. As well, her teachers felt that she needed more balance, to spend more time with friends, to be a kid. She had completely different ideas.

'The school wanted me to get involved in other things and I just wasn't interested in that,' she says. 'They weren't used to someone like me who didn't want to socialise. I don't think they really knew how to handle it. So I spent a lot of time in the office talking to teachers, which was just a nightmare for me.

'I kept thinking, Is it that big a deal, just wanting to come to school to do my work and go home for training? I remember thinking I wasn't harming anyone by being such a loner, so what was the problem? But obviously they thought it was a problem, or that I had problems, and I couldn't seem to convince them otherwise.'

To add to the mix, there was trouble brewing at home. Alyssa's family had always been an isolated little group, since the children never saw their grandparents on their mother's side, and rarely their grandparents on their father's, something that had helped make young Alyssa even more self-sufficient. But Therese and Glenn had been gradually becoming more distant with each other, Therese busy with their eldest, Brooklyn, and the two younger children, Christian and Samantha, as well as her own career, and Glenn tied up with his work at the gym, leading the adventure treks, and with Alyssa's training. Now, however, Therese wanted to move to Wagga Wagga in country NSW to take on more study, and neither Glenn nor Alyssa wanted to go. In the end, Glenn stayed behind in Toowoomba, living in a small room off the gym, and Alyssa pleaded to be allowed to stay with him.

'The business was going through a bit of a slump at the time, and I couldn't afford to rent another place,' says Glenn. 'But Alyssa begged us not to make her move. So finally I made her promise to stay for one term down there with her mum, her sister and her brother. She agreed, packed her bags and went down there. But the next time I went there to visit, she had her bags packed, ready to leave. She knew exactly what she wanted. So we had to let her come back with me.

'We lived together in that room, the size of a small living room, with no cooking facilities and not much else beyond two beds, a microwave and a TV. We showered at the local pool and survived on either microwaveable food or take-outs. If I had to go away, Alyssa stayed at a friend's. I think that really created damage to our family, and after that Alyssa was never as close to her mum, while I was never as close to Brooklyn. It was very sad. I was always determined to be completely different from my dad and to do better than my parents had with us, but here I was, repeating the same cycle. We both loved our kids and spent many years ensuring we reversed that damage as best we could. And even though our relationship didn't survive, we are really close to the girls.'

To distract herself from the difficulties at home and trouble at school, Alyssa threw herself even more determinedly into her training, getting ready for the trek to Everest Base Camp. She boxed as hard as she could, trained with heavier weights and ran faster and further than she'd ever done before. To prepare for her first venture into serious altitude, she and Glenn also researched an altitude centre that had just opened in Brisbane, where athletes could train in a chamber of thin air as if at altitude. They went over one day with a friend who was into competitive cycling, and checked it out. From then on, they visited once a week for a few months to run on a treadmill in thin air to get themselves used to the kind of altitude they would face in Nepal.

Alyssa also started paying more attention to mind-training. Glenn had always put up little motivational messages and positive-thinking notes around the house – his dad used to do it too, he said, but never stuck to them – and now she started doing the same. She began writing down phrases she read that she liked, and maxims she came across that she believed could serve her well in her life.

'A determined person doesn't find it hard to succeed,' she wrote in her diary, 'they find it hard to stop trying.' 'Don't tell me the sky's the limit when there are footprints on the moon.' 'Wanting something is not enough. You must hunger for it.'

In any spare time she had, she read books about Everest climbers, watched documentaries about their exploits and expeditions, and sat and gazed at photographs of Everest. She simply couldn't wait to get going.

'I think in some ways, it was easier for me to focus on my next adventure, instead of worrying about what was happening with school and at home,' says Alyssa. 'There was nothing I could do to change things or to help them, they had to work it out themselves. So I just kept concentrating on my training, physically and mentally, what was coming next, and what I could control.

'And while getting that boxing title was a thrill, I was still very focused on the next big trip Dad and I were going to do. Everything else was secondary to our trip to Everest Base Camp. I was counting the days. I just couldn't wait to see Everest for myself.'

PART TWO

The Call of the Sky Goddess

CHAPTER 6

Everest, the Rugged Giant

'There are no beautiful surfaces without a terrible depth.'
– FRIEDRICH NIETZSCHE

Mount Everest: the highest point on earth and a sight that strikes wonder into anyone who sees it, and terror into those planning to climb. A brooding triangular hulk, dwarfing the other giants of the Himalayan range, it stands a majestic 8848 metres above sea level, with its summit carved in two by the international border between Nepal and Tibet. It's a snow-covered, cloud-draped peak that has captured people's imagination since time began.

The Nepalese name for Everest is Sagarmatha, meaning Goddess of the Sky, while Tibetans know it as Chomolungma, or Goddess Mother of the World. It wasn't until 1865, with both countries closed to foreigners, that it was christened Everest by the Royal Geographical Society, after the British surveyor-general of India.

Everest first caught the attention of the wider world in 1921 when a British expedition set out to reach its peak, not knowing whether humans could survive in such rarefied air over 8000 metres. They discovered a possible route from the Tibetan side and returned the next year, managing to climb to 8326 metres – the first time anyone had ever been recorded as being so high.

One of that expedition's members, expert mountaineer George Mallory, was completely captivated by the view of Everest towering above him. He wrote in his journal: '. . . like the wildest creation of a dream, Everest, a rugged giant, a prodigious white fang, a colossal rock plastered with snow. From a mountaineer's point of view, no more appalling sight can be imagined.'

In 1924 the group returned and, just 245 metres from the summit, Mallory and engineering student Sandy Irvine left their team members to strike out alone. They were never seen again.

Seventy-five years later, in 1999, Mallory's frozen body was found by a new expedition sent out to find the pair. It seemed he'd been roped to Irvine when one of them slipped, sending both to their deaths. No one will ever know whether they died on their way to the top, or were the first to conquer Everest and perished on their way down. Intriguingly, Mallory's snow goggles were in his pocket, which might suggest he was descending at night when he fell, and nowhere to be found was the photograph of his wife – something he'd pledged to leave on the summit.

After the Second World War, Nepal opened its border to outsiders, and in 1950 Tibet came under Chinese rule and was closed off to foreigners, so the race to reach the top of Everest resumed via the southern Nepalese side. Finally, it was a team from the British Commonwealth who made it, and on 29 May 1953 Edmund Hillary, a New Zealand beekeeper, together with local Sherpa Tenzing Norgay, were the first officially to go where no man had gone before.

'We looked around in wonder,' Hillary recounts in his book, *View from the Summit*. 'To our immense satisfaction, we realised we had reached the top of the world!' In typically understated Anglo-Saxon fashion, Hillary then stretched out his arm to shake Tenzing's hand, but the Sherpa threw his arms around him in an almighty bear hug.

Seven years later, a Chinese and Tibetan team summitted Everest via the northern ridge for the first time, and in 1979 China opened Tibet back up to overseas climbers. Since then, there have been all manner of milestones. The first woman, Japanese Junko Tabei, climbed the summit in 1975, Italian Reinhold Messner and Austrian Peter Habeler were the first to climb without oxygen in 1978, and Tim Macartney-Snape and Greg Mortimer were the first Australians, reaching the top in 1984 without oxygen via a completely new route. In 1990, Sir Edmund Hillary's son Peter summitted Everest, the first father and son to make it. Seven years later, in 1997, Brigitte Muir became the first Australian woman.

Over 4000 climbers have now made it to the top of Everest, helped by advances in weather forecasting and knowledge of conditions and routes, better equipment and communications, warmer lightweight clothing and well-run commercial expeditions. At the start of each climbing season these commercial outfits all pitch in to pay for Sherpas to put up ropes along the route and ice ladders over crevasses, but getting to the top is still never an easy feat.

Only a little over a third of the climbers who attempt the summit make it, and a 2006 report in the *British Medical Journal* put the death rate of those who try at one in ten. Of course, some years have been much more tragic than others. In 1996 fifteen people died, eight of those on a single day due to a terrible storm that engulfed the higher reaches. In 2006, eleven lost their lives, and in 2012 eleven perished, making climbers, superstitious at the best of times, even more nervous about expeditions in any year that ends in a figure divisible by six. Then, in 2014, 16 Sherpas died in an avalanche and, in 2015, 24 died on Everest in an earthquake.

The causes of climbers' deaths on Everest vary hugely. Most have been caused by exhaustion, particularly when people give their all to get as close to the summit as they can, but just don't have enough strength left to climb down safely. 'You have to remember, the peak is only halfway there!' says Brigitte Muir.

Some have had heart attacks: a complication of altitude is that the blood becomes thicker, making people more susceptible to heart problems and strokes, as well as to frostbite. But even tiredness can be lethal. Depleted of energy, many tend to stumble, make bad decisions, and act with less care than they should. As a result, accidents claim more lives. There are few other places on earth where a broken leg can prove fatal. Teammates may have only enough energy to get themselves down; helping someone else who is significantly disabled down to safety in time to save their life may be impossible.

While some who die are given a rough mountain burial, which involves being covered in stones by their fellow climbers, others ask in advance for their bodies in such cases to be pushed over crevasses. When either is too difficult, a number are simply left where they fall. It's not unusual for climbers to come across frozen, mummified corpses just off the main routes to the top.

Altitude-related illnesses, also known as acute mountain sickness or AMS, can also become extremely serious, extremely quickly. Its effects can start being felt generally over the altitude of just 3000 metres – well under half the height of Everest. It's for this reason that Everest is such a long slog. Anyone attempting the climb usually has to allow two to three months for their body to adjust to the altitude, so they stay at Everest Base Camp for a while, then climb to Camp I, then back to base, then back up to Camp I again to spend some time there, then down to base for a rest, back up to Camp I, then on to Camp II and back down to base . . . in a long series of ups and downs called 'rotations'. Although it can seem an almost endless grind, it's absolutely necessary. If a climber doesn't acclimatise well or quickly enough when gaining altitude, the body doesn't adjust to the reduced oxygen and changes in air pressure and the results can be deadly. And, of course, the higher the climber goes, the riskier it is.

'Unfortunately it is difficult to get experience of what it is like climbing above Camp III (8300 metres) without climbing Everest,' Dr Andrew Sutherland, a medical advisor on Everest expeditions, told the *British Medical Journal*. 'Climbers invariably do not know what their ability above 8300 metres is going to be like.' Some people are simply affected much worse than others, and there's no way of predicting how anyone will fare at a high altitude until they get there. In addition, climbers who cope well one time, may find the next time they don't, and may be at a loss for a reason why.

People can have headaches and bouts of vomiting as a result of hypoxia, a lack of oxygen reaching the body's tissues, or experience loss of appetite, breathlessness, and an inability to get warm. In severe cases, they may have impaired cognitive function and slurred speech, and can suffer a cerebral oedema – fluid on the brain – or a pulmonary oedema, a potentially lethal build-up of fluid on the lungs. If the person doesn't realise they're experiencing symptoms of AMS and doesn't descend fast enough, it can develop rapidly. Hallucinations can follow, which have led to some even jumping to their deaths, believing they can fly.

In the so-called Death Zone, above an altitude of 8000 metres – on Everest or on any other of the world's fourteen mountains above that height – the atmospheric pressure is about a third of that at sea level, with only about a quarter to a third of the normal rate of oxygen in the air. Humans simply can't survive for more than a couple of days in this zone; no amount of acclimatisation or extra oxygen will stop the brain swelling or the lungs filling with water.

If a normal sea-level dweller were to be dropped by helicopter into that altitude, without acclimatisation, they would only be able to stay conscious for three minutes at most. Even climbers who have gone through the proper acclimatisation are generally so weakened, it takes them around forty-five minutes to walk 100 metres, and they often have to breathe three to four times more rapidly than they would normally – something that contributes hugely to exhaustion levels. Onlookers sometimes find it hard to understand why some people turn back within 50 or 100 metres of Everest's peak. It's because, while only a small distance, it will take the kind of effort they know might kill them.

'All the time you're in the Death Zone, your body is actually slowly dying and deteriorating,' says famed American Everest conqueror Dan Perfet. 'So you have to limit how much time you spend there, especially on the summit. You really don't have much option; you're living on borrowed time.' To stay more than twenty minutes on Everest's summit is generally considered perilous.

Then last, but certainly not least, there's the weather. Up on Everest, it's a different type of weather entirely. The winds can gust at up to 281 km an hour, pretty devastating considering that the fiercest catastrophic level of hurricane at sea level, Category 5, is only 252 km an hour. From late October until the end of January there are almost constant hurricane-force winds blowing more than three out of four days and, for one day in every four, routinely a hurricane at least of a Category 1 magnitude. The jet stream, as the westerly wind at the summit is known, is said to sound like a large plane taking off a few metres away, and eases off sometime in April or May, giving climbers a short window to the summit. Australian Andrew Lock, one of the most accomplished mountaineers on the planet, and one of the few men to have climbed all fourteen of the world's mountains over 8000 metres, describes Everest as having 'a summit perpetually shrouded in wind-thrashed cloud'.

In addition, on Everest's summit, the temperature can drop as low as -41° C, but generally tends to fluctuate between -35° and an almost balmy, by comparison, -20°. During the windy winter months of December to the end of February, the wind chill factor is constantly around -100°. Throughout the summer monsoon season, from the start of June to the end of September, there is almost daily snowfall.

Besides the regular dangers such weather extremes on Everest present, they can also trigger avalanches, with the risk to climbers of being crushed to death, swept over edges or buried alive under hundreds of tonnes of falling snow. Changing temperatures can also cause shifts in icefalls and walls, and send blocks or columns of ice, called seracs, hurtling down the sides of the mountain. These may range from the size of a large TV set up to the mass of a twenty-storey apartment building. As well, crevasses can suddenly open up beneath mountaineers' feet to create dizzying gaps in the earth hundreds of metres deep, and a glacier can, in a moment, be transformed from a stable pathway into a deathly slippery slide.

And while those ropes and ladders can be a godsend, they can also be treacherous. Many experienced climbers avoid them like the plague – there are a number of ropes that are frayed and decayed, and some ladders aren't fixed firmly enough into moving ground – and a wrong choice has sent many a summit hopeful to their death.

Many of those who die on Everest perish as a result of a combination of factors. For instance, American Scott Fischer, an extremely competent climber and guide on one of the fateful 1996 expeditions, died of a mixture of frostbite, exposure and AMS during the storm that lashed the top of the mountain, and a massive drop in barometric pressure.

Despite – or perhaps because of – the myriad dangers and all the deaths, Everest still remains one of the last great challenges for humankind, cloaked in reverence and romance. Many people dream of one day making it to the top, whether purely for adventure, to test oneself, gain the sense of achievement, or for fame and fortune.

But why climb in the face of such overwhelming odds against success?

No one's been able to answer that question better than George Mallory himself. When asked why he wanted to climb Everest, his explanation was curt.

'Because it's there.'

CHAPTER 7

Love at First Sight

'When the going gets tough, the tough turn up the volume.'
— ALPINE MOUNTAINEER MARK TWIGHT,
KISS OR KILL: CONFESSIONS OF A SERIAL CLIMBER

When Alyssa and Glenn Azar arrive in the Nepalese capital, Kathmandu, on a direct flight from Sydney in late November 2007, they're assaulted by a kaleidoscope of colour and noise. The roads are streaming with hooting motorcycles, taxis and rickshaws, and the streets are a jumble of Buddhist monks in bright saffron robes, Hindu sadhus with painted faces, hustling souvenir touts, families out for a stroll and tourists looking bewildered at the incredible level of activity going on everywhere, all to a soundtrack that's almost deafening.

For most visitors, their first visit to Kathmandu is an incredible culture shock. Ten-year-old Alyssa feels she's landed in a different world. Compared to sleepy Toowoomba, and the only other overseas place she's visited, PNG for Kokoda, the atmosphere is electric. There are simply so many people, all of whom are rushing around at what looks like a million miles an hour, hundreds of vehicles jamming up all the streets, and buildings, both ancient and modern, everywhere.

For keen trekkers and climbers, however, after the first sense of shock has subsided, Kathmandu is a nirvana. The city is surrounded by four major mountains, Shivapuri, Phulchoki, Nagarjun and Chandragiri, and symbols of Everest are everywhere, from the trekker clothes stores to the names of restaurants, from the souvenir shops to the touts constantly approaching visitors to offer guides for the Annapurna region, through western Nepal and up to Base Camp itself.

Kathmandu's Thamel neighbourhood is where most travellers congregate, with its western coffee shops, restaurants, bookstores and internet cafes, but the city is nearly 2000 years old and there are plenty of richly authentic sights to see off the main roads and through the maze of tiny backstreets and alleys of the ancient capital.

Alyssa and Glenn have already decided to spend a few days in Kathmandu to acclimatise to the height slowly, since it's exactly double the elevation of their hometown. It also seems a shame to rush through without taking a while to unwind and see some of the major attractions. For Alyssa, it's a revelation. Coming from a regional city in Queensland, she's never seen monuments so old, so beautiful and so revered, or met locals so friendly.

Again, she attracts a huge amount of attention. Locals approach her constantly to touch her blonde hair, even at the airport, and, while Glenn keeps a watchful eye on her, she finds it intimidating at times to be approached by strangers. But they do it in such a friendly, charming way, always smiling, and she soon begins to relax.

The pair visit the old royal palace in the central Durbar Square, the Hanuman Dhoka, founded in the mid-sixteenth century, and the Tribhuvan Museum, with its displays of the lifestyles of past kings. They photograph the four red towers of Lohan Chowk, each representing one of the four ancient cities of the Kathmandu Valley, but the highlight of their sightseeing is a trip to the iconic Buddhist hill temple of Swayambhunath.

A UNESCO World Heritage site, its centrepiece is its stupa – a mound-like structure containing holy Buddhist relics and the ashes of monks – with 365 steps to the top. From there, a view of the whole city unfolds as the prayer flags flutter, the prayer wheels spin and dozens of monkeys play. Alyssa is enchanted. This is exactly as she'd imagined Nepal.

The next day, they wander through the Jawalakhel Handicraft Center and watch Tibetan refugees make their beautiful carpets, along Kupondole Road to see the craft cooperatives, and look at the weavings of Mahaguthi. In the evenings, they eat vegetable curry and dal bhat, the rice and lentil soup that's a staple of Nepal, to get their stomachs used to the local fare ready for the trek ahead.

On their last night, they eat at the Rum Doodle, a restaurant in Thamel which has become a magnet for trekkers, climbers and Sherpa guides alike. The entrance features a series of large white 'footprint' cut-outs with messages and love songs written by past diners. Behind the bar is the largest collection of autographs of Everest summitters in the world, from Sir Edmund Hillary to Reinhold Messner, Rob Hall to Naomi Uemura. Alyssa has read about the restaurant, and knows it as a place where all who climb Everest call in. She can barely contain her excitement; it makes her feel as though, at last, she's really on her way.

And the next morning, she and Glenn are. They pick up a flight in one of the small aircraft that fly the forty-minute journey to the small town of Lukla in north-eastern Nepal, the start point for the trek to Everest Base Camp up the southern route. Alyssa's heard a lot about the flight – and none of it good. With Lukla perched in the Himalaya at 2860 metres, it's right on the edge of a towering escarpment and has one of the shortest airstrips in the world. After a series of fatal crashes, its Hillary–Tenzing Airport has also been billed as one of the most dangerous airports on earth.

It doesn't take long for Alyssa to see why. Pilots fly there without the help of radar guidance systems, and so rely only on being able to see where they are and where they're aiming for. In an area notorious for sudden onslaughts of bad weather, gathering clouds, snowstorms, raging winds, mist and fog, all causing terrible turbulence, flights are only confirmed at the last minute – and then frequently cancelled. At the old Kathmandu domestic airport, a sign above the check-in counter used to read: 'Passengers Please Note: In Nepal we do not fly through clouds, as here they often have rocks in them!'

Alyssa and Glenn try to ignore the slightness of the two-engine plane as they climb into its cramped interior. Its engines whine as it heaves itself out of the smog covering Kathmandu and up into the Himalaya proper. It's a clear day and Alyssa stares spellbound out the window at the green folds of the mountains below. They look never-ending, twisting and rolling, rocky and chaotic, with the odd little village clinging to tiny flat spots on the sides. In the distance, far off on the horizon, she can see even higher mountains, with blue-tinged, snow-capped peaks. Everest is somewhere out there, she thinks to herself. Maybe one day . . .

She's lost in her own daydreams until she hears the crunching of the plane wheels being lowered and the engines squealing in protest. She peers at where the plane seems to be heading and sees a flat shelf on a mountain's edge with a tiny strip of tarmac rising steeply, and ending at a high brick wall.

At that point, sitting there in that tiny plane, looking at how small the airstrip is and how high the mountains are, she can see why it's been branded the worst place to land in the world, and is considered the most worrying part of the whole Everest Base Camp trek. Everywhere she looks, all around her, are towering peaks. In complete contrast, the airstrip looks like a very short piece of dental floss. Their plane lifts and falls, screeches to the start of the strip and then lurches, bounces, and slams back down again. The engines roar as the pilot reverses the thrust to slow down as quickly as possible with the wall at the end looming up. It finally veers off to the right just as it begins to look as if it'll go straight through, and pulls up to a halt.

The pair clamber unsteadily out of the plane and a tide of porters rush over, wanting to carry their bags. Alyssa still feels a little shaky as she and her dad smile and thank them but say they're fine. They know exactly what they're doing.

* * *

Alyssa and Glenn have already pinpointed their route from Lukla to Base Camp after reading extensively about how beautiful the trek can be. When the idea of visiting Everest Base Camp first occurred to Alyssa, she also researched the alternative trip to the base for the north-ridge route, through China's Tibet. For that trip, however, there's not much trekking involved; climbers drive from Kathmandu to the Tibetan border and then drive slowly over a few days, in order to acclimatise to the altitude, all the way to the base, which is the starting point for the other popular climb. The southeast ridge from the Nepalese side is still the route more frequently used, and Alyssa is eager for a good trek to that base camp.

The route meanders its way up to the camp, which sits at an altitude of 5380 metres, 2520 metres higher than Lukla. Glenn has already fixed up a local porter-guide for the nineteen-day round trip and they rendezvous outside the airport in Lukla and then head straight off, eager to be away and into the Himalaya as soon as they can.

They follow the road at first, past numerous tea houses and cafes and locals selling carpets and trinkets. Soon, however, the buildings peter out, the road becomes little more than a broad stony track, and the ridges roll high above the patchwork of green fields tended by the villagers along the way. Alyssa breathes a sigh of relief. These mountainsides are what she's really here for. She sets a cracking pace and the pair pass a couple of other groups of walkers with yaks trailing behind, laden with equipment, food and camping gear, and led by local Sherpas. She gives the yaks and their fearsome-looking horns a wide berth. She's heard how bad-tempered they can be at lower altitudes and how they can accidentally bump you, particularly when they're struggling with wide loads.

Very soon the path drops down into a narrow valley, with a brilliant blue glacial river below. It's only a couple of hours before they come to their first stop: the small village of Phakding. They check into a small guesthouse, eat some lentils and rice for dinner, and then sleep soundly on the narrow iron beds.

The next day the trek really begins, with a six-hour walk to the village of Namche Bazaar. Alyssa's up early, keen to move on. She and Glenn both take an acetazolamide pill, Diamox, in the hope of preventing altitude sickness, and set out with their guide. The route here climbs upwards, high above the river, and there are sensational views ahead to snow-capped peaks, particularly the world's sixth highest mountain, Cho Oyu.

Alyssa marvels at the views and keeps looking out for her first glimpse of Everest, but so far it's hidden. She stops every so often to take a photo and have a snack from her ration pack of energy bars. She can feel the beginnings of a headache, however, and feels vaguely anxious that it might be the start of altitude sickness. She's never been to these kinds of altitudes before – she's around 1200 metres higher than she was on the Kokoda Track, close to Mount Bellamy – and her heart sinks with the thought that maybe she won't adjust quickly. She sips from a water bladder in her pack, in case the headache's from dehydration instead, and presses on.

The extreme cold has taken her by surprise, too. That's another completely new experience. In the jungle at Kokoda it was warm and humid during the day, but here in the mountains the temperature dips as low as -20. She's enjoying the cold, but it is uncomfortable. She grits her teeth a little harder. She knows she'll get used to it in time.

For, above all else, she's anxious to prove to her dad that she's capable of the trek. She's trained hard and set goals for herself, but she is still keen to show him how dedicated she is. He's always been her biggest supporter and has believed in her since she can remember, and she needs to demonstrate that she's physically and mentally up to it, and that she will be able to manage at altitude. It's also going to be her longest stint ever away from home, and, secretly, she's not sure how she'll cope with that. She hopes she will manage, and doesn't want to show any sign of vulnerability. She knows this is going to be another life-changing experience, but in the meantime she tries to concentrate on the beauty of the scenery to keep her mind occupied. Hopefully sometime soon she'll get her first glimpse of Everest. That will make it all worthwhile.

It finally happens just as the pair reach the top of the hill leading into Namche Bazaar. Suddenly the great snowy peak of Everest looms up in the distance. Alyssa's heart skips a beat. She stops dead in her tracks and stares and stares. She's spent so much of her young life looking at photos of Everest, but it's so different to be actually standing there looking at the real thing. It feels incredible, breathtaking. She can almost hear her heart racing, and she immediately knows it's an image she'll carry with her for the rest of her life.

Glenn sees the excitement on his daughter's face and smiles to himself. This is turning into a shared experience he knows he'll cherish forever. He has little idea, however, what an impact it is having on his daughter, and what a momentous turning point it is going to prove for her.

By the time they reach the village of Namche Bazaar, Alyssa's headache is gone, and she's relieved and filled with excitement about the area. As the administrative centre of this Khumbu valley region,

Namche is an old town perched on steep, crescent-shaped hillsides, and while it started as a trading post for locals to barter yak cheese and butter for agricultural produce grown lower down, now it has cafes offering western food, hot chocolate and cakes, and tea houses to stay in with hot showers and laundry facilities.

Alyssa falls in love with the place immediately. She's still getting used to Nepalese food, and while that's happening quickly – she's having to eat so much to keep up her energy levels at this altitude – she welcomes being able to eat the kind of food she is used to.

The pair stay in Namche a couple of days, exploring its trekking shops, visiting the large and noisy market and smiling genially every time Alyssa is approached by locals curious to see such a young girl passing through. She watches them too, with big, round eyes. She's amazed how everyone works so hard, and yet seems so happy. One woman scrubs clothes in a bowl for hours, but smiles constantly. Alyssa is fascinated that people have so little, yet seem so much nicer than some people she knows back home who have infinitely more. She feels she's learning so much about life, every day.

The main reason for the extended stay, however, is to help with the acclimatisation process. The key, Glenn knows from his medical training, is to ascend slowly and gradually and, unsure of his daughter's capacity for adapting to such heights, he's keen to not rush. He's also aware that Alyssa is so excited about this trip, and wants to do it so much, she may well not tell him if she's feeling ill. He watches her closely for any sign she's feeling off-colour, but she seems to be taking it all in her stride. He's incredulous. He would never have thought a kid could cope so well with so many different challenges.

Yet even as he reassures himself that she's managing well, he suddenly develops a violent headache and starts to feel feverish. When the headache grows worse, he realises it can't be the altitude; it must be a relapse of the dangerous strain of malaria he contracted on one of his many visits to PNG for the Kokoda Track.

He doesn't say anything to Alyssa to worry her, and only hopes he'll be able to hold out until they reach Base Camp and then make it safely back to Australia. But on their last night in Namche Bazaar, it hits him with full force. He realises that the strain of being at altitude is taxing his red blood cells and has triggered another bout of the deadly sickness, and he can do nothing to stop it.

He sits up the whole night, his temperature high, his body clammy, almost delirious with fever. Alyssa sits by his side, giving him warm drinks and planning to find a doctor as soon as daylight breaks. It's nerve-racking, but she tries to stay calm for her dad's sake. She feels quite helpless, and can see her dad barely has the strength left to move. Suddenly, she knows she's out of her depth – after all, she is still just ten years old – and it's nerve-wracking to see the rock she's always depended upon crumbling before her eyes. But she reminds herself that Namche is the kind of place where there's bound to be a doctor who can speak some English and, as soon as dawn breaks, she ventures out of the tent to find help. It comes quickly.

The local doctor takes one look at Glenn and suggests a helicopter to take him back immediately to Lukla from where he can fly back to Kathmandu and go straight to hospital for treatment. The pair fly back to the city, this time barely glancing out of the window at the mountains below. That's fine, Alyssa thinks to herself. She's resigned to getting back to Kathmandu as quickly as possible for her dad's sake.

But, quietly, to herself, she resolves that she'll be back one day. Already, she's realised that she prefers the mountains to the jungle, that she loves the cold rather than the warmth and that, in the moment she stood and looked at Everest for the first time, it was love at first sight, and her life would never be the same. And, like with any love affair, she can't wait to return and feel that thrill and excitement again. But next time, she resolves to herself, she'll make it all the way to Base Camp. Then, one day, who knows? Perhaps she'll even continue on and up to the very summit of Everest itself, to touch the roof of the world.

CHAPTER 8

Everest's First Dynasty: Edmund and Peter Hillary

Peter Hillary, part of the most famous Everest climbing dynasty in the world, first sighted Everest when he was eleven, only one year older than Alyssa Azar was on her first trip to Nepal.

Born eighteen months after his father Sir Edmund Hillary's history-making first Everest ascent, his childhood was filled with the stories of his father's great adventures. He grew up travelling the world with his dad, climbing New Zealand's highest peak, Mount Cook, and spending a year in Nepal, trekking and climbing in the Himalaya. In 1966, his father took him to see Everest.

'That was the first time I'd ever seen Everest,' says Peter Hillary. 'People pointed up towards the big mountain, and I remember the excitement everyone had. It was infectious. I'd heard all about it from my father, of course, and soon you start wondering what it would be like to actually climb something like that.'

But, unlike Alyssa, he didn't immediately feel the physical pull of the summit. 'No, I think I just thought that was Dad's deal,' he says now. 'But later, as I got more into my teens, it started to appeal a lot more. I started going on journeys of my own, getting into the

Himalaya and climbing, and then I started thinking about it more. Eventually, I became hooked, and decided I really wanted to climb the big one.'

Of Alyssa, he says, 'Everything about her seems to suggest she possesses great fortitude. And passion. The key thing you need is to have the fire burning inside you, you need to really want to get out there and get to the top.'

Peter Hillary certainly has that in spades, and he ended up climbing on Everest five times, summitting twice. The first time he reached 8300 metres on the exceedingly difficult western ridge, and then summitted in 1990 from the southern route, becoming part of the first father-and-son duo – separately – to ever reach the top. He summitted again in 2002 as part of a National Geographic Society expedition to celebrate the fiftieth anniversary of Hillary and Tenzing's climb, along with the Sherpa's son, Jamling Norgay. In addition, he's climbed many other of the world's highest mountains and has trekked to the South Pole and landed in a small plane on the North Pole, in the illustrious company of astronaut Neil Armstrong.

Like Alyssa, he always longed for a life of high adventure. 'I've always loved being involved in challenging endeavours and going to places that I know will involve a lot of hard work,' he says. 'I think to a certain extent, you've either got that drive or you haven't. I'm one of those people who've always had that.'

Indeed, that's one of the reasons Alyssa, from her childhood reading about her mountaineering and trekking idols, so respects both him and his father. Sir Edmund, who died in 2008, was a quietly spoken man with immense reserves of determination to succeed against all the odds. His son is cut from exactly the same cloth.

'They're both pretty amazing people,' says Alyssa. 'They both seem humble but they've both achieved so much. Sir Edmund was a beekeeper but he was the first man to make it to the top of Everest.

That's huge! I love that side of it, that it was his drive to get there which made him so successful. No one at that stage knew whether it would even be possible to get up there. Mallory might have been to the top, but he didn't live to tell the tale. So climbing Everest in those kinds of conditions would have been enormously challenging.

'Peter Hillary has also gone on to do so much, and to have adventures around the world. His books about his exploits have always really inspired me. When he talks about how necessary it is to have the fire inside you, that's exactly how I feel. I don't know what I'll be able to achieve in my life, but I know I have the drive, and I'm willing to put in all the hard work it might take.'

For Hillary believes that when you get results, there are few better feelings in the world. He loves the challenge of climbing mountains, the camaraderie of his fellow climbers, the adventure, the not knowing what each day might bring, and then, finally, hopefully, the accomplishment of reaching the goal.

Naturally, he's had his share of tragedies along with the triumphs. He's fought for his life through storms, avalanches and accidents. In 1984 he was climbing Everest's dangerous west ridge when two of his teammates, Australians Craig Nottle and Fred From, lost their footing at 7800 metres and disappeared down a steep slope to their deaths. Hillary abandoned that expedition immediately.

In 1995 he was climbing the world's second highest mountain, the notoriously dangerous K2, when he predicted a change in the weather. He turned back just a few hundred metres from the summit, but others decided to go on to the top without him. Soon after, a violent storm descended and killed seven members of his expedition.

'In a place like the Himalaya, you have a lot of challenging experiences,' he says. 'There are times when you have to concentrate on your own survival and you're thinking much more about the possibility of getting down safely than getting up. But then you have other times you can describe as a "textbook" ascent. Some of the climbs can be technically less demanding, but conditions can easily push you to the edge.'

As for Alyssa, he hopes her dream to climb Everest will come true, and she'll be able to make it to the top. Some young people can be incredibly mature for their age, he believes, and what matters much more than someone's relative youth on a mountain are their individual qualities.

'It's still about the blaze within someone, that's what will push them on when things get difficult,' he says. 'It's also their dedication and the amount of preparation they put into it. I try to stay away from encouraging climbs on big mountains where the main motivation might be a record, like the youngest to do it or the oldest, but for many people, it's not about that. It's about the passion and the ambition and the appetite for challenge. And as long as they have a strong grasp of reality too, and know the dangers, then they might well be successful.

'But it's mostly about that fire, and she seems to have plenty of that.'

CHAPTER 9

The First Trials

'To walk through life in a comfortable way is still not my goal.'
– SWISS ROCK CLIMBER AND MOUNTAINEER UELI STECK

With Alyssa now nursing a dream of one day returning to Everest to climb to its summit, her life suddenly felt as if it had fresh purpose.

Glenn had recovered well enough from a few days in hospital in Nepal, then a week in hospital in Brisbane, to return home, and he certainly seemed amenable to returning to the Himalaya one day. For him, that trek towards Everest Base Camp had been a great one, despite having to abort the last part, and a good experience for them to share, as well as an excellent trip to possibly add to the Kokoda one he would be offering through the company he was planning to set up, Adventure Professionals.

'I thought it would be a great trek to do again,' he says. 'Nepal, we'd found, was an amazing country, with incredible cultural diversity. There was so much to see and do. And on the trek, it was amazing to be able to walk through all those villages with all these great views of Mount Everest and the surrounding peaks. I thought it was fabulous and, while it was embarrassing to have this ten-year-old bouncing around, and me not able to make it, it only added to the trip to see what an impact it was having on Alyssa.'

Therese and the children had, in the meantime, returned to Toowoomba, and the family was back together again. Therese was pleased to welcome Alyssa back in one piece, was thrilled she'd had such a good time, and relieved both she and Glenn were home safely. 'I didn't mind so much her going to Everest Base Camp because she'd done Kokoda, and I felt Kokoda was worse in many ways. It just felt like a wilder place and so many more things feel as if they can go wrong.

'Everest was a long way, and I knew she was going to be away for three weeks, which is a long time. But I was still more comfortable with it as she'd had a little bit of experience and there were plenty of ways to get her out if there was any trouble. When I looked at her photos, I felt reassured. Every photo of her in Nepal, she had a big smile on her face.'

There was lots of interest in Alyssa's trip from her friends at school and she gave a couple of presentations on Everest, Nepal and the trek to Base Camp to different classes. There were more calls from the media too, and she was again interviewed about her latest adventure. Everyone asked her what she was planning to do next. She just shrugged her shoulders and smiled.

But every evening she was back at the gym, training for whatever would come up next, and then on the internet at home, looking to work out exactly what that should be. Therese was hoping her daughter might be more content at home after having had such an adventurous few years, and told her to concentrate on school. She didn't really have too much time to grow restless, in any case. Glenn was working harder and harder for the new adventure business he'd bought into in Brisbane with the fellow ex-soldier, setting up Everest Base Camp treks now as well as the Kokoda trips.

In April 2008, he and Alyssa returned to Nepal with the aim of further checking out the Base Camp trek, and hopefully making it all the way. This trip ran a great deal more smoothly and, this time, as the pair trudged out of Namche, Everest immediately appeared on the horizon. Alyssa thrilled at the sight all over again. She knew its curves, the shape of its peak so well, it all felt terribly familiar. It seemed to add a spring to her step. The next village was Tengboche, high on a knife-edged ridge with fabulous views again. Alyssa and Glenn stayed overnight, aware that they still needed to acclimatise to the 4400-metre height. Alyssa didn't sleep well, however; she was too excited about the trek and reaching Everest Base Camp.

The next day, the pair finally reached Gorek Shep, at 5200 metres, the last village before the camp. They slept there another night and then walked straight into the camp. It took just two hours. Alyssa looked at the grey, stony patch of land, dotted with bright yellow tents, with real awe. One day, she felt, she was going to be here, ready to actually climb Everest as she'd vowed. She knew it. She just hoped it wouldn't be too long to wait.

She and her dad wandered around the camp. In truth, there was not a lot to see: the tents, a few figures washing pans, strings of fluttering prayer flags. Everyone seemed to be out, either practising on slopes nearby or training for the big climb up Everest itself. But it was enough to fire Alyssa's imagination. She was absolutely certain she would return.

* * *

Back home again, and Glenn was finding it increasingly difficult to run things from Toowoomba. In the end, he and Therese agreed to move the family to Brisbane.

Alyssa wasn't used to city life, missed the hills she'd grown up around, and found it hard to adapt to the change. She transferred to a Brisbane high school, the girls' school Corpus Christie College at Nundah, later to become Mary McKillop College. But she was struggling.

'I didn't enjoy that school at all, and I never felt as though I fitted in,' she says. 'I think I just wasn't interested in a lot of the things most kids were interested in. I went to school for the sake of going to school, just to learn, whereas most of the other people there went to socialise, which is a side I never enjoyed. Also, I wasn't really sure I wanted to go to an all-girls school any more.'

Alyssa ended up moving to Kelvin Grove State College, where the atmosphere was a little more relaxed. She still didn't exactly enjoy it, but disliked it a bit less. She distracted herself by attending the gym and training every spare moment she had.

Never a chatty kid, over the next few months she became even quieter and more withdrawn. All her family noticed it, but they just assumed it was a stage she was going through. One day, Glenn drew her aside and asked her what was really wrong. She finally told him: she was being bullied again at school. The other kids saw her as the odd one out, and they were being merciless. She was once more being targeted on social media, being picked on and derided.

'It turned out she was being ostracised because she didn't play an instrument or do ballet,' says Glenn. 'She was different from the rest. She boxed and worked out and was having all these adventures that got her publicity, and the others didn't like that so much. It meant she was copping a lot of flak. Parents would see a story about her in the newspaper and they'd say to their kid, Look what's she's doing, and I can't even get you to clean your room! Even on radio, someone would interview her and joke that their child just sat on the couch all day. It was meant in good humour, but it built up a bit of resentment among some other kids. Also, she's pretty quiet, and doesn't really defend herself, which only encourages them. But it was starting to affect her.

'Bullying, particularly on social media, is pretty hard to counter and so I talked to her about how she could not let it bother her.

As a twelve-year-old, she couldn't control other people, but she could control her reaction to them. I told her it was a bit sad if she was going to let other people stop her doing things she liked doing because it made them uncomfortable. I tried to explain to her that in life, people often judge you by their own limitations, and that teenagers, particularly teenage girls, sort of sit in a safety bubble. They like to be the same as everyone else and any kids who come outside that bubble and are different, they'll just try to pull them back in to make themselves feel comfortable.'

Alyssa listened quietly and nodded. She made a mental note to herself to start toughening up. She couldn't let things like this get in the way of her dreams. 'There was a lot of drama in high school and gossip and all that kind of thing, and I just wasn't interested in any of it,' she says. 'I didn't really see the point. So I found it difficult to get involved. I suppose I was a bit different and obviously I'd travelled to third world countries and seen certain things that a lot of them hadn't, so I guess they had a different perspective on things. But I'd been having a rough time at school, and I was getting a bit negative and unhappy. Dad felt that wasn't like me, so I decided I needed to change my attitude.

'I always felt, even from a young age, that no matter how small you are, what age or what gender, you can accomplish anything, and those who put you down are just too scared to go for their own dreams. I tried very much to remember that.'

To cheer her up, Glenn suggested the pair go on another adventure. An old soldier mate of his, Kyle Williams, who'd figured out the logistics for the Townsville to Brisbane charity run all those years ago, had suggested summitting the ten highest peaks in Australia in one trip, a circuit he dubbed 'The Aussie 10'. It could prove a great adventure trek, he said. Glenn was immediately interested. Of course, they'd be nothing like the Himalayan peaks, with the highest being Kosciuszko at just 2228 metres, merely a pebble or two over a quarter of Everest's height. But they do offer spectacular alpine trekking and they're all within the Kosciuszko National Park in NSW's Snowy Mountains, part of the same Great Dividing Range that gives Toowoomba its curves. Since all the peaks, including Mount Townsend at 2209 metres, Mount Twynam at 2195 metres and Rams Head at 2190 metres, are within 12 km of each other as the crow flies, the whole trip with its 50 km hike would only take a few days, but it would be tough.

Alyssa brightened immediately and trained with even more vigour. Glenn suggested they keep this trip quiet, with no press, to try to avoid giving the bullies any more fodder.

* * *

A few weeks later, the pair drive down to the Charlotte Pass in the heart of the NSW Snowy Mountains, and meet up with Williams as their guide, as well as a couple more friends who've decided they'd like to come along. It really seems this could be another trip for the schedule of the adventure business: a challenging trek on Australia's most spectacular mountain range, with the country's only mainland glacial lakes as a stunning backdrop.

Alyssa celebrated her twelfth birthday in November 2009, just before they set off, and is looking forward to such an impromptu, spontaneous getaway. She didn't even have time to research it beforehand but, being local, it is pretty easy to arrange and she's excited at the thought of another adventure. There's a great deal of snow and ice around. She's seen snow on the Everest Base Camp trek, but she's never experienced walking through it. At each step, she sinks deeper and deeper into the snow and, since she is still quite small, the others joke that they might soon lose her completely. And they almost do. At one stage they're standing on the side of a freezing cold river, working out the best way to get across, when the ice beneath Alyssa's feet gives way and she slips in. She's hauled out, soaked to the skin and shivering from the freezing water, but takes it in good heart, and laughs along with the others. There's nothing for it then but to take off her sodden tracksuit pants, knowing there's no chance of them drying in the cold, and trek in her compression shorts, raising the eyebrows of other groups who pass them, wondering why on earth such a young girl is out on such a chilly day in so few clothes.

At first her legs feel deathly cold but eventually they go pleasantly numb, and from that point on she feels much happier. Besides, there's an old mountain-climbing expression that you need to get comfortable with being uncomfortable. She decides this experience is only helping prepare her for all the discomfort to come in later years, and the thought cheers her immensely. Several hours later, she walks the winding track up Mount Kosciuszko as her seventh peak. By now, she is really feeling it. The climb is steep and much harder than she thought it would be.

But finally, she reaches the top – the highest point in Australia. She looks around with a feeling of huge satisfaction. She feels proud to have made it with such comparative ease and knows that, despite the problems she's been facing, she hasn't lost her love and passion for adventure.

The next three peaks are comparatively easy, and Alyssa is cheered by the experience. She starts feeling positive again about her life, and being among mountains has helped put everything back into perspective. Somehow, she always finds the experience of height conducive to clearer thinking, and trudging upwards ever life-affirming. Tackling the Aussie 10, and succeeding, has now put her back on track and heading in a positive direction. She feels happy and excited all over again about what she can achieve in the future, as well as being proud of her past achievements. This time, she hasn't experienced a new culture, but is returning a new person.

On the way back, she realises that, in climbing Kosciuszko, she's ticked off one of the famed Seven Summits, the highest peaks on each of the seven continents. She starts daydreaming about tackling the other six, including Everest. It's starting to feel more and more possible.

CHAPTER 10

Everest's First Australians: Tim Macartney-Snape

Australia's best-known and most acclaimed mountaineer, Tim Macartney-Snape, spent his youth climbing all over Australia, first in the Victorian Alps at the age of fifteen, and then, after his HSC exams, hiking and climbing in the NSW Snowy Mountains and Koscuiszko in his own inimitably challenging version of a schoolies week celebration.

Koscuiszko and its surrounding peaks held him in such thrall that the next winter he returned, this time on skis. 'But I faced ferocious conditions – a fierce blizzard and boilerplate ice [ice so hard, it's impossible to pierce],' he says. 'For me, it was a very valuable part of my mountain apprenticeship.'

It was all great training in preparation for one of the biggest challenges of his life: a historic attempt on Everest in 1984 – twenty-five years before Alyssa Azar would tackle the Aussie 10.

Back then, everything was against him and his four fellow Australian climbers. Everest figured much less in the public consciousness than it does now, and it was hard to raise money for expeditions. In addition, they were planning to climb by a new route from the Tibetan side that no one had ever attempted before – without oxygen cylinders. Few took the tiny team of just five people seriously, and even fewer imagined they had any chance at all of success.

But Macartney-Snape, together with Greg Mortimer, Lincoln Hall, Geoff Bartram and Andy Henderson, planned to give it the best they possibly could. 'I wanted to do it because I had this dream,' says Macartney-Snape today. 'It was something I found really exciting. And I knew that with enough drive and passion and excitement, we might be able to pull it off.

'If Alyssa's going to succeed, she'll really need that same inner drive and excitement at meeting her challenges too. I hope she has it. Without that kind of passion, she won't ever get beyond Everest Base Camp.'

For their expedition, the little band arrived in Beijing, China, in July 1984, drove to Chengdu and then flew to the Tibetan capital, Lhasa. From there, they were driven over the rocky road to the base of Everest, having to jump in boats to cart their gear over sections that were flooded by the monsoonal weather.

Their climb started badly. They hauled much of their gear up to a camp they made higher up, but were then forced down by heavy snowfall, raging winds and the bitter cold. By the time they were able to climb up again to be reunited with their equipment and stores, rats and birds had eaten much of their food, an avalanche had ripped some of the tents to ribbons and their climbing gear was so completely buried by snow they were unable to locate it.

As a result, Macartney-Snape was forced to continue the climb in cross-country ski boots, while Mortimer and Hall were nearly buried by another avalanche. Then Hall developed respiratory problems. They were forced to retreat back down the mountain.

It wasn't until late September that the bad weather broke temporarily and the five set out again, but then had to shelter for four days in a makeshift snow cave when the monsoonal gales returned. Soon after, Bartram started suffering a violent headache, blurred vision and dizziness and, recognising all the symptoms of a cerebral oedema, or fluid on the brain, had to descend. And then they were four.

In another break in the weather, they continued up through the snow, ice and shifting rock. Hall was the next to hit trouble, unable to keep his hands and feet warm. Having lost parts of his toes after being stuck on a ridge in a snowstorm for two days on an earlier climb, he took shelter and decided not to continue.

The remaining trio then pushed on, battling freezing temperatures, exhaustion, and air so thin it took all their efforts to keep breathing. Adversity struck again when Henderson broke a crampon. He was forced to take off his outer mittens to try to repair it, and felt his fingers instantly freeze. He knew he was now suffering frostbite and couldn't continue. The last two went on, stopping every few steps to struggle for breath, knowing the summit lay just before them.

Finally, at dusk on 3 October 1984, Tim Macartney-Snape and Greg Mortimer made it to the top of the world. 'It was the hardest day of my life, but the view from there was absolutely incredible,' says Macartney-Snape. 'It was hard to believe we'd made it.'

It was even harder to believe, however, they might make it down again alive. After twenty minutes on the summit it was dark, and the pair climbed down to join Henderson, still nursing his fingers, and then further down to meet Hall, who'd been working hard to set up sleeping bags and melt ice on a burner for them to drink. By the time the sun rose again, Henderson's hands were frozen in a curled position and Mortimer was behaving erratically, showing signs of either extreme exhaustion or, even more worryingly, cerebral oedema.

The little group started down the mountain, Mortimer at one point suddenly catching a crampon in his trousers, tripping himself and rolling down the slope towards a sheer drop before just managing to stop himself by plunging his ice axe into the snow. They finally reached the base intact – although Henderson later lost parts of all his fingers – much to the astonishment, and acclaim, of the rest of the international climbing community.

The fact that such a small, unassisted group had successfully climbed an uncharted route, and without oxygen tanks, conferred on them an unrivalled place in the history of Everest. As one climbing veteran declared, 'The Aussies pulled off the mountaineering coup of the century!'

Now, pondering Alyssa's dream of making it to the top of Everest, Macartney-Snape says it's still a very tough call. 'For a young person, it's a long time away from home. In addition, you're not so physically aware of yourself as when you're older, and not quite as well versed in pacing yourself. Then there's the challenge of having sound judgement about the weather and what the conditions are likely to be in deciding whether to go up or stay put, while all the time resisting the pressures from sponsors and other people's expectations. She has to make her own decisions, and her own choices in the mountains.'

But despite those considerable hurdles, Macartney-Snape says he would encourage Alyssa to follow her heart. 'I love it when young people decide to follow adventurous pursuits,' he says. 'It's sad when they don't. So many of them spend so much time on computers now, and while it's wonderful that the digital revolution has put so much information at our fingertips, we have to be reminded that the virtual world is only a product of the real world, and is so much poorer than the real world. That's the world that's really fascinating.

'It's great when youngsters like Alyssa want to get out there and experience real life and the rewards of challenging themselves. It's wonderful that they do, and gives me so much more hope for the future that people are still inspired to do things like climb Everest.'

In 1990, six years after Macartney-Snape's ascent, he returned to Everest with the idea of being the first in the world to climb the mountain from its true start in the sea, at the Bay of Bengal, to its summit. It took him three months but, attempting the summit solo, without oxygen, light-headed, dehydrated, plagued by bouts of diarrhoea and nausea, and nearly falling to his death at midnight when stopping to adjust the movie camera he carried, he finally made it.

In 1993, he was made a Member of the Order of Australia (AM) for services to mountaineering and international relations.

As a veteran of so many Everest adventures, he's now keen to offer Alyssa the benefit of his experience. 'Be very, very careful up there,' he advises. 'Listen to yourself and your own feelings and what your body's telling you. Be mindful of what's happening to you. Don't rush into things, and if you're not feeling good, get down.

'Be mindful of changing conditions as the weather is still the single biggest factor on the mountains. The weather has caused a lot of fatalities because conditions can get bad and everything gets more difficult. That's when it's easy to compromise yourself, get lost and get cold and stumble. But if you know it's getting bad, get back down. That's sometimes a hard decision as you've spent so much money and time and effort getting there, but that's when people die. And that's failure on all fronts!'

Having been in so many life-and-death situations himself, and survived, Macartney-Snape is keen to neither overstress nor downplay the risks. 'It's good to be afraid, but you need to be able to control your fear and still find yourself loving being there,' he says. 'Be aware of what's around you, and enjoy the experience, and love it.

'Because if you're not loving it, it's time to leave. You can always come back again later, but if you make the wrong decision when you're there, you might not be able to.'

CHAPTER 11

Dare to Dream

'The greatest battle is not physical but psychological. The demons telling us to give up when we push ourselves can never be silenced for good. They must always be answered by the quiet, steady dignity that refuses to give in. Courage. Suffer. Keep going.'

— UK WRITER GRAEME FIFE

With Alyssa Azar back on course with her Everest dream, it was now Glenn's turn to falter.

He'd been working hard as a partner in the adventure company in Brisbane, while still managing to continue running, from there, his Fighting Fit gym back in Toowoomba. The demand for the trips was increasing every year, especially for the Kokoda Track over the Anzac weekend, and in just one year the company led no fewer than thirteen trips over Kokoda. At one point, they had a total of 120 people on the track at once, in six different groups, with Glenn helping to organise the whole expedition and leading one of the parties.

Some of their clients were high profile, too, including former Australian cricket captain Allan Border, rugby league's Mal Meninga, *Sunrise* TV host David Koch, the Brisbane Lions rugby team, the Hawthorn AFL team, and the heads of the National Australia Bank. Even future prime minister Kevin Rudd and future treasurer Joe Hockey joined them on a trek in 2006, and formed one of the most unlikely friendships in history.

Hockey didn't seem to appreciate Glenn's sense of humour too much, though. 'I remember sitting and having a conversation with Joe Hockey at 4.30 one morning,' Glenn says. 'Someone was talking to him and the light was shining in his eyes off their head torch and he got a bit annoyed. He said, Can you turn your light down, it's shining in my friggin' eyes – but not in quite such polite language – and it's giving me a headache. In the army, when someone says they've got a headache, it's a really common line to say that a head like that should ache. So I said it without thinking, and he really got the shits and walked off. I thought, Oh, well – there goes my chances with him!'

As well as all the people wanting to go to Kokoda, there was also a growing number signing up for his Everest Base Camp treks and the new hike Kyle Williams had pioneered with Glenn and Alyssa, the Aussie 10. He had plans for expanding even more in the future, with a few vague thoughts about possibly taking a group over to climb Africa's highest peak, Kilimanjaro.

But, somehow, the money didn't seem to be coming in. 'I'd been working as hard as I could, but we just didn't seem to be getting the financial rewards,' Glenn says. 'I couldn't understand it. But I carried on working, harder and harder. Then the Global Financial Crisis hit and in 2009 everything fell apart. I'd never had a lawyer look at my agreement with the company, I'd just joined on a handshake. A lot of people lost a lot of money and I lost everything. I was on the border of becoming bankrupt.'

In 2010, Glenn moved the family back to Toowoomba and decided to start all over again. 'I met with a couple of friends of mine who own big businesses and I met with my accountant and the lawyers and they drew a line and said, This is what bankruptcy could look like. It's borderline as to which way you go. But if I'm really bad at one thing, it's quitting; I'm not a good quitter. I thought the only way was to fight my way out of it, and I knew overcoming setbacks like that can only ever make you stronger.'

The gym was still going extremely well, with a large number of regular clients and his boxers winning four Australian titles, five Queensland titles, three national Golden Gloves titles, and numerous regional competitions. So Glenn took a long, hard look at the kind of programs he was offering, and decided to increase them.

'For a long time, I just taught boxing and did fitness training at the gym,' he says. 'But now I was really desperate so I started a boot camp and called it Overhaul. It was a real military-style boot camp, the way we did it in the army. I ran it as an eight-week program and thirty people signed up for it, which is what we lived off for the next two months.

'People did that program a few times and then I created another boot camp program. Slowly, I started to advance that business. There are two things that make people achieve things in life: inspiration and desperation. For me, it was desperation. They say that's a really good motivator and it was. This was about survival. But it taught me a lot about being knocked down and then having the courage and strength to get up and start again, and I think seeing that was also a great lesson for Alyssa. She could see from my example that you have to work hard to achieve the things you feel are worthwhile, you have to dare to dream, and then work hard to make your dreams a reality. I think she's always taken that lesson to heart.'

Then Glenn also started his own adventure company, Adventure Professionals, and this time made sure everything was drawn up by lawyers. He started organising trips again, but this time through his own company: Kokoda, Base Camp, Aussie 10, and yes, maybe one day soon . . . Kilimanjaro.

* * *

Alyssa also had her mind on Kilimanjaro. She'd wanted that to be her first big expedition after Kokoda but, because of the age limit, she'd been forced to put it aside. But now she was dreaming again about the Tanzanian peak, and talking about it to her dad, hoping it could be scheduled in as her next adventure, in 2011, when she'd be thirteen.

She was back in hard training and started keeping a diary of her workout routines, her goals and how she planned to reach them. Everything now was geared to Kilimanjaro, with the thought that it would be a great step on the eventual road to Everest. Together with Glenn, she devised a cross-training program, involving three boxing sessions a week plus exercises like squats, sit-ups, push-ups and burpees. She was also running three times a week, and on weekends put on a weight vest or carried a backpack weighing 10–15 kg and did a three-hour bushwalk with Glenn and any of his clients who might be in training for one of his expeditions.

There was also a mental training element to her life now. She wrote out even more inspirational quotes and put them everywhere. She started reading more, too. Glenn gave Alyssa a book he'd read and really enjoyed, *Warrior Training: The Making of an Australian SAS Soldier* by Keith Fennell who, as a member of the SAS, was deployed on many missions around the world. It gave an insight into the training and mindset of SAS soldiers, and talked about what makes high-performing individuals and teams tick. She devoured the book in two days, then immediately started reading it again. If she was going to succeed at the kind of challenges she wanted to set herself – Kilimanjaro, Everest and the rest of the world's biggest mountains – it was this kind of mind-training, as well as all the physical stuff, she believed she needed.

As well as getting into the gym by 5.30 every morning, returning after school and then trekking every weekend, she started the long process of making sure her mind was fit enough for the work that lay ahead. 'Without the right mental approach and determination, it doesn't matter how physically strong you are,' she says. 'You'll just never be strong enough. That book, *Warrior Training*, just struck such a chord with me. I felt like I'd been waiting to learn the kinds of lessons about building up your mental toughness. It was the one gap in my armour and I was now able to start filling it.'

When Glenn finally agreed to take her to Kilimanjaro, she was over the moon. Her mum Therese was not so sure. 'I thought after Kokoda and Base Camp and the Aussie 10, she might have got it all out of her system,' she says. 'But no, she hadn't. Several times, I considered saying, No, she shouldn't do it, but I'd have felt pretty guilty. Naturally I felt nervous about the idea of her going over to climb a mountain in Africa, but I knew Glenn wouldn't let her come to any harm.'

Glenn knew the Aussie 10 had whetted Alyssa's appetite again, and he was always keen to support anything she wanted to do – within reason. He knew how much she wanted to climb Kilimanjaro and it did seem another good candidate for him to add to his adventure company's trip list. He also knew, on the other hand, that he was likely to receive criticism again as a parent for allowing a young girl to do something so potentially dangerous.

'But I've always felt strongly that we shouldn't mollycoddle kids,' he says. 'In my opinion, a lot of parents are too precious. I think sometimes that even though they don't realise it, they're helping their kids fail. We have to help our kids live their own lives and encourage them to really achieve their own dreams, however big.

'I knew she would ask about Kilimanjaro again, and sure enough, she did. I was determined to make it possible for her. But it is an expensive trip. It costs a few thousand dollars just to get there. So I told her to wait a little while and then we'd put it on in July 2011 when she was fourteen. She was impatient, but she knew she'd have to wait till we could afford it.'

One evening, he was asked to give a public talk about leadership and military teamwork models. During the talk he said how necessary it is to encourage kids to do adventurous things, rather than try to put an invisible ceiling over their heads, and described some of the adventures he'd undertaken with Alyssa.

'You know,' he declared a tad flippantly, 'if she ever wanted to climb Mount Everest, I'd support her. I wouldn't want her to do it, but I would fully support her if she wanted that enough. It's not always about what you want to do as the parent, or what you want your kid to do. It's about their dreams, and helping to make them come true.'

Glenn didn't think any more of it, but unbeknownst to him, there was a young girl listening from outside.

Alyssa didn't tell him she'd heard, but threw herself even harder into training for Kilimanjaro. Besides, she was looking for all the distraction she could find, as school wasn't going any better now that she was back in Toowoomba. She was trying to settle in at her new school, St Ursula's College, but it wasn't a great fit. Her teachers worried that she wasn't taking part in any of the school activities; that all she seemed to do was attend her lessons and then go straight off to the gym. They'd have preferred her to become involved more in school life, to spend more time with her classmates and to have a much more balanced life.

Alyssa simply didn't see the point. 'They were always complaining, but I just didn't have the time to fit anything else into my life,' she says. 'I was too busy with my training and getting my homework done in the gaps between it. I didn't want to be doing stuff around the school. My mind was on training for another climb, hopefully Kilimanjaro this time. By the time I got to school, I was often tired and had to try to focus. That automatically drove me away from what everyone else was doing, which they didn't like.

'They weren't used to someone like me, who didn't want to socialise and didn't want to do all that stuff. I don't think they really knew how to handle it.'

Her parents were called frequently to the school to discuss their problem child, and while Therese tried to smooth everything over, Glenn was outraged. He understood the teachers believed they were doing their best by Alyssa, but he knew his daughter and defended her, protesting that she was making all the right choices for herself.

Although she again became a target for bullying over the internet by others at the school, this time she tried not to let it affect her and vowed to help others also struggling. Just as she and Glenn had collected money for the local hospital with Kokoda, they decided to try to raise funds with their Kilimanjaro trip towards Kids Helpline, a phone counselling service that helps youngsters with their problems, including bullying. Alyssa did some publicity for the upcoming trip to increase its profile and raise some money through sponsorship for the trip and extra for the charity, and the personal bullying grew worse. She received a volley of texts and barbs on social media from people saying they hoped she'd fall off the mountain and die.

'I cut off a lot of social media I looked at so I just wouldn't see it,' she says. 'I didn't see the point in having it if it was going to be negative. Instead, I just used my energy to focus harder on the trip. It was hard for me to understand why that kind of thing would happen, but I guess some people just didn't like me or what I was doing. By the end, though, I just thought I'd use it to make me stronger, and sharpen my focus, and harden my resolve, and I found that worked.'

Watching on, her aunt Tanya Azar was highly impressed by how she was coping. 'She said at times she didn't know if she could cope with it,' she says, 'but she showed incredible strength. She said that helped her move forward. She's very young, but she's an old soul inside, and very wise for her age.'

But the bullying and the difficulties with teachers did make Alyssa start thinking about alternative ways of going about her schooling. She researched home-schooling and distance education, which would allow her to do lessons over the internet instead.

She reasoned that would be a good way to escape the bullying, and would allow her to finish her school years in peace, spending more time on her favourite subjects, English and history. At the back of her mind, though, there was an even more compelling reason.

'I loved these adventures so much, but I was impatient to do more and try to get to Everest more quickly,' she says. 'It was great doing a trip every two years, but I knew if I was serious about climbing Everest, I'd have to increase my training and do more climbing and trekking more often. It was taking time out from school but I kept thinking that if I could organise my own schoolwork, I'd be more free to travel when I had the opportunity.

'Even though I was still just thirteen, soon turning fourteen, I was on my way to Kilimanjaro, knowing that it would put me at a higher altitude than I'd ever been before. It was going to be a big challenge, and I'd then be able to see how I might react to higher and higher climbs in the Himalaya. I was keen to see Africa, I was eager to climb its biggest mountain, but everything was already geared towards that ultimate dream of Everest.'

She simply had no idea how hard Kilimanjaro would prove.

CHAPTER 12

Everest's World Record-holder: Dave Hahn

Is Mount Everest any place for a teenage girl? According to Everest veteran Dave Hahn, the American who holds the world record for the greatest number of successful climbs to the top for a non-Sherpa, the answer to that is: Maybe . . .

If she's mature for her age, physically strong and mentally tough, then it could be the mountain on which she can learn a great deal about both herself, and life in general. But if she's not up to the challenge?

'You don't want the mountain to have the tone of death and destruction for its climbers, but anyone who goes there has to keep in mind what the full consequences can be for any mistakes or bad decisions,' he says. 'A girl of that age might be physically able, but it's a lot to expect of a young girl to be able to size up all the risks and still be okay.'

It's impossible to dismiss Hahn's scepticism out of hand. After all, he is one of the most experienced Everest climbers who's still alive to tell the tales. With fifteen successful Everest summit ascents to his name, some heroic rescues and three Mallory and Irvine search expeditions, including being part of the 1999 team that found Mallory's body, he now works as one of the world's most revered high-altitude mountain guides.

However, even he failed to make it to the top on his first attempt in 1991. On a climb of the north side without oxygen, he was forced by bad weather to turn back just 310 metres from the summit. Three years later, he made it all the way – but it very nearly cost him his life.

'I knew I'd go back to Everest as it was such a profound experience the first time,' Hahn says from his home in New Mexico. 'But that climb in 1994 was probably one of the more difficult things I've ever done and was my closest brush with death. That was the biggest hole I've ever dug for myself.

'I ended up climbing continuously for sixty hours. I summitted by myself at ten minutes to five in the afternoon in a cloud, then I spent the night trying to get down. Eventually, I ran out of oxygen in a snowstorm and I reached a point coming down at night where I couldn't find my way any more. I was climbing by my headlight in the storm and I couldn't figure out how this ledge connected to the next.

'So I told my teammates on the radio that I would hunker down and wait till daylight, which was just a few hours off. But all the time I waited there, I knew if I fell asleep, I would die or wake up without feet or hands. So the real challenge was to stay awake and keep moving my hands and feet all the time to save them. I remember surviving that and then remembering, Oh, yeah, I went to the summit too!'

Yet it wasn't a triumph he could savour for long. When he reached Base Camp safely, he discovered that others from his expedition were close to the summit and one, Australian Mike Rheinberger, who was on his eighth attempt to get to the top, was in terrible trouble. He'd persevered up the north ridge despite the late hour and had reached the summit just before dark, but was too exhausted to make his way back down. He spent the night there and by the time the sun rose the next morning, he was too weak to descend.

Everyone tried to help, but in vain. 'He died, and watching that drama play out through the telescope and listening to it on the radio profoundly changed my perception of that climb,' says Hahn. 'It made me realise how lucky I had been at so many junctures.'

That wasn't the only disaster Hahn saw played out over his years on Everest, either. In 2001, he was part of a party who gave up their bid to reach the top to rescue five climbers – three Russians, an American and a Guatemalan – who'd been stranded overnight at an altitude where no one expected them to survive. Hahn and his fellow expedition members gave the near-comatose climbers oxygen, drugs, water and food in a rescue carried out higher than anyone had ever considered possible, even as others clawed their way past to reach the summit. For that, Hahn, with two others, received a medal for heroism from the American Alpine Club for selfless devotion at personal risk or sacrifice of a major objective.

The next year, he was guiding an expedition that had turned back 90 metres from the summit down through the Khumbu Icefall. He and four others were standing on a tricky ledge waiting to descend the next stage when they heard a noise 'like a 90-mile-per-hour subway train, like a dragon getting ready to blow fire at you'.

It was an avalanche of tonnes and tonnes of frozen ice coming from somewhere around 1800 metres above them. Everything began to shake and quiver. 'I guess I thought we were dead, so I was calmer than I should have been,' Hahn says. But all at once the ice slopes above the little group disintegrated, collapsed and finally, happily, disappeared into a void below them.

Later that year, he cheated death again when he was dispatched to help an injured climber on a mountain in Washington, D.C.

and the helicopter in which he was travelling crashed. He survived unscathed, so rescued the pilot and then went off and saved the climber. For that, he received yet another award.

In 2007, he was part of another dramatic Everest rescue. Hahn and Sherpa Phinjo Dorje stumbled on a female Nepalese climber who'd been left for dead on a steep slope about 550 metres from the summit. She was semi-conscious, suffering severe cerebral oedema, had run out of oxygen and was too weak to move. The pair risked their own lives to push and drag her back down to Camp IV at 7920 metres, and then carry her down on a sled and lower her by ropes to Camp III at 7300 metres.

'Everest is dangerous, but it's an incredible mountain,' says Hahn. 'It means a lot to me as it's the highest, it has a shape that pulls you in and it's always challenging, as well as having an enthrallingly rich history.

'It's never a given that you're going to be able to summit; I can't ever count on summitting it again. You have to be strong enough and lucky enough, and everything has to come together. Over the years, there've been times when an Everest expedition is like a meat grinder, and you come away from it shattered mentally and physically. I've watched people die up there and tried to save people. It's a place of epic experiences.'

In the past, Hahn has taken two young people up Everest, a seventeen-year-old American girl in 2009, and a sixteen-year-old American girl in 2011. Neither made the summit, both deciding to turn back despite being achingly close.

'I think Everest is a lot tougher for a young girl or boy than anyone else,' says Hahn. 'I couldn't even tie my shoelaces at Alyssa's age! It's okay for someone of that age to go to an event or a big contest for a day, but it's something else when it takes two months to complete. It's a lot of money and time away from your home and your family, you have to sit out bad weather and cope with false starts and it's tough to hear on the radio about people dying and people rescuing others in trouble. That's hard for any climber, but even more so for a teenager.

'At that stage, they have fewer life experiences to draw on and there's a lot of pressure on them to succeed. Someone that young will be climbing on a big stage, everyone knows about it, there'll be a lot of publicity, and you Facebook and blog your progress and you get a lot of people following you to urge you on. In those circumstances, it's difficult to keep perspective.

'It's hard to summit Everest, but it's still harder to decide not to summit when the circumstances aren't favourable. That's hard personally, and even harder to explain to others. You need the ability to turn around short of the summit if necessary, and if that's not possible, then Everest isn't a good place for a girl her age . . . or even a fifty-year-old!'

PART THREE

The Road to Mount Everest

CHAPTER 13

Climbing Kilimanjaro

'If you aren't in over your head, how do you know how tall you are?'
– T.S. ELIOT

On 20 June 2011, fourteen-year-old Alyssa Azar steps onto a plane to Nairobi, Kenya, her heart beating fast. Glenn is already in Tanzania, completing an earlier climb of Kilimanjaro with a couple of clients, and she's travelling with a member of the eight-strong group ready to take part in his second trip.

She tries to sleep before the plane stops in Dubai to refuel, but she's far too excited. For the tenth time, she goes over her list of equipment: sleeping bag, climbing gear, sunscreen, insect repellent, lip balm, handwash, wipes, tissues, energy bars, snack packs, microwaveable packs of roast beef and gravy, and tins of beans, spaghetti, tuna and diced peaches.

She checks her itinerary again. This is going to be an eight-day round trek, and on the seventh day they will hopefully reach the summit of Kilimanjaro, the dormant volcano that's the highest freestanding mountain in the world at 5895 metres above sea level. She's nervous about how well she'll handle that kind of altitude too; it's 531 metres higher than she's ever been before, on Everest Base Camp. In addition, she knows that you ascend much more quickly with Kilimanjaro than with the trek to Base Camp, so that will impact the body harder too. And then there's all the ice and snow close to the top, probably far more than she's seen on the Aussie 10.

But she's been training hard, and feels ready. She's taking nothing for granted, she knows she's been getting stronger and stronger, and she's determined to get out there and enjoy every moment of what she's doing.

Alyssa is the youngest person taking part in the trip, and her travel companion is, at fifty-six, the oldest. Cath Beutel has never been on a trip like this before, and she's just as nervous as Alyssa. It's always been an ambition of hers to climb Kilimanjaro, and she has far less experience of heights than Alyssa does. The pair have met a couple of times previously on walks Glenn arranged for training but, as they chat on the plane, Beutel is taken aback at how clearly, and forcefully, Alyssa can articulate her goals in life and how determined she is to achieve them. She's also struck at how young Alyssa is – only a couple of years older than her grandchildren – and thinks silently that most parents would be delighted if their children had just a tenth of that kind of drive.

By the time the plane finally arrives in Africa and the pair board the connecting flight to Kilimanjaro airport in neighbouring Tanzania, Alyssa is exhausted. She's beginning now to feel sleepy, but she won't let her eyes close. She's concentrating on the view out of the plane's window, hoping that she'll see the snow-streaked cone of Kilimanjaro rising out of the flat Tanzanian savannah that, up to Mount Meru 80 km to its west, has always been traditional Maasai country. The plane goes round the volcano as it's too high to fly over, and she's heard it often gives passengers a once-in-a-lifetime look at the summit and into the crater from the air. In the event, though, she's disappointed. The summit remains resolutely hidden by clouds.

The plane lands and Glenn's there to greet the pair. He hugs his daughter. He looks tired. The trek up the mountain is much harder than many people credit – 40 per cent of people who attempt it don't make the top, and the climb routinely takes lives each year through altitude sickness, heart attacks, slips and rock falls, killing tourists and guides alike. 'But it's very beautiful up there,' he tells his daughter. 'It's well worth it!' He drives them to join the others at their lodge in the middle of a coffee plantation in Arusha, the nearest town to Kilimanjaro. There, he delivers the official briefing to the trip and then they all relax, most going off to bed for an early night.

The next morning, Alyssa's up before dawn, too excited to sleep in. Kilimanjaro is going to be her second of the world's Seven Summits. She's already climbed Mount Kosciuszko, the highest peak in Australasia; this is the highest peak in Africa, and then there'll be only five left on the most common list of the seven: Mount McKinley in Alaska, the highest in North America; Aconcagua in Argentina, the highest in South America; Mount Elbrus in Russia, the highest in Europe; Mount Vinson, the highest in Antarctica; and, of course, Everest, the highest in Asia, and the world.

The group have breakfast at the lodge, then drive to the Lemosho Glades, the starting point of their climb, to meet their guides-cum-porters over morning tea. Glenn's chosen the Lemosho route over the five other routes up the mountain, mostly because of its beauty, remoteness and the great views it offers of Kilimanjaro. There are other much easier routes, but this group is fit, happy to test themselves and eager to ascend by a way that makes it unlikely they'll meet other trekkers. As they arrive, their local African porters sing them a beautiful song of welcome that touches everyone. Alyssa is moved. She now finally feels she's in Africa, and part of another culture.

It's a slow pace at the start, with everyone looking around at the scenery and trying to spot the buffalo, elephants and monkeys that the porters say have been seen along this stretch. It's through lush, fertile rainforest, with towering trees, ferns and thick bush, and occasional clearings for views. After an hour and a half they stop for lunch, then move off again along the narrow, undulating earth track that juts upwards for a steep climb every now and again, then flattens out. Sections through jungle, shaded by a canopy of trees, remind Alyssa of Kokoda, but then she remembers where she really is and feels excited all over again at being in Africa and walking up the side of its highest mountain.

One of the trekkers is businesswoman Sonia Taylor. She's intrigued that such a young girl is taking part, and asks Alyssa about her school, her sisters, her brother and what kind of training she does. She's a little surprised at how Alyssa politely answers but doesn't give too much away, and that she never starts any conversations. But she can see the young girl does listen, and takes in everyone else's conversations.

The group reaches their first campsite in plenty of time, a clearing surrounded by high trees called Forest Camp, or Mti Mkubwa – 'big tree' in the local language, Kiswahili. By the time they arrive, the porters have already unpacked, erected their tents and started cooking dinner. The trekkers sit around a fire drinking ginger tea and eating popcorn, waiting for dinner to be served in the mess tent and listening to the sounds of the rainforest. Alyssa's happy and relaxed, although she still feels a faint qualm about how she'll fare at altitude. At the start of the day they walked past a sign warning people to only tackle the climb if they were physically fit, to be aware of tiredness and heart conditions, and to drink four to five litres of fluid a day. Also up there was the ominous instruction: 'If symptoms of mountain sickness or high altitude diseases persist, please descend immediately and seek medical treatment.' Alyssa doesn't sleep well.

The next morning they rise early, have hot Milo and breakfast and then start walking again. Once the track leaves the forest, it climbs steeply through tall savannah grasses, heather and volcanic rock swathed in lichen, the path crossing a number of small streams. There are fewer and fewer trees due to the decreasing amount of oxygen in the air. As the track reaches higher on the Shira caldera, one of the three historic areas of volcanic activity on Kilimanjaro, the day grows hotter and dustier. Alyssa has a small headache most of the day, but drinks as much water from her supplies as she can, hoping it's from dehydration rather than the altitude.

They're now at about 3600 metres, and up on the top of the Shira ridge spectacular views of Kilimanjaro suddenly unfold. Alyssa immediately feels better. From there, the trail drops gently to the next stop, Shira Camp. That afternoon, as she's unpacking her gear close to a stream, a bee swoops past her, almost brushing her cheek. 'That,' someone tells her, 'is lucky. It means someone is talking about you, and while it might not be nice, it's lucky it didn't sting you . . .'

Day three is a trek across the Shira Plateau to Shira Two Camp, at 3800 metres. Alyssa notes how the shrubbery is becoming gradually sparser and sparser, until the terrain becomes exposed, giving way to alpine desert. But unlike most treks, when you rarely see your end goal until you're almost upon it, all day there are stunning views of Kilimanjaro and its summit, Kibo. Alyssa decides she's in love with Africa, this amazing continent with beautiful mountains in settings so incredibly different from the Himalaya.

One of the other women on the trek is Ana Ivkosic, who has taken the place of someone who dropped out at the last minute. This is the first time she's met Alyssa, and she's staggered by her determination and mental strength. She herself is finding the trek quite intense, but she notes how Alyssa never grumbles and, while she's not talkative by any stretch of the imagination, she listens to what people say in a way that most teens don't.

The night is spent at Barranco Camp, and everyone wakes the

next morning to icy temperatures, with all the drink bottles frozen solid. Alyssa shrugs on her cosy pink fleece, ties a scarf around her neck and then warms up with the steep walk uphill to the Lava Tower, a 90 metre–high volcanic plug – formed when magma hardens on an active volcano creating a lava neck – sitting at 4600 metres above sea level. At this spot, lava flows from the three volcanic craters Kibo, Shira and Mawenzi coat the ground, and it's here the band stops to have lunch. Then there's a steep descent and a small uphill walk, until finally there's the long, winding meander down the valley.

Alyssa walks with her dad at the back of the group, and Cath Beutel is struck by the closeness of their relationship. She feels it's lovely to see a bond like that between father and daughter, and while she knows they share the same love of adventure and climbing, she can clearly see the mutual love and respect they have for each other too.

Neither are particularly demonstrative about the affection they feel for each other, but they do form a very tight unit. 'We've always been close and, out of my four children, she's the only one who's been interested in walking, fitness and adventures,' says Glenn. 'But she's always been someone who bites off more than she can chew, and then she'll chew like hell!'

In turn, Alyssa says her dad is one of her real heroes. 'I really admire him,' she says. 'He's always believed in me and, ever since I was young, told me and my sisters that our size or the fact we were girls never mattered; we could achieve anything we set our minds and hearts to. He's always been like that. He's the person who lifts people up and tries to inspire them to follow their dreams. He got into thinking about positive quotes and mindsets, and he's made that a big part of who I am, too.

'We do clash at times. We're both strong personalities and when we want something, we go after it 100 per cent. We're both pretty stubborn. We'll argue about decisions, about things we want to do, stuff around the house, the usual things, and disagreements can last awhile sometimes. But he has a great work ethic and perseverance, and they're things I try to copy. He's always passionate about what he does, which really inspires me.'

Day five is a much easier four-hour, fifteen-minute walk, but it does include the one and a half hour trek up the Barranco Wall, with a scramble on hands and feet at the end. Alyssa's been particularly looking forward to that, and enjoys the sudden rush. She still has a small headache though, and later in the afternoon starts feeling sick. As the group moves down to the Karanga Valley campsite, beneath the icefalls of the Heim, Kersten and Decken glaciers, she secretly worries she might not be okay for the summit. But she hides it well.

Day six is the one she's really looking forward to. Everyone is woken at 4 a.m. and they start at 5.15 with a three-hour walk, first uphill and then down into a long valley, before descending to Barafu Camp on a small, flat, exposed area on the ridge. It's quite bleak and icy but they have an early lunch, then try to sleep for three hours until dinner. After that meal they rest again, then get up at 11 p.m., have some Milo and start their ascent to the summit, the Kibo Crater.

It's a long, slow shuffle in the dark with their head torches lighting the way on the mountain. Everyone struggles to breathe, although the guides don't seem to be troubled at all by the fact that, at that height, every breath contains 50 per cent less oxygen. Instead, they continually sing to the group to keep them going as they trek along lots of switchbacks, between the Rebmann and Ratzel glaciers. It's pretty hard going. Alyssa feels like she's experiencing some altitude sickness; eating is difficult and she feels full all the time. She also feels dizzy and nauseous, as if she wants to vomit – but her body won't let her.

Others in the group have no idea she's feeling under par. She hasn't mentioned, or shown, that she's having even the slightest difficulty. Glenn, however, knows his daughter well, and realises she's doing it tough. An hour on, her head is by now throbbing in pain, her breath is rasping in her chest, and the air feels so thin, every gasp hurts. At any moment she feels she might throw up and collapse in a heap on the rocky ground.

Walking beside her, Glenn pauses. 'Are you okay?' he asks her worriedly. 'Do you want to stop?'

In some ways, yes, she wants to stop more than anything else in the world. She wants to stop climbing ever higher, to where she knows she'll have to work even harder for every breath, to where the tightness across her temples will clamp itself like an iron fist and squeeze until she'll be blinded by the light, to where every step will feel like she has a tonne of lead tied to each foot.

But she looks up at him, summons all her strength and smiles. 'No, Dad,' she replies, as evenly as she can. 'I'm good.'

She knows if she doesn't beat Kilimanjaro, she won't be allowed to go on to try for the roof of the world.

Her dad, however, doesn't look convinced. 'You look like you're going to be sick,' he tells her. 'You're incredibly pale.' She nods, mutely, but continues walking. He sighs. 'Okay, then,' he says. 'If you want to carry on, be sick and then let's get on. We don't have much time.'

Alyssa nods again. Although the climb is proving a massive challenge, she's worked too hard and dreamt too long about conquering such peaks in training for Everest to stop.

Five hours later, the group hits the first milestone, Stella Point at the crater rim at 5730 metres. They all shout and high-five each other and hug, then sit down for a rest. It strikes Alyssa that they may have been celebrating a touch too soon – it's still another hour to the actual summit. She steels herself for the last big push, and discovers it's extremely tough going. Her fingers feel frozen and they sting like hell but she tries hard to think of other things. This last stretch is proving the hardest trek she's ever done.

Finally, at about 6.30 a.m. on 1 July 2011, the group scuffles up to the true summit and a big wooden sign: 'Congratulations! You are now at Uhuru Peak, Tanzania, 5895 metres, Africa's highest point, world's highest free-standing mountain.' They reach it just as the sun is rising in a glorious orange haze, slowly lighting the peak and the wide green savannah below.

Alyssa stands and marvels as the view slowly comes into focus out of the darkness, knowing it was well worth the struggle. Up there, it certainly does feel exactly like its nickname, 'the roof of Africa'. She sits down with the rest of the group to watch the sunrise. She's tired and feels emotional, and has a headache, but she's too happy to care. She poses with her dad, and then the guides, for a few photos, and everyone else takes photos too. She's thrilled to have climbed to the top of her second of the Seven Summits. She can hardly believe it.

Alyssa phones her mum from the summit on Glenn's satellite phone. Therese is amazed she's been able to phone from the summit of Kilimanjaro – especially when she can't even get mobile phone coverage in Target in Toowoomba – but is delighted to hear from her, and relieved. She's happy her daughter sounds so happy, but immediately suspects this won't be the end of the adventures.

After half an hour on the top, the group then walk the three hours back down to Barafu, have a short sleep, then have lunch before descending to Mweka Hut and receiving their certificates to show they made it.

As the group is walking out that afternoon, Alyssa sidles up to Glenn. 'Dad,' she says. 'I want to talk to you about something.'

He looks at her, not having any idea what might be coming up. 'Yes, Alyssa?'

She takes a deep breath. 'Last year, I heard you say something, and I wondered if you meant it.' She pauses and he nods, urging her to go on. 'Well, I heard you giving a speech to a group and you were saying how they should encourage kids to do adventurous things.'

Glenn steals a look at her. He now has a feeling he knows what she's going to say. She doesn't look at him.

'You said that if I ever wanted to climb Everest, you'd support me. You wouldn't want me to do it, but you would fully support me if I wanted to enough. You said how kids could sometimes have big dreams, and it was up to parents to help them come true . . .'

He grins at her. He knew this day might come, but he didn't expect his own words to be quoted back at him, or for it to come so soon. Everest was a big mountain for such a little girl, but hell, he couldn't fault her determination, nor her commitment. She battled sickness up there, but still carried on. He nods.

'It'll be a lot of hard work and training and money,' he says finally. 'You'll also have to climb other mountains first to make sure you're up to it. But yes, if you still want to do it in a couple of years, I'll do everything I can to help.'

Her face immediately lights up and she whoops with delight. He laughs to see her so animated.

'Thanks, Dad!' she says. 'That's great. I can't wait!' And then she speeds off, already trying to work out what's likely to be the earliest year she'll be allowed to try.

CHAPTER 14

Everest's First Australian Woman: Brigitte Muir

Twenty-two years earlier, Australian climber Brigitte Muir was, like Alyssa Azar, climbing Kilimanjaro, also as her second of the Seven Summits. She'd previously climbed Alaska's Mount McKinley, the highest peak in North America, and she too dreamt of one day climbing Everest. Eight years later, at the age of thirty-eight, she became the first Australian female ever to summit, after four dramatic attempts.

Her first in 1995 she called off at 8200 metres because her husband and climbing partner, Jon Muir, fell ill. On her second try, shortly afterwards, she was close to the top but was abandoned by her two climbing partners when she stopped to change the batteries in her failing head torch. Unable to see in the dark, she was forced to wait till sunrise to make a move – by which time she didn't have enough oxygen to reach the summit and get back down again.

She returned in 1996, that terrible year on Everest when eleven people lost their lives in a single night, caught by cataclysmic weather conditions. She'd been sitting in camp waiting it out, hoping for a break in the storms when the news came from higher up of a disaster of epic proportions.

But in May the next year, 1997, she finally stood on top of the world, becoming not only the first Australian woman there, but also the first Australian – male or female – to have successfully climbed each of the Seven Summits. But the joy of her triumph didn't last long. She very nearly didn't make it back again after a severe attack of bronchitis on the mountainside, complete exhaustion and 'an eternity of suffering'.

Yet today, she wants only to encourage Alyssa in her quest. 'I'm very supportive of any person who wants to get out there and challenge themselves and inspire others to follow their heart,' she says. 'I've always believed it's important to live our dreams, rather than dream our lives. But you always have to go into such things with both eyes, and your heart, open.

'People tend to learn what they need to learn on big mountains. Alyssa's climbed other mountains, so she's been keen to put in the time to develop her experience and gut instincts about what's right and wrong. You can't always follow your guide on places like Everest. It's always important to trust yourself.'

Alyssa is a long-time fan of Muir. 'She attempted Everest a few times, but when she didn't succeed she just kept on going,' says Alyssa. 'That really resounded with me, especially since she is a woman. She's a great example for me to follow.'

Muir grew up in Belgium, where she discovered caving as a teenager and fell in love with outdoor adventures. She moved to Australia in 1983, and in 1988 began her own quest to climb each continent's highest mountain. She says she simply loves pushing herself, hearing the crunch of snow beneath her feet and the feeling of achievement when she reaches a summit and successfully comes down again.

Now based in western Victoria, she doesn't climb mountains any more, choosing to challenge herself in different ways: motivational speaking, painting, writing, making documentaries and raising funds for charity.

'I'd been climbing mountains for thirty years and seen a lot of friends die,' she says. 'Then in 1999 I went to Makalu, the fifth highest mountain in the world, close to Everest, and a very good friend of mine, Danish climber Michael Joergensen, died coming down from the summit. After that I couldn't get back on the mountain. I'd loved mountains since I was a little girl, but I'd achieved my personal goals and wasn't learning any more. I didn't need to challenge myself on big mountains. I needed to move on to something completely different.

'Alyssa is only young, but I don't think wisdom has an age. It's important she listens to her body, especially at altitude. I don't think anyone really gets into their stride with altitude until their late thirties or forties. When I first started climbing, I'd get headaches and would have to go down. But after doing that, my body would remember what it was like to be at high altitude and would switch on. You just have to be very patient out there.'

She believes Alyssa's age will put her at a disadvantage as far as stamina is concerned. In all Muir's years of mountain climbing, she's discovered that older people often fare much better than the young. 'A lot of younger people burn out quickly,' she says. 'That's also a good lesson to learn with patience. High altitude is a waiting game and it can be as tedious as watching paint dry. You get cold and tired and fed up.

'But you have to learn to live in the moment, look at the beauty around you, watch the incredible sunrises and sunsets on the mountain and feel a part of them, and appreciate everything around you. Everest is a very dangerous place, but it's also a very beautiful one. It's very special.'

Her words strike a real chord with Alyssa. Making four attempts on the summit is a wonderful example of the kind of determination that is sometimes necessary to achieve such a worthwhile goal. And to hear Muir talking about taking the time to drink in the beauty of Everest makes her yearn even harder for the Himalayas. She wants so much to be back there, looking up at Everest, it actually physically hurts.

CHAPTER 15

Setting the Goal

'Don't bend; don't water it down; don't try to make it logical; don't edit your own soul according to the fashion. Rather, follow your most intense obsessions mercilessly.'

– FRANZ KAFKA

When Alyssa Azar arrived back in Australia from Kilimanjaro in July 2011, her mind was made up. She was still only fourteen, but she now knew with more clarity than she'd ever known anything that Everest was in her sights. Everything, from here on in, would be focused on getting to the top of the highest mountain in the world.

'I loved that whole experience of Kilimanjaro,' says Alyssa. 'I loved Africa and it was great to be having another adventure on a whole new continent. I loved those mountains. The mornings were always cold and dusty and the people were so friendly and gorgeous. They were amazing, and it was a great experience.

'I was pleased how I went with the altitude as well. I definitely felt it, but then my body did get a bit more used to it as we went along. And that made me even more hopeful about climbing Everest someday soon.'

Again, there was a lot of media attention on her after reaching the top of Kilimanjaro by one of its most challenging routes and raising over $70 000 for Kids Helpline, but at every opportunity she mentioned her end goal. 'I'm going to climb Everest,' she declared to the world. 'I like to test myself against nature and that will be the toughest test of all.'

Usually, after arriving home from a trip, she would settle in and take her time, letting her heart decide where in the world she'd be off to explore next. But this time she knew there was no more thinking to be done: it was time for the big one. 'I enjoyed the trips I had done, but there was something about aiming even bigger that attracted me to this mountain,' she says. 'Once that dream began, I knew this was my next trip. No question about it.'

It was then that a friend discovered that if she summitted Everest before the age of eighteen, Alyssa would be the youngest non-Sherpa female in the world ever to reach the top. She'd have smashed another world record, along with her Kokoda one.

The idea of another record was appealing, but Alyssa refused to let that be her main motivation. 'It's not about records, that doesn't concern me too much,' she says. 'It's about dreaming big, challenging myself and going for something. Yes, if I achieve my dream I will be the youngest non-Sherpa female and the youngest Australian ever to summit Everest but, for me, it's about my passion for climbing, not the record.'

If she stood any chance of success, however, she knew she was going to have to prepare carefully for the climb. Before she even set foot on Everest, she'd have to climb other high peaks to hone her skills and improve her capacity to work at altitude, and to learn more about rock and ice climbing. And she didn't want to allow anything, or anyone, to stand in her way. Everything on her personal timetable was now drawn up to focus on training hard enough to one day tackle Everest.

One of her major obstacles, she believed, was school. So when she returned from Kilimanjaro she didn't return to the classroom. Instead, she started distance education. It meant she'd be able to do her lessons in her own time over the internet, just with conference calls and occasional trips to Brisbane, which she could fit in around her training and in the periods she wouldn't be away trekking or climbing.

Therese wasn't keen on Alyssa leaving school so young. 'I would have preferred her to have stayed at school, she knows that! You worry, What if she got an injury and couldn't do everything she wanted to do, and then, without a good education, was unable to achieve in other areas? You don't want your kids to miss out on anything, and we all go through those years where we hate high school. I thought it'd be better for her to finish school, but she was sure this was what she wanted.

'Also, I know distance education is hard to do on your own. You have to be really motivated to do the work in your own time, and set deadlines. Mind you, if anyone can do it, Alyssa can. She's good at setting herself a task and doing it. She's never had a problem with that. It's a lonely mission she's on. There won't be many people on that mountain . . .'

But Alyssa's life still wasn't without its problems. Glenn and Therese had separated again, and Glenn moved out to a house nearby. The children were each asked where they wanted to live, and Brooklyn, now sixteen, Christian, seven, and Samantha, four, opted to stay with their mother. Alyssa went to live with Glenn, and agreed to stay with her mum whenever he went away. The two youngest would come to stay at their father's every second week or when their mum, now working as an emergency nurse and studying pharmacy, was working shifts. Brooklyn, interested in studying photography and beauty therapy, would visit, and Glenn went to see her, but she said she didn't want to stay.

'It was sad,' Glenn's sister Tanya says. 'Glenn was doing a lot of work building his brand and business and was away a lot, and he wanted to give the family everything he could. But at the same time, it was hard for Therese. There was a lot of pressure on her, especially with Christian, and she's really smart and really determined and driven as well. And Alyssa and Glenn had always had a massive connection from when she was very tiny, so she felt that too.'

The break-up of the family was distressing for Alyssa, but she tried hard not to let it affect her. She'd always been close to Christian and Samantha, and missed them being around, although she still spent a lot of time with them when they did come to stay. Samantha was always happy to see her and play with her, and she used the time with Christian to build even stronger bonds. He adored her but he could be difficult, and his autism meant he could suddenly get terribly upset for no discernible reason. Alyssa always made an extra effort to be patient and attentive. That was often tested; she had to watch him continually to make sure he didn't run off, or hurt himself. But the pair always had a lot of fun together. 'We get on really well,' she says. 'We both love hanging out together. And however hard it is for the rest of us, you have to remember that it's much, much harder for Christian. Looking at how he copes with some of life's difficulties, I'm filled with admiration for him. I think he has really taught me a lot, and helped me become a better person.'

As for the break-up of the family, she's philosophical. 'It is hard but people have to decide what's best for them,' she says. 'I try not to let it get to me. Brooklyn and I were old enough to decide what we preferred to do, and we all mix based on schedules. Really, it works better with the climbing if I'm with Dad. It's easy access to training and Dad and I work a lot of it together. I still spend a lot of time with Dad, and see loads of Christian and Sammy, and I do catch up with Mum, so I'm happy that's worked out. Having my climbing, and all the training and planning that goes into it, is a great way to direct my energy into something positive.'

Glenn struggled, however. 'To be brutally honest, it's probably the worst thing I've ever been through,' he says. 'We'd grown apart over the past five to six years and we'd separated a couple of times.

But it doesn't get any easier. I look back at me and Therese and think, Wow! We didn't really know each other. Therese's not interested in the gym and adventure travel; she's very clever and loves to study and reads textbooks and gets a lot of pleasure out of them. And, well, I would imagine I can be pretty hard to live with.

'I get something into my head and just go for it – Alyssa's very, very similar to me there.'

* * *

With Alyssa's course now set, she nominated 2014 as the year she'd make her attempt on Everest, when she'd be seventeen.

She knew the climb and the other peaks in the run-up would be an expensive undertaking, so she hoped she'd be able to attract some sponsorship to help with the costs. In January 2012, just after her fifteenth birthday, she sent out a press release through Glenn's Adventure Professionals. 'I love adventure and testing myself to my limits, so I've signed up to attempt the summit in 2014,' she wrote. 'I'm not that fussed about records, or holding the title of being the youngest person to achieve something. I just love to climb mountains and test myself. It's when I'm out against nature that I seem to have the most fun.'

Website and graphic designer Daniel Borg, who'd been on one of Glenn's 2009 Kokoda treks and had since started working with him on his website, met Alyssa at Glenn's launch of Adventure Professionals. He heard about her Everest quest, and contacted Glenn, offering to sponsor her through his company, the multimedia studio psyborg. He thought her obvious determination to make things happen, as well as her youth, would make her a great ambassador for his brand.

'I had a lot of confidence and trust in Glenn after having been to Kokoda with him,' says Borg. 'so I'd heard about Alyssa's adventures and I thought I'd like to support her, even if nothing ended up happening. I could see how confident and goal-oriented she was, and how she'd taken on her dad's belief system that you can do anything if you work hard enough, and believe. I thought that kind of mental strength worked well with my company's slogan, "Part Mind, Part Machine". And she's young and cool, and our branding just fits well together.'

He became Alyssa's first sponsor and also helped her set up her own website, and design business cards, a logo and a letterhead. She was thrilled. 'It feels, with psyborg's help, my trip is really taking off,' she says. 'To have someone like that come on board and believe in my dream . . . I couldn't thank him enough.'

The fresh wave of media interest also brought other unexpected attention. She started getting messages of support, and she printed some of them out, thrilled that she was having an impact, however small. 'Alyssa, you are an inspiration to other young kids,' one read. 'There should be more of you out exploring the outdoors. It makes me proud . . . Good luck on your summit attempt.'

With her website up and running, she started blogging about her life and her plans for Everest. She'd always loved writing in her diary, and while it was strange to think of other people reading about her life, she enjoyed putting her thoughts down on paper. A voracious reader, particularly of books about anyone doing anything heroic or adventurous, she also loved writing about what she'd learnt from them. And then she set out a preparation schedule that included another Kokoda trek, rock and ice climbing in New Zealand around its highest mountain, Mount Cook, the mountain Island Peak or Cho Oyu in Nepal and then, finally, Mount Aconcagua in the Andes in Argentina, another one of the Seven Summits. By then, she reasoned, she should be ready.

'I'm a big believer in daring to dream and then doing everything physically and mentally possible to achieve those dreams,' she says. 'You only live once, right? I know what I've signed up for, and it's totally on my head. I'm so excited that I want to get up each day and push myself.'

Alyssa now went to Glenn's gym three, sometimes four times a day to train. She also started doing CrossFit, the strength and conditioning program that aims to improve muscular strength, cardio-respiratory endurance and flexibility, and is practised by many military units, police squads and professional athletes worldwide. It's based around Workouts of the Day, or WODs, posted on the founding company's website, to increase functional fitness – training the body to be able to carry out real-life activities in real-life positions, not just lifting weights on machines that set up perfect posture first.

For Alyssa, a typical daily workout included standing-start jumps onto a raised platform, push-ups, kettle bells – the bell-shaped weights that are swung around the body – rowing on a machine, pull-ups and skipping. She augmented that with more running, boxing and walking with either a heavy pack on her back, or strapped into a harness dragging a tyre around behind her. Competitive boxing she opted to give up in order to concentrate on her overall mountain fitness.

'CrossFit will probably be the best thing I can do for my climbing,' she says. 'It doesn't just give me muscles and strength, it also trains my body how to properly use that strength, and gives me a lot more endurance. Rather than just lifting weights, it involves every movement I'll need to be strong enough to pull myself up a mountain.'

Glenn helped her draw up her training schedules, and very soon she became used to the feeling of soreness she woke up with every day. She started welcoming it as a sign she'd been working hard, and making progress. He also helped her time herself running 5 km, and then 7 km, so she'd be able to judge how quickly she'd be able to improve on her personal bests.

She made her workouts even harder with an elevation training mask, which looks just like an old-fashioned gas mask, to restrict her breathing. It has three different interchangeable nose pieces with which you can control the flow of air, to mimic the difficulty of breathing at high altitude. She started using it daily, sometimes when doing kettle bells or boxing, and sometimes when she ran, particularly on the treadmill. She hoped it would condition her lungs by creating pulmonary resistance, and strengthen the diaphragm. Anything she could do to get herself altitude-fit, she'd try.

She took a part-time job waitressing at a local cafe to earn extra money for her trips, and in her spare time, she studied climbing and its technicalities. She practised all the knots used with rope climbing, and got to know all the climbing devices, like ice axes, crampons – the spikes screwed into boots to give them traction on ice and snow – and carabiners, spring-loaded metal loops used to connect different components.

She also carefully researched each of the mountains she'd be tackling and devoured books and DVDs on climbing, and on Everest. She wrote out her goals and motivational quotes she found and posted them up where she'd see them, and put photos of all the mountains on her bedroom walls, as well as on her computer and phone. 'I believe if I focus and give this major goal everything I have, I will achieve it,' she says. 'Having images of my goals everywhere makes it very real and forces me to focus on my goals whenever I see them. It's very inspirational and means positivity becomes almost second nature, making success even more likely.

'I've always believed that if you're going to do something, don't do it half-heartedly. Give it everything you've got and really commit to it. Give yourself every advantage and never sell yourself short. You are more capable than you think!'

Glenn's gym was getting busier by the day, but Alyssa always found space to work out on her own, or she occasionally joined in others' activities. Glenn and Alyssa were both surprised by the numbers now flocking to the gym. When Glenn started training others, he was only the second personal trainer to operate in Toowoomba who wasn't employed by a gym, and now there were hundreds. Still, he seemed among the most successful.

'The more, the merrier,' he says. 'You have to remember that only between 5 and 7 per cent of Australians take some kind of professional fitness training. So some people might say, Why get into an industry that involves such a small percentage of people? I say that means 95 per cent of the population are potential customers! Gyms aren't for everyone. Some people like to swim and go bike riding, but it's all about getting people moving.

'And it can be so rewarding. I've had clients who come looking so unhealthy, they can't run three laps of the gym – and it's not that big. So to see them get on track and then looking so healthy and feeling so good, it's great. I was talking to a guy who was running for local politics. Physically, he was overweight and looked bad. He said in his role, he was always eating and drinking. I said, Come and see me! But he said at his age it wasn't worth it. I asked him how old he was, and he said forty-five. I said, Mate, you've probably got another forty years to go, you don't dare throw in the towel so soon!

'People who exercise might live longer, but they also live *better*. Who'd want to spend the last ten years of their lives in bed? You do hear of people in their forties who die of heart attacks doing exercise, but it's rare. It's all about feeling good within yourself. I'm all about helping other people achieve things, that's what makes me tick and I use my own personal errors as examples. I don't hide from the things I've done wrong. It's pretty cool to be able to achieve a goal yourself and it's pretty cool to help others to do the same thing.'

Glenn's Adventure Professionals was also doing well, with his trips growing more and more popular. The Kokoda Track remained his favourite. Glenn knew 2012 was going to be a big year, since it was the seventieth anniversary of the World War II Kokoda campaign. Alyssa asked if she could come along, and he was pleased she was so keen. He agreed and she nominated his April 2012 Kokoda trip to be her next adventure, her next training session for Everest.

She'd be in good company. Even though there were now around thirty operators running treks on Kokoda, Glenn's trips were still heavily subscribed. 'There are some really good operators that have come in, but there are also some real cowboys out there who just throw trips together with minimal insurance or backup and just hope nothing goes wrong,' says Glenn. 'Nearly every trip you come across another group coming the other way unprepared, and something always happens that makes you wonder.'

One time, he ran into a man with a group of high school kids. He stopped Glenn and his medic and told them that one of the girls was really sick. The medic took a look and said, 'I could be wrong, but I suspect she has meningitis – you need to get her out of here ASAP.' The man replied that he was planning to wait another day to see if she'd come good. Glenn was horrified. 'I think that's a dangerous game,' he told the man. 'You need to get her out of here as fast as you can.' He then had another thought, and asked him if the kids were insured. 'I don't know,' the man replied with a shrug. 'Maybe their parents have got insurance as part of their program.'

'It's amazing,' says Glenn. 'Some people don't have insurance, don't have an evacuation plan, they just hope nothing goes wrong. We ended up organising the evacuation for him.'

Another time he chanced on two Brits walking on their own, trying to do the track quickly in four days. One was fine and he and Glenn had a chat about the military history of the area. Then the other arrived, stumbling and sounding incoherent. 'Mate, are you going all right?' Glenn asked him. 'No,' he answered. 'No, not really.' Glenn asked him if he needed some help, but immediately his friend stepped in. 'He's fine,' he insisted. 'He'll be okay.'

Glenn was still concerned, and asked them if they had a satellite phone with them. They didn't, but the one who was coping well said there were CB radios along the track. 'But none of them are working,' Glenn said. 'You could be in trouble if you don't have a sat phone.' 'No, I've been here before,' the man retorted. 'Then you should know not to come here without communications,' snapped Glenn. 'This is a really tough jungle.' But the man wouldn't listen, and hustled his friend away.

The pair headed off but Glenn saw the one who was struggling had fouled himself, and looked on the brink of collapse. He knew the pair weren't even through the worst of it yet: there were still some big hills to go. The tough guy could well be playing with his friend's life. So Glenn raced back up the hill to them, and got one of his party to take the strong one aside before he fronted up to the one in trouble. 'Look, mate, do you want to get out of here?' Glenn asked him. He nodded mutely. 'Have you got insurance?' The man shook his head. 'Well, it's going to cost you about five grand.' The man shrugged. 'I don't care,' he said. 'I just want to get out of here.' So Glenn called a chopper and left as he heard it approach.

But apart from the people who tried to trek Kokoda when they obviously hadn't done any exercise for years, or those who arrived with a few cans of food and a great deal of misplaced hope, or even those carrying tonnes of tins of beans and no can-opener, it was always a trip Glenn relished.

'One of the things I love about Kokoda is that you don't have phones – apart from the satellite phone for emergencies – and people can't contact you,' he says. 'And out there, it's so peaceful and quiet, I solve the world's problems. Sometimes I can't see a way out of problems and I feel I can't take any more pressure, but you get out there into the jungle, with no mobile phones, no internet, and just walk through trees and talk to people, and somehow you get some real clarity and realise your problems aren't that big a deal.'

Over the years, he's taken a huge variety of people out there. There have been fourteen- and fifteen-year-old kids who have gone with their parents, and he's watched some amazing relationships develop. The kids started interacting with their parents as young adults, he says, and their parents started responding differently to them.

'A lot of people need to have their boundaries pushed a little to realise how capable they really are. For a lot of people doing Kokoda, it's the first time they've even camped. And it can be life changing – for good or bad! We call it the Kokoda Curse. Women sometimes do Kokoda, then come back and get divorced. One woman cried on top of every mountain, and at the end of it she told me her husband had organised an intervention for her when she'd told him she was going to Kokoda, with his parents and her parents. They told her she had kids and was being irresponsible going there, as she could die. It was incredible. But by the end, she said she felt so much stronger.'

Glenn's favourite trip was in July 2011, when he went over to lead a trek of Afghanistan veterans who'd all been badly affected by their time there, whether with severe physical injuries or Post-Traumatic Stress Disorder. One of the men was Damien Thomlinson, a former commando who'd lost both his legs after the vehicle he was in drove over a Taliban bomb. His mate Scott Palmer dragged him from the wreckage, tourniqued his wounds and saved his life, but was then killed in a chopper crash a week before he was due to return to Australia. Thomlinson was joined on the trek by Palmer's father – whose last conversation with his son had been about doing Kokoda together one day – and the whole Kokoda trek was filmed by Channel 7's *Sunday Night* program.

It was hard, a lot harder than they'd imagined. 'Damien's got prosthetics but the computer that controls them locks if it senses that he's falling, and the steps on Kokoda are so high, every time he tried to take a step his leg locked. So he took one leg off and used crutches,' says Glenn. 'But he'd lost half of his shoulder and triceps so he didn't have the strength in his upper body. Half the time we'd start walking in the dark while everyone else was asleep, and they'd overtake us very early in the morning. He would then walk until his arms fatigued and he couldn't lift himself any more. Then the locals would make a stretcher and they and some of the other soldiers would stretcher-carry him across the track.

'We would get in late at night and they were long, hard days. Some of these soldiers would carry two backpacks while the others would carry the stretcher. They really showed what being a soldier was about – and we made it across the track. It got quite emotional at times. But that was a really cool thing to be a part of.'

* * *

Glenn and Alyssa set off for Kokoda in April 2012 with a full contingent of trekkers intent on commemorating the seventieth anniversary. Alyssa's eager to return; she was so young the first time and this trip will be much more about the history. She also feels she knows much more about the mindset of soldiers, since learning the lessons of *Warrior Training* and knowing them almost by heart.

In the meantime, Glenn has actually written to the book's author, Keith Fennell, telling him how much he liked his book. Fennell wrote back to thank him, and the two started communicating. They have plenty in common, having both served in the army and having similar interests. Slowly, a friendship has steadily been building, with Alyssa watching on with interest.

This time on the trek, she's much more relaxed: she's confident she'll be able to do it, although she knows it's never easy. Also, she's started helping her dad with the organising, as they have around fifty people trekking across a few groups, and she's keen to learn more about what leading adventure treks involve. One day, she hopes, she might be leading treks herself.

'It's wonderful to be on the track in the anniversary year and over Anzac Day,' Alyssa says. 'I knew it was going to be the best Kokoda experience I'd ever had. Being on the track where our diggers fought is very humbling.

'It's funny, though, because there are so many people from all parts of Australia, I didn't think any of them would really know me. I thought I'd just tag quietly along, helping Dad. But instead I get bombarded with questions: Do you remember this? Do you remember that? It's a very different experience to what I'm used to, but it's an enjoyable trip at the same time. Of course, I'm older now too, so I don't get anything like the same reaction from the local villagers, so it's nice to have a bit less attention there!'

Watching on, Greg Chamberlain, a friend of Glenn's who used to work at the gym and is now running another group for him, wonders how Alyssa will cope with the group dynamics. He knows her as a very quiet girl back home who spends a lot of time working out on her own.

'But she mixes very well with everyone,' he says. 'We have people on that trip from fifteen to fifty-plus and she gets on with them all. Normally girls her age would have trouble with that, but she doesn't. As they trek, some in the group make up funny songs about people in the group, and everyone sings them to a well-known tune they nominate, to keep themselves going. She joins in with all that. At the same time, she's like a little sponge. She listens to others and watches how we lead the treks, and soaks it all up. She's pretty impressive.'

The weather is worse this time, however, and that's a challenge. Eventually, everyone gives up on trying to keep themselves, their clothes and their gear dry. Alyssa merely welcomes the rain and damp as another way of getting used to discomfort.

'It's all about discipline,' she says. 'Discipline is going through pain to achieve your goals and become who you want to be. I'm willing to do maybe what others aren't to get where I need to go. Sometimes things get very tough and you need to have courage and discipline to get through those times. If a goal is worth achieving it won't be easy, but it will definitely be worth it.'

Every new hurdle Alyssa gets over, she celebrates it as another achievement in her bid to get up Everest. 'I have shown myself that nothing is impossible,' she says. 'I am just a fifteen-year-old girl from a small town in Australia, but I was always taught to believe in my dreams and to become bigger and better.

'My goal of climbing Everest comes from my pure love of the mountains, nature and adventure. But I have to say, if I could encourage anyone to go out and truly live and believe in the "crazy" and "impossible" dreams they have, that would be very fulfilling for me.'

CHAPTER 16

Everest's Youngest Australian: Rex Pemberton

There were always plenty of people keen to tell Alyssa Azar that her plan to climb Everest was crazy and that she was far too young to attempt anything so monumental. Often, she'd retreat to her books both about and by people who'd managed to summit, and watch films over and over again about their triumphs over adversity. She also kept a close eye on other people who had attempted the climb, and followed their progress carefully.

One in particular captured her imagination. Sydneysider Rex Pemberton was just twenty-one years old when, in 2005, he became the youngest Australian ever to climb to the summit.

Pemberton grew up rock climbing with his dad and brother from the age of eight and ascended his first mountain, in South America, at sixteen. Then, inspired by the achievements of fellow Australian Jesse Martin who, in 1999 at the age of eighteen, had become the youngest person ever to sail solo around the world unassisted, he wanted to conquer Everest.

'I've always believed in following my passion and seeing where it would lead,' he says now. 'And Everest was where it led. I knew it would be tough, and I prepared mentally and physically. I read a lot of books, watched a lot of documentaries, learnt all I could about the mountain, and hoped I'd be okay.'

During his climb, Alyssa followed his progress closely, especially when a massive avalanche destroyed sixty tents at Camp I and Pemberton lost a lot of his oxygen and climbing gear. As he continued on up, bad weather arrived, and forced other members of his expedition team down. The monsoon season had arrived late, and strong winds blasted the mountain every day. But Pemberton kept going.

'I suppose I identified with him a bit more than many others as he was quite young too,' says Alyssa. 'I was willing him on. I felt he had a lot of determination, and I really wanted him to succeed.'

And finally he did. On 31 May 2005, he reached the summit and became the youngest Australian ever to do so.

Although, like Alyssa, he'd worked hard on his preparation, he freely admits he was very lucky too. 'There were moments I felt really, really bad,' he says, 'and I thought, What am I doing here? This is ridiculous! You do a lot of soul-searching up there. It's such a wild environment and I was away for three months, which is a long time.

'But I'd put in an enormous amount of effort and work beforehand, and I never wanted to give up. At some stages you do think, I could just give up now and go back. That would be so easy to do. But you just put one foot in front of the other, and hope that things will get better and the weather will improve. I was totally driven to achieve the summit.

'The hardest thing was the weather and working out the right time for the summit push. We sat and waited for two weeks with bad weather and you start thinking, Maybe the mountain isn't going to let me go. That was tough. The physical effort is exhausting, but that mental strain is much worse. Then finally the weather gave me a very small window to make it and I just went for it.'

Pemberton admits his youth did make it harder for him. Others in his expedition were wary of him, wondering if he'd be up to it, and keen not to be held back by such a young man. 'So I had a lot to prove and that can be a dangerous thing,' he says. 'I was watched very closely by others until they realised I could make good decisions. We all know that one bad decision can cost you your life up there – and endanger the rest of your team.

'In the mountains, it's your mind that will break first. It's 40 per cent physical strength and 60 per cent mental strength. It's so easy to give it all up. That takes the pain away and the hurt and the cold and the tiredness and frustration about the weather.

'I also think maybe being young wasn't to my advantage when we hit the Death Zone. Acclimatising was difficult and I think having so much nervous energy didn't help. I got altitude sickness before I even got to Base Camp! I had to calm myself down and let my team go ahead, and then start later. It didn't help that I was nervous about what lay ahead, especially as I'd never been above 8000 metres before. There's also a lot of outside pressure when you're young, especially when you have sponsors behind you.'

But then again, Everest is incredibly difficult for everyone, regardless of age, he believes. He's heard of many extremely experienced climbers who won't go near Everest. Then there's the complexity of picking the right expedition and guide to go with. The one you end up with might not be anything like as passionate and determined to get to the top, as they might have been there twelve times already.

These days, Pemberton is on another quest: to climb the Seven Summits. From his base on the west coast of the US, and through his own company, RPMP, he's an adventurer who has delivered more than 250 of his Reach for the Summit corporate presentations to over 35 000 people around the world, talking about planning and preparation, goal-setting, motivation, teamwork, risk management and overcoming obstacles – all in the context of climbing Everest.

Because Everest, and the lessons it imparts, are never far from his mind. 'But I don't mind at all if Alyssa takes away my record as the youngest Australian to make it, as well as becoming the youngest non-Sherpa female in the world to get to the top,' he laughs. 'If someone beats my record, that will fill my heart with joy! I just want to spur on any young Australians going out and having adventures.

'I think girls are just as tough as boys. You have to have the skill and preparation behind you, but you also need the right wind and temperature and the right day up there, and the courage to utilise that lucky window.

'It's all about following your passion. Life is a gift, and you only get one shot at it.'

CHAPTER 17

Climbing in Ice and Snow

'May your dreams be larger than mountains and may you have the courage to scale their summits.'

– US WRITER, POET AND MOTIVATIONAL
SPEAKER HARLEY KING

While Alyssa Azar knuckled down to her training, her dad was keen to support her all he could without overly encouraging her. He knew how dangerous Everest could be, and wanted to make sure she knew it too. On his next trip to Everest Base Camp, he returned not only with an Everest calendar for her, but also every book and DVD he could find on everything that had ever gone wrong on the mountainside.

'I wanted her to understand the worst-case scenarios, not the best,' he says. 'It's easy for her to imagine herself sitting on the top of this mountain and it's all glorious and the weather is beautiful, but that's not reality. I hope that happens, but there's a good chance it's not going to. But I know Alyssa. If she gets something in her head it's going to happen, with you or without you. If I'd refused to help, it might have held her back a year or two but it was never going to stop her doing it.'

Alyssa, in turn, watched every DVD spellbound, pored over every book. She wasn't put off in the slightest. 'It just makes me realise how well prepared I have to be for every possibility,' she says.

'But discouraged?' She laughs. 'No, not at all. It made me feel even more excited for when I'll finally have a chance to climb.'

While Glenn continued to keep the dangers at the forefront of his daughter's mind, he also admired her resolve. In addition, a friend's daughter went to a party celebrating the end of Year 12 and was hit by a taxi and killed. At the funeral, the girl's mum told Glenn how much she regretted all the times she'd forbidden her daughter to go out and do things.

'So part of me thinks about all those things,' says Glenn. 'I know other people probably wouldn't understand that, and if something happens to Alyssa it will be so hard to bear, but you don't always have the rest of your life to do things.'

Alyssa wanted to work on her rock-climbing skills, so Glenn bought her the special climbing shoes, chalk and the chalk bag she'd tie around her waist to keep it in. She'd been watching some of the best rock climbers in the world on YouTube, particularly Frenchwoman Catherine Destivelle, who climbed solo and without ropes. She raced up the side of steep rock faces that looked so smooth and sheer, it was impossible to see any features that could possibly act as hand and footholds. With her fingertips searching out minute dents and cracks, she looked like a spider as she scuttled her way up, seemingly effortlessly.

There was an indoor rock-climbing wall locally, and Alyssa became a regular visitor when Glenn finished work every day and was free to belay for her – holding the ropes that secured her if she fell. Every time, she became a little better. He then drove her over to Brisbane to try out the walls there. It wasn't long before she'd conquered all of those too.

But they both knew if she stood any chance at Everest she'd also need some experience, and expertise, at rock climbing outdoors in the ice and snow. There were a number of courses on offer in New Zealand, around its Southern Alps. The cost, though, was high: $5450 for her plus a companion to go with her. So far, Glenn had financed all of Alyssa's expenses from either his own pocket, through her sponsor psyborg, from donations to her quest via her website or from people calling after hearing about her story in the media, but there wasn't much spare cash for this trip.

'I'd made a promise to her to support her, but we were a bit blown away by the cost,' he says. 'But I said I'd do everything I could to raise it, and she should just focus on the climbing and the training. Then someone sent me a link to the crowd-funding site pozible.com, through which you appeal for donations for funds for a project.'

The pair put up a photo of Alyssa and called the project 'The Road to Mount Everest'. They explained how they needed $5450 for the rock-climbing course to get Alyssa ready. From the day the request was submitted to the international site, set up to encourage creative or daring projects, there were sixty days for supporters to pledge funds. If the total wasn't reached by the deadline, no one needed to pay up. If the total was reached, then people were obliged to come good on their donations.

Slowly but surely the money trickled in – from locals in Toowoomba who'd heard so much about Alyssa through the local newspaper and radio, from people around Australia who'd been impressed with what they'd seen of her on TV, heard in interviews on radio or from visiting her website, and even a few donors from overseas. Some gave $10; one gave $400 and a good luck message. Every day, Alyssa and Glenn checked the total. On the fifty-ninth day they realised they were just $100 short. If they didn't raise that final amount by midday on the sixtieth day, they wouldn't be able to claim the $5350 others had offered. With just ten minutes to go, Glenn paid the final $100 himself.

'It was wonderful,' Alyssa says. 'I was so grateful. We both think lots about giving back and supporting charities when we can, and the gym also sponsors kids' sports teams. I've been lucky to have opportunities in life, and there are a lot of people a lot worse off than us. But it was so great for all these people to come forward and play a part in helping me realise my dream.'

With the funds, the pair booked a winter climbing course for her in New Zealand, where she'd have the chance to learn first-hand about real rock, ice and snow climbing around the country's highest peak, Mount Cook. Glenn knew this would be the make or break for Everest. Either she'd hate the experience and come back and want to forget all about Everest, or love it – and be even more spurred on to go. He reckoned it was a gamble worth taking.

In addition, he decided the course, in August 2012, would be the first trip Alyssa would make without him. He'd always loved trekking, but had never been into climbing. Besides, if he were to climb with her, he knew he'd be making decisions as her father, rather than on her chances of success. He wouldn't be able to help himself. Instead, he arranged for a couple of friends who'd been on some of his previous expeditions to accompany her. He wanted to give her, as much as he was able, the experience of climbing mountains without the comfort and reassurance of his presence, as just a taster of what it might be like on Everest with people she didn't know well.

Alyssa's grandmother, Carmel Clark, visited for Glenn's birthday and was taken aback all over again at how mature the fifteen-year-old appeared. She simply couldn't believe Alyssa's dedication. 'I saw her getting up at 4 a.m. to go to the gym,' she says, 'and then she'd go back three more times for more sessions! She's always been a bit of a loner, but now she seemed even more so. She's not interested in parties or boys; she has too much to do, she says. But then she comes home and plops on the lounge with her iPod like any other kid and is always looking at her phone. But she really isn't like any other kid at all . . .'

* * *

Eight-year-old Alyssa making history as the youngest person to ever complete the Kokoda Track.

ABOVE: Alyssa and older sister Brooklyn trying out Glenn's first Fighting Fit gym.

BELOW: Alyssa, aged ten, on her way to Everest Base Camp.

ABOVE: Resting on Mount Kilimanjaro.

LEFT: Alyssa and her father Glenn at the summit.

Sixteen-year-old Alyssa takes on Manaslu in the Himalaya.

ABOVE: The mighty Aconcagua in the Andes, Argentina.

BELOW: Alyssa on her second visit to Everest Base Camp in 2012.

Alyssa's gruelling training regime: boxing with Glenn (above), abseiling (below left), an essential skill for climbing and descending mountainsides, and dragging a 16 kg kettlebell (below right) to build strength.

She sleeps in a hyperbaric chamber that mimics high-altitude conditions and trains with a special mask to build her lung capacity.

RIGHT: Part-way up the Lhotse Face, a significant point on the climb.

BELOW: On top of the world! Alyssa on the summit of Mount Everest, May 2016.

Alyssa is simply raring to go on her next adventure. Nothing, it seems, will put her off. She flies over to Christchurch on New Zealand's South Island with Glenn's friends Brock Casson and Rob Appleton and they hire a car to drive to the alpine village of Aoraki/Mount Cook. There they meet their climbing instructor and are taken to stay in a mountain hut in the Upper Tasman Glacier area of the Southern Alps. It feels like the middle of nowhere. Every day they go out for seven hours at a time – they tackle ice walls, inch their way up the snowy side of Mount Aylmer at 2699 metres and traverse the Hochstetter Dome at 2827 metres. It has the same kind of atmosphere as the Himalaya, with slabby rock, glaciers and snowfields, only on a significantly more manageable scale.

The idea is to get them used to all the tools they will need to use, and so the trio end up doing a bit of everything. They are getting used to long hours out in the snow, understanding the gear they have, wearing crampons and using ice axes, and learning about avalanche safety and glacier travel and how to stop yourself when you're falling. For Alyssa it's physically a lot tougher than trekking. She's carrying all the clips and the ropes and the carabiners, and her boots are a lot bigger. But she can't get enough.

When they arrive back at Mount Cook village they do some rock climbing, learning how to rope up with each other, abseiling, decision-making and risk analysis at altitude. Alyssa knows this kind of technical climbing tuition will really help with her mountaineering. One day she might like to try pure rock climbing, when people go out – usually without ropes – to climb sheer rock faces. But that's a very different discipline. On the mountains, you're usually weighed down with clothing and equipment and can spend months there. With rock climbing, you're usually home and dusted and back in your own bed the same day.

Casson, who's previously been on the Kokoda Track and on the Everest Base Camp trek with Glenn, isn't sure what to expect of

Alyssa. It seems a tough course for anyone, let alone a fifteen-year-old girl. But the first day proves the greatest test. They're climbing in the mountains and are three-quarters of the way up when a blizzard suddenly hits. It's snowing, windy, cold and wet, and takes everyone by surprise. Very soon, they're soaked through and shivering, but still clinging on to the mountainside, inching their way up through the sleet. Alyssa, however, doesn't falter. She continues climbing slowly, deliberately, without missing a beat. Casson is amazed. After a while, he forgets he's climbing with a teenage girl and treats her as a complete equal.

The trio spend time practising climbing while roped to each other, setting anchors and belaying for each other, and learning how to understand and predict sudden weather changes – a lesson that might have stood them in even better stead before the blizzard struck. It's a lot of information to take in at once, but Alyssa seems to be able to absorb it without problems. It's also pretty uncomfortable – as they climb from the sun into the shade the temperature suddenly plummets, but there isn't time to adjust any clothing under the coils of rope. They have to put up with being boiling hot one minute under all their gear, and deathly cold the next. Alyssa doesn't mind. She's heard it can be exactly the same on Everest on some of the exposed rock faces at different times of day, and welcomes the chance to weather both extremes.

Appleton also notes how well Alyssa seems to be coping. He knows that once you get out in the elements, it's completely different to the controlled environment of an indoor rock gym. But he's impressed by how she never complains and just gets on with things. He comes to the conclusion that she's unique, and that she's definitely got the mindset to succeed.

Another challenge comes when the three are roped together for a climb. The two men suddenly blanch at the thought of their lives being held in fifteen-year-old hands. But Alyssa seems so switched on, and so confident about using what she's just learnt, that they both find it easy to trust her, and relax.

When Alyssa flies back to Australia, Glenn meets her at the airport, his heart in his mouth, wondering how she's found the experience. He doesn't have to wait for long to find out. One glance at her beaming face tells him. He doesn't know whether to be pleased or dismayed.

* * *

Alyssa had only a week at home before she joined her dad's next Everest Base Camp trek in November 2012. The days between the two trips were frantic, and she sat up till 2 a.m. most nights to finish her school assignments. They had to be done, she knew, as part of the whole deal. Still, she managed to fit in training at the gym and a couple of long runs. If she missed her training in the morning, she'd catch up at night, even if it meant back-to-back sessions, or stayed up late at night in order to do it. Sometimes she even slept over at the gym so she could exercise at 2 a.m. and then again when she woke up at 5 a.m, sleeping only in between sessions.

The only indulgence she allowed herself was two days off her strict nutritional program, on which she ate only lean proteins and vegetables. She treated herself to muesli with yoghurt and honey for breakfast, her favourite food – tacos – for dinner, and an ice-cream. For most kids her age that would be pretty normal fare.

'Sometimes it does all feel a bit overwhelming because there's so much to be done,' she says. 'But I'm seeing huge advances in my training, with my endurance, strength, balance and even mindset all improving. It's exciting to see how strong I can grow, and that keeps motivating me even when things get tough.'

Her collection of motivational quotes was growing daily. They were plastered up everywhere she looked, and flashed up each time she glanced at her phone. They came from a huge variety of places and authors. There was Shakespeare, from Henry VI: 'Let me embrace thee, sour adversity, for wise men say it is the wisest course.' There was the Roman poet Horace: 'It is courage, courage, courage, that raises the blood of life to crimson splendour. Live bravely and present a brave front to adversity.' There was Mahatma Gandhi: 'Strength does not come from physical capacity. It comes from an indomitable will.' Basketball star Michael Jordan got a guernsey too: 'My attitude is that if you push me towards something that you think is a weakness, then I will turn that perceived weakness into a strength.' There was even talk show entrepreneur Oprah Winfrey: 'Where there is no struggle, there is no strength.' But her favourite was from Sir Edmund Hillary, the first man on the summit of Everest: 'It's not the mountain we conquer, but ourselves.'

'I don't just copy them out, I live by them,' says Alyssa. 'We all go through tough times that you think you might not come through. You always have moments where you doubt yourself, and where positivity drains away. Sometimes I struggle to keep positive and I feel alone and that it's all too hard. But in my heart, I know it's not and that I'm capable of anything if I'm willing to work hard enough. Quotes like those really help me in times when it all gets too difficult and they help motivate and inspire me.'

* * *

The trip to Everest Base Camp comes up almost before she knows it, and she feels her excitement mount. It's been seven years since she was last in Nepal, and so much has happened in the interim. This time she'll be making the trek knowing that, hopefully, it will be her last practice run for when she walks to Base Camp again as the start of her assault on Everest.

Knowing that, she wants to perform even better on the trek than she did in 2005, to prove to herself that she's up to going much further. Most of all, she wants to be at altitude again, to test herself.

She decides not to take the pills to prevent altitude sickness until she absolutely has to.

One couple taking part in the six-person trip have met Alyssa before at the gym. When they all arrive in Nepal, however, they can barely believe the difference in her. She completely transforms from a loner they often can't get two words out of at the gym into someone who talks passionately about Nepal and Base Camp and Everest, and never shuts up. Both Nat and Zac McDermott are amazed. They realise suddenly how much Alyssa knows about Nepal and Everest, and conclude it's obviously her sole goal in life to get up that mountain.

In Kathmandu, Alyssa celebrates her sixteenth birthday with a dinner at a restaurant popular with climbers, the Northfield Cafe. She can think of nowhere she'd rather be to mark it – except, perhaps, on the top of Everest. The worst part of the trip for her is going to be that flight to Lukla, and the landing on that tiny airstrip. She's dreading it, but it passes again without incident. Then she allows herself to relax and enjoy the trek, back among her beloved mountains.

It feels so good being back; it's almost like coming home again. This time, the weather is clearer and she can see Everest from so many places, which she relishes. She keeps gazing over at Everest and thinking, Soon, I'm going to be up there climbing! It seems crazy to her that one tiny idea she had about climbing that mountain has shaped who she is, who she's become and where she's going, but every achievement, she realises, starts with a small idea which can then be fanned by hope and nurtured by determination. She considers those who've managed to climb to the summit. If they can, then why can't I? she thinks. What makes them special? She resolves to just climb one step at a time. That's all she can do.

Also on this trek is Sonia Taylor, who took part in Alyssa's Kilimanjaro trip. It's her second Everest Base Camp trek and she's pleased to see Alyssa again. Although she's now a year older, Taylor sees that, despite becoming so much more talkative when they arrived in Nepal, she's still the same girl afterwards: keeping to herself, rarely starting conversations, but politely responding to questions. But with three teenage boys herself, she knows that kids of that age can sometimes be engaging, and other times it's like pulling teeth.

Most of the time Alyssa's walking she has her earphones in, listening to music, but when she's not walking, she writes in her journal and reads books, most notably her much-loved *Warrior Training*, the book she's adopted as her major motivator, with its SAS-style training and lessons on mental toughness.

Sometimes she needs it too, as rarely do such treks come without difficulties. By the time the group reaches Namche Bazaar, where she and Glenn had to abandon the rest of their walk the first time back from Base Camp, Alyssa's started feeling sick and light-headed, and is forced to take the altitude medication. She shrugs, and vows she'll train even harder back at home in the hope she'll do better next time. The next day, she gets up and it's business as usual.

After two days in Namche, they set off again, heading for Tengboche, five to six hours away. The path climbs up to the airstrip at Syangboche that services the Hotel Everest View – the highest hotel in the world at 3880 metres – and provides another fabulous view of Everest. Alyssa feels like she's seeing an old friend again.

When she can finally tear herself away from the view, the group climb again, then descend into the village of Khumjung to visit Sir Edmund Hillary's Khumjung School built in the 1960s for the locals as the first big project of his charity, the Himalayan Trust. Alyssa looks in through the classroom windows at the children hunched over their desks and smiles, glad that visitors are giving back to the area. They then all hike back to the main trail for the collection of tea houses and stalls of Sanasa and then on through smaller villages that feel a lot less touristy. With the breathtaking panorama of Everest and peaks like Thamserku, Kwangde Ri and Ama Dablam in front, the track goes down further to the lowest spot in the Khumbu at Phunki Thunga and then climbs again to Tengboche, high on a hill above two rivers, with more glorious views of Everest and neighbouring peaks, including Lhotse, the fourth highest mountain in the world.

Everyone then climbs over stones inscribed with the Buddhist prayer, 'Om Mani Padme Hum', to visit the town's picturesque monastery, adorned with fluttering prayer flags. It is here, Alyssa knows from her reading, that Everest mountaineers stop off on their way to the mountain to light a candle in the hope of a successful, and safe, expedition. It's also where Tenzing Norgay was once sent to become a monk.

After a night in Tengboche, they walk the five hours to Dingboche, climbing ever higher. Alyssa makes note of the altitude at every stop, mentally checking herself to see how she's faring. There is the occasional downhill stretch to rest the legs, but the respite never lasts for long. She can feel the altitude having some effect; walking is becoming more difficult and she doesn't have as much energy. She makes sure she's drinking plenty of fluids and eating, even though she doesn't feel like doing either.

They stay two nights in Dingboche, at 4530 metres, and by the time they set out, Alyssa is feeling much better. They are now heading for Lobuche, another five hours away. The last part is always the hardest: up a steep, slippery, muddy climb to the settlement standing at 4940 metres. Here they stay in rooms in a rudimentary stone hut that's a lot colder and less comfortable than any of their other accommodation so far. But no one minds. Everest Base Camp is so close now, only a day's walk away. Alyssa doesn't sleep much. She's far too excited.

They start off early the next morning for Gorak Shep, a tiny village sitting at an altitude of 5164 metres on the edge of a frozen lakebed, but barely stop to look. They are too intent on reaching Base Camp, between another hour and a half and two and a half hours away, at the daunting altitude of 5364 metres.

Alyssa sets a cracking pace and they reach Base Camp far earlier than they'd imagined. At the first sight of the place she stops dead in her tracks, as awestruck by the sight as she was the first time. It is a chaotic jumble of multi-coloured tents, all grouped on different parts of a stony plateau with a huge variety of flags flapping in the wind around them. Everywhere there are little clusters of trekkers and climbers milling around, dressed in big down jackets, talking, moving into other people's tents and entering some of the larger tents that Alyssa knows serve as mess halls for the various expeditions.

Yaks stand motionless under staggering mounds of equipment, and Sherpas sit in groups, talking and laughing, holding tin cups of steaming tea. There's a near-palpable excitement in the thin air. Alyssa hugs herself. She's conjured up the memory of this sight so many times, but actually being here again is incredible. It's fascinating to simply stand and watch, and to imagine these people getting ready to go off and climb Everest.

Although you can't actually see much of Everest from Base Camp, you do see the start of the climb, and the beginning of what's called the Khumbu Icefall, one of its most dangerous stretches. Alyssa gazes at it, thrilled and mesmerised, knowing the next time she clamps eyes on it, it will be to actually start her own climb. She wonders, yet again, how that will actually feel.

But it's on the way back from Base Camp, when the group reaches Gorek Shep again, that Alyssa hits her greatest difficulty. It appears she's contracted a stomach bug from something she's eaten, and she throws up violently. She quietly goes to bed in the hut where they're staying without mentioning it to anyone, to try to cope with it herself. But it doesn't subside and she's up and down all night long. At one point, Nat McDermott sees Alyssa climb out of her sleeping bag just as the temperature hits -20°, put on her shoes and head off yet again for the toilet – only to find it occupied by someone else. McDermott follows her to check she's all right, and discovers her trying to open a window to throw up through so she won't disturb anyone. She feels desperately sorry for the young girl.

But Alyssa takes it all without a murmur of complaint or self-pity. She feels there is nothing to do but accept it as good practice – the same kind of thing could happen on her way to the summit of Everest.

The next day she looks pale and exhausted, and everyone's heart goes out to her. But Alyssa puts on a mask of cheery indifference and just gets on with the job at hand, saying blithely that what doesn't kill her will simply make her stronger.

CHAPTER 18

Everest's Hero: Dan Mazur

To be successful on a climb of Everest, you need to know how to suffer. You need to be willing to suffer, embrace the suffering, and make the suffering work for you. Otherwise, you shouldn't even get out of that plane at Lukla.

So says Dan Mazur, one of the world's most successful Himalayan mountaineers and the man best known for abandoning his own attempt on the summit to save the life of Australian Lincoln Hall.

'A lot of high-altitude climbers talk about Everest as a sufferfest,' he explains. 'Because you really suffer up there. There's the cold, the snow, the wind, the ropes that aren't fixed, the accidents, the tragedies, the deaths, even that time a bunch of foreigners got into a fight with the Sherpas. There are so many different things that can go wrong, and you really have to be prepared to suffer, to know how to suffer and to keep going despite everything.'

American-born Mazur has been visiting Nepal for twenty-five years, and for over eighteen has been organising and leading trekking and mountaineering expeditions. He had his first experience of altitude at Alyssa's age – seventeen – when he climbed peaks in Montana's Glacier National Park, on the Canadian border. From that time, he was hooked.

'I love the beauty of climbing, the scenery up there, the thrill, the excitement of it and sharing it with other people,' he says. 'Then there's the part where you get to deal with the local people, and meet them and learn about their culture.'

Many people know of Mazur from May 2006 when he was leading an expedition of three climbers up Everest. They were only a couple of hours from the summit when, at 8600 metres, they came across Lincoln Hall, who'd finally reached the top twelve years after his first attempt as part of the 1984 expedition with Tim Macartney-Snape and Greg Mortimer. He was on the way down the previous day and had fallen sick and been left for dead. His team was convinced he'd already died and had wanted to cover him with stones in the makeshift burial that's customary on Everest, but it wasn't possible where he lay, on a spine of rock covered by a 2 metre–wide snowbank.

But as Mazur and Jangbu Sherpa came up the crest of a ridge, they were startled to see Hall very much alive, sitting cross-legged on the top. The pair looked at him, dumbstruck. Hall was the first to speak. 'I imagine you are surprised to see me here,' he said levelly. Mazur asked him if he knew how he'd got there. 'No,' replied Hall. 'Do *you* know how I got here?' 'No, I don't,' replied Mazur. 'Do you know your name?' 'Yes,' he said. 'My name is Lincoln Hall.'

Thus began one of the most daring rescues in the history of mountain climbing. The four gave him oxygen, liquids and food, and tried to keep him warm in temperatures 20 to 30° C below zero. They remained at his side until reinforcements arrived to help bring him back down the mountain, abandoning their own hopes of reaching the summit. Mazur saved his life yet again when Hall, hallucinating, went too close to the edge of the ridge, thinking he was on a boat or an aircraft. Mazur pulled him back from the drop each time, and then roped him to the precipice for safety. It took ten to twelve Sherpas and thirty-six bottles of precious oxygen to help Hall out of the Death Zone and back to Base Camp.

The heroism of Mazur's actions was particularly celebrated in the light of the death just over a week earlier of British climber David Sharp, who got into difficulty lower down the mountain, but who was ignored by around forty people who continued to tramp past him on their way towards the summit. But Mazur always tried to shrug off the hero tag. 'The summit will always be there,' he says. 'There is always another chance to go for the summit, but Lincoln only has one life – this is for sure. You just can't leave a guy like that. You'd think about it for the rest of your life.'

Hall has always been a hero to Alyssa, not just for his extensive experience in climbing mountains but his gift of then writing about them in such compelling terms in his books. 'He was always one of my great favourites,' says Alyssa. 'I love his books and you feel you get to know him through them.

'It was an extraordinary rescue by Dan Mazur, too. That would have been so hard, when someone can't really contribute to getting down the mountain, and Lincoln was delirious some of that time, and had been fighting the Sherpas who'd been trying to help. It shows how, when things go wrong at that height, everything is different, and you never know what's going to happen.'

Mazur counts himself the lucky one for having been able to play a role in Hall's rescue, also revering the man. 'Oh my God, he's my hero,' he says. 'What an amazing man! I was so lucky to have got to meet him, and then to get to know him later.'

Hall died six years later in 2012, but far from the mountainside. At the age of fifty-six he finally succumbed to mesothelioma in hospital in Sydney.

Mazur says he doesn't deserve any plaudits for deciding to help Hall, who has seven acclaimed books about expeditions, mountaineers and explorers to his credit. 'People talk about the rescue but just because you go to Everest, it doesn't mean you'd be a different person to the one you'd be in your hometown,' says Mazur. 'I suppose some people might drive right past someone in trouble by the side of the road with the bonnet of their car up, waving for help. Others would always stop to help. The same thing goes for Everest.

'Some people go up there but are still keen to help others while others are very focused on their goals and won't stop. Everyone's different. No two snowflakes are alike; that's what makes the world interesting.'

Mazur ended up reaching the summit the next year, and went on to climb seven of the world's 8000-metre peaks. Since then, he's taken on a role in the support team as the man waiting in the last camp before the top, to try to help get climbers to the summit. He also spends a lot of time raising funds for the Mount Everest Foundation for sustainable development in Nepal and Tibet, building hospitals, schools, and environmental projects. One day, if everything's going well, he'll attempt the summit again, he's sure. But until then, he's just happy helping make others' dreams come true.

Besides, most people need all the help they can get. 'I do love it up there, but it's really, really dangerous,' he says. 'I've seen many people die, which really takes the heart out of you. The worst thing you ever have to do as an expedition leader is to phone the family of one of your members to tell them that something's happened to their loved one.

'I've heard some people say that since more people attempt Everest now, it must be easy. Well, it isn't. No one can ever say that. There have been advances – for instance, we have much more sophisticated weather forecasting tools now, but you still have to interpret the results. And the kit is so much better than it was in the 1920s and 1930s of those first expeditions, and so you don't see so much frostbite any more. It's among the older generation of climbers that you see so many missing fingers and toes.

'But there are so many elements that are still unpredictable. The weather is really powerful up there, it's huge. While you're there, too, you have to give it 100 per cent focus. As soon as you let down your guard and relax a bit, that's when something happens, like a storm comes in or an avalanche occurs. You have to be watching all the time.'

Success on Everest comes in three equal parts, he believes. One is the weather, the second is mental toughness – feeling you *should* be there – and the third is physical fitness. On top of all those is patience, being ready to wait out bad weather and problems, and not be affected by them.

'You have to do a lot of waiting on Everest for the weather to improve or ropes to be fixed and you have to be able to keep your spirits up until it's time to go again. You need to have patience as well as the ability to rest and relax when you can, and keep your mind off what's coming and not worry about it, as that can sap your energy.

'Then when you get going, you have to be steady, methodical and plodding, and make sure you don't get nervous as that will rob you of your concentration. You also need to be able to handle altitude sickness, and know when it's serious or when it may pass. One in ten people need extra time to acclimatise, one in twenty seem to be almost allergic to altitude and can't handle it at all, and for the rest of us, it can change on different climbs. You just never know. It's different each time.'

Mazur remembers when he was seventeen and going on a long hike in the mountains with a heavy pack, accompanied by people he didn't know well. That was difficult, he says, but Everest is much, much worse. 'The suffering you go through on Everest is on another scale altogether,' he says. 'It's a very tricky mountain, and so, so dangerous. Everest has to be respected. Everest rules. It's still in charge.'

CHAPTER 19

Pushing Your Body to the Limits

'To be the best, you have to work overtime.'
– US WORLD CHAMPION BOXER FLOYD MAYWEATHER

January 2013 arrived in a flurry of activity for Alyssa Azar. It was only fifteen months before she'd start on her Everest climb, and she was determined not to waste a day she could be using to get fitter, faster and stronger.

She sat and wrote down everything she was going to be doing over the next year, and ranked each activity from one to ten; ten for when she was good at something, and one for when she wasn't. She then resolved to work extra hard on everything she perceived to be a weakness in her armour. For example, she wasn't good at pull-ups, so she planned to put in extra practice every day. She skipped well, so she could continue at that without too much hassle. And burpees – a drop into a plank and then jumping back upright – well, they were no one's favourite exercise. She vowed to do them more often, and repeat them over and over, usually with a push-up in between.

Every time she ran or rowed on the rowing machine, from now on she'd also wear a 10-kg vest to improve her endurance, while the altitude mask had already become a regular companion.

'The aim is to improve myself step by step,' she says. 'It's exciting how you can turn a weakness into a strength with a lot of work – no matter how much it sucks! I am determined, but I think I get that from both my parents; they have a pretty amazing work ethic. I think the motivation has to come from within, and it's great to have an aim. It doesn't have to be climbing Everest! It can be as simple as doing a run, taking a yoga class, going for a bike ride, anything.'

She was asked to give some talks to local groups about her extraordinary life, and how she kept so motivated, and was then invited to address a few company seminars as a paid speaker. Ironically, considering all she'd been through, she classed those as among the most nerve-racking moments of her life. The first talk was to the financial group OBT Financial, about goal-setting – a subject on which she was, by now, an expert. They loved hearing her story, and immediately came on board as sponsors, by signing up as official members of her summit club. She received a couple more invitations from others, and slowly but surely, her confidence began to build, and along with it, the funds for her next trips.

The first trip of the year came in January: a weekend rock-climbing course near Brisbane, and the chance to practise some of the roping techniques she'd learnt in New Zealand. The Saturday started with tuition about different knots and devices to tie them on to, and how to set up anchors properly. It continued with a trek to the summit of the old volcanic plug Mount Ngungun in the Glasshouse Mountains, and rock climbing up the side, abseiling and belaying others. That day finished with an abseil of 40 metres off the side of the summit with all her bags and gear. Then there was the trek down and out, the drive back to Toowoomba, and some schoolwork she'd left to the last minute to complete, before bed, finally, at 4.30 a.m.

Despite only a couple of hours' sleep, it was then an early start and a drive straight out to the cliffs at Brisbane's Kangaroo Point for some abseiling from anchors they'd set up on the cliff tops, followed by several hours of theory, talking over the concepts and going through exam questions. She was then able to abseil for another three hours, as she was assessed on her ability to use different techniques and belay devices. It was an exhausting two days. 'But it felt good to be taking another step of action towards Everest,' she says. 'I was feeling so excited for what the year would bring.'

It was set to be an extremely busy one. Already, she'd scheduled in another Aussie 10, this time with the added challenge of completing it in twenty-four hours. The rest of her wish list had changed after the route up Cho Oyu was closed by the Chinese authorities for a while. Instead, it became a trip back to Nepal to climb Island Peak at 6170 metres, then over to Argentina to climb another of the world's Seven Summits, the 6960-metre Aconcagua, and then back to Nepal for an attempt on Manaslu, the world's eighth highest peak at 8165 metres.

In the meantime, she started on a program of long trail runs and pack walks with plenty of hills through Toowoomba's bushland, including up and around the undulating MacKenzie Trail. She started off wearing the 10-kg weight vest and carrying a pack weighing 5 kg. Gradually more sandbags were put into the pack and the weight increased to 15, 20, 25, then 30 kg. One day, Glenn went to watch her train and helped her take off her pack, then struggled as he tried to put it into the car. 'How much does that weigh?' he asked his daughter. She shrugged. 'I don't know.' He weighed it when they got home. It was now 42 kg, and rising.

It gave him pause for thought. The main reason there'd never been a woman admitted into the elite SAS unit in the army was that everyone had to routinely carry 50 kg of equipment with them, and women generally weren't able to. But for Alyssa, that could well be another career option at some point in the future.

She also switched on her iPod and ran up and down the escarpment along horse trails and bike tracks, around Prince Henry Heights and on the four-hour round trip over Tabletop, dragging a 20-kg 4WD tyre behind her from a harness she strapped around her torso. That was a training idea she and Glenn got from a documentary about Rex Pemberton, who prepared for Everest by dragging tyres up and down sand dunes. It was a good endurance exercise and was never easy, but when the weather was dry, it was a great deal more manageable than when it was wet in the middle of winter and the mud came up to her ankles and coated the tyre. She always timed herself, or asked Glenn to time her, to make sure she was getting faster every week.

'She has to find the right balance between strength work and cardio,' Glenn says. 'But she can't afford to be too lean when she tackles Everest as it's so cold, and people do lose a lot of weight up there.'

She cut a lonely figure in the hills on her own. Some locals would feel for her, and kids would ask to hang out with her. But they didn't understand that she liked being on her own. 'I don't really hang out with other people,' she says. 'When I'm not busy, I like to chill out alone and just think. I am a bit of a loner, really. To a lot of people that's negative, but to me, it's who I am. It actually helps when you're out in the mountains for months at a time, and you have to be on your own and in your own headspace.'

One person she was building a relationship with, however, was Keith Fennell, the writer of her much-admired *Warrior Training*. Glenn had asked him if he'd like to run a couple of challenges for his adventure business, and Keith said he'd be happy to, setting up a series of Special Forces challenges to develop participants' teamwork skills, mental toughness and self-belief. Alyssa had emailed him a few times about her quest, and he'd replied with tips and suggestions of exercises she could do to improve her psychological strength. One day, they planned to get together for a training session so he could assess how she was doing, and perhaps pinpoint any weaknesses he saw.

Alyssa had so much going on, sometimes she couldn't sleep at night, too busy going over everything that bubbled to the surface of her mind in the dark. When that happened, she'd go to the gym or off for a run, even if it was past midnight. Doing that, she found she went into a zone in her own head where all her worries disappeared. Usually by the time she was finished, she could then, finally, sleep, even if she just curled up on the floor of the gym. At least it meant she was there, ready to start a fresh workout at 4 a.m.

Often she trained so hard, she had to stop and vomit into bushes by the side of tracks. Then she just carried on. Her program at the gym also continued at an ever-increasing intensity, so she'd often have a bucket close by in case she had to stop there too.

'I don't mind it at all,' she says. 'It's good practice for when you're on Everest. There, you might throw up because you're affected by the altitude, and might have no energy left and feel terrible, but you just have to carry on. There's no alternative. So while I'm training, if I throw up and have nothing left, I'll get more used to carrying on training and keeping going. Yes, I know it seems weird, but it all has a purpose . . .'

* * *

Nepal's Island Peak was set to be Alyssa's next big climbing trip, but finances were tight, and she and her dad decided to drop it in favour of bringing the Manaslu climb forward instead. It was set for October 2013, and Alyssa continued with her brutal training regime.

In between, Alyssa gave an increasing number of talks to business groups, to companies, to the Toowoomba Chamber of Commerce and to various conferences in Brisbane. There were some lunches to raise money for her quest, with Alyssa speaking at those too. Naturally quiet, she found it hard, but her audiences responded well to this young girl pouring out her heart about her dearest ambition.

Often she was asked what she'd be taking with her to the top of Everest. Her answer would always be the same: as well as an Australian flag, she'd be taking a photograph of her little brother, Christian. Because of his autism, she'd say, it was unlikely he'd ever have the opportunity to go himself, and she didn't want him to miss out. He seemed to understand the idea of Everest, as he'd seen the flag fluttering on Toowoomba's Picnic Point hill. 'And although it's not something he'd ever want to do, there are lots of other things he can't do, which is hard for him,' says Alyssa. 'So I think putting the photo of him up there is something that'll mean a lot to me. And I'll take a photo of the flag there, and his picture, and show it to him. It'll hopefully be a great surprise for him.'

That was a sentiment that enormously impressed Queensland coffee magnate Phil Di Bella, who came on board as a sponsor after reading about her on social media and then meeting with her and Glenn. 'I was surprised what a good speaker she is,' he says. 'She's very quiet, she doesn't talk much, and she's not terribly animated, but she has an intenseness and focus about her that's very engaging. You can see the tenacity in her eyes. She's comfortable in her own skin, scans the room, and then speaks with great confidence and passion.'

Di Bella started his coffee business in 2002 at the age of twenty-six. Back then, everyone told the Brisbane barista he was mad to enter such a competitive industry. He ignored the naysayers, holding fast to his belief in himself. 'There's only the future,' he'd say as his mantra. 'Don't worry about what happened in the past.' His willingness to back himself paid off: he now owns and runs one of Australia's biggest specialty coffee companies, with about 2.2 million people a week throughout the country drinking his coffee, and in 2013 made number fifteen on the *BRW* magazine Young Rich List. He has huge respect for other young people similarly backing themselves to achieve. He does a lot of work for youth charities, and sponsors a number of young people. Alyssa is among his most prized.

'What immediately struck me about her is how determined she is, how thoughtful and how passionate,' says Di Bella. 'But she doesn't come with a lot of hype. She's not Muhammad Ali, she's more a Mike Tyson in his young days. She doesn't say much, but what she does say is meaningful. She has that mental toughness, as well as a physical toughness, coupled with real endurance, and she's wise beyond her years.'

When two years ago he launched a canned coffee energy drink, Espresso Kick+, Alyssa became one of its ambassadors. Since then, they've been in monthly contact, with Di Bella mentoring Alyssa and helping her with media exposure, as well as organising fundraising events for her.

Mountain Designs, a company selling outdoor clothes and equipment, also came to the party, going through Alyssa's list of the gear she needed, and providing much of it for her. 'We stumbled upon Alyssa a long time ago as a customer of ours and we got to know her through all her amazing adventures,' says company spokesperson Tyng Huang. 'She was pretty young then, so in a sense, we've grown with her. She's still young, and we decided to sponsor her as we love her willingness to give things a go. We're not just about hardcore outdoor activities; we're also about getting out there and challenging yourself, and Alyssa's a perfect example of that.'

Apart from those occasional bonuses, Alyssa and Glenn focused on financing each trip before it happened. 'We do that through sponsors, some people donate, if I do a talk, people will pay for that and that will help,' says Alyssa. 'We do a bit of everything, really. Mountain climbing can be very expensive. As I'm getting to my goal, the trips mean longer periods of time away, they're more involved, the gear costs a lot more. And my dad helps fund a lot of it as well. A branding company is now trying to help us get bigger sponsors.'

The grand total cost of an assault on Everest, Glenn has calculated, will be around $150 000, including the costs of sending Alyssa on two training climbs beforehand, with airfares, insurance, permits, the cost of joining an expedition, Sherpas and equipment. Everest alone would be $70 000. 'If all else fails, I'll remortgage our house to pay for it,' says Glenn. 'We can't get all this way to fall at the final hurdle.'

Some people suggested Glenn and Alyssa should approach mining companies in Queensland who were keen to improve the public perception of their work by giving back to communities. But Alyssa wasn't keen. 'They might even give me the cash in one hit,' she says. 'But I'm not comfortable having such a strong link with mining. The companies have got a lot of money, but many people feel they're killing the land. And if anything goes wrong, I wouldn't want to be trotted out for them.'

The rest of Alyssa's living expenses were quite minimal. She wasn't interested in clothes, jewellery, make-up, boys or going out, like most teens tend to be. Her clothes were stored in a suitcase in her bedroom, and her cuttings were in plastic bags. The only decorations were a few artefacts she had from Nepal – photos, the Everest calendar, Buddhist prayer flags, a gauze prayer scarf and some letters from people she treasured, and had framed. One was from elderly Kokoda veteran George Palmer, whom she'd previously met at a dinner for veterans and Kokoda trekkers. 'You are certainly a very brave young lady to be taking on these future trips,' he wrote.

After all, Alyssa felt she didn't need much: most of her hours were spent in the gym, training, or speaking to try to raise more money. She also studied at home, either at Glenn's or at her mum's, where she occasionally stayed.

Glenn and Therese's separation was proving tough for everyone. It was tricky juggling lives between the two homes. Alyssa now saw less of her mum and older sister, but Therese would try to provide just a little more balance in Alyssa's life by buying her, every birthday and Christmas, 'girly' presents, like jewellery, handbags and make-up. Alyssa was seeing more of her younger siblings, though, since they came to stay so often. Glenn had been working hard on his businesses, but now he decided to re-prioritise.

An old army mate of his, Ritchie Gibson, who'd qualified with him as a physical trainer, served with him in East Timor and had been a volunteer on the support crew of the Townsville–Brisbane run, had a chat. He'd long been an admirer of Glenn for his ability to keep reinventing himself and liked the way he seemed to have little to no fear of failure. In turn, he'd come to have enormous respect for Alyssa, too.

'They're both people determined to achieve, despite any obstacles or roadblocks in the way,' he says. 'Not many people in life inspire me, but Glenn's definitely one of those. Once he's made up his mind to do something, nothing stops him. And Alyssa's grown up to be exactly the same.'

After the army, Gibson became a business entrepreneur as well as getting into motivational speaking and goal-setting. It was in this capacity he came to gave Glenn a hand. He told him that men spell love with the letters M-O-N-E-Y; they see it as all about a house and providing for their kids, and actually spending time with their family comes last. Women and kids, on the other hand, spell love T-I-M-E.

'I could see the sense of that,' Glenn says. 'When I train people, I ask clients their priorities. They usually say number one family, number two health and fitness and number three career. Then I make them look at their diaries – and they soon realise they're living their life as if the reverse is true. It's all about work, and family comes third. For busy blokes, if it's not written in their schedule, then it has no importance. They never write in a time to take the kids to the park. If they did, it would change their core business, and the way they look at their life. I realised I was exactly the same.

'The kids would come to me and I'd got into the habit of saying, We'll go to the park, but I just have to do a few things first. So I'd do all those things, one thing would lead to another, and it'd be time for afternoon naps, and *then* we'd go to the park. People knew I was always available on the phone or email, so they'd come first.'

So he took the decision to change the way he does things. 'Now I never answer the phone or emails on a Sunday,' he says. 'My kids come first. If we're going to the park, we'll go there first. When I turn my phone back on, I might have a huge number of texts and messages and emails, but I've come to the conclusion that it's good to be uncontactable sometimes. We're all living at a million miles an hour and constantly multi-tasking, and it can't be good for our brains.'

On the weeks Christian and Samantha come to stay, Glenn picks them up from school and then stays home with them, rather than returning to work. He plays with them, reads to them, baths them and watches *Dr Who* with Samantha because it's her favourite show in the world. 'I'm very close to them,' he says. 'I feel like I've had a second chance with Sammy. She seems to be really artistic and she's won art awards already at school. She loves to draw, and whereas other kids might draw flowers or trees, she draws pictures of Alyssa on the side of mountains.

'With Brooklyn, we've drifted a little since the separation and that affects me a lot, so I'm trying to get closer to her. She's always been very different to Alyssa. She is a nurturing soul and amazing with her younger brother and sister. She has a deep caring side to her and also a very artistic side that I hope she fully explores one day.

'I love spending time with Brooklyn when I get the chance, and

I encourage her to reach for her dreams. One day I know she'll find her "thing" and nothing will hold her back.

'Christian is different because of who he is and the problems he has, but he's an amazing little human in his own right. He has challenges, he needs medication and anything that can go wrong goes wrong for him, but he knows the name of every adult who works at his school, whether they have something to do with him or not, and he celebrates every train track and flag he sees. I've always said to people, I don't know if I would change him if I had that option now, because that is who he is. But you do worry what life is going to be like for him when we're no longer around.'

After the final separation came formal proceedings, and the divorce was set to be granted towards the end of the year. It saddened Glenn enormously but both he and Therese were working hard to stay on good terms.

'Alyssa has no time for boyfriends,' he says. 'Maybe she looks at her mum and my relationship and thinks all relationships are bad . . . But hopefully she'll grow out of that.'

* * *

The 24-hour Aussie 10 challenge comes up in May 2013 and Alyssa is pumped. It will mean doing the whole circuit in one go, non-stop, with no camping or resting, so she sees it as a great mental and physical challenge. In the Himalaya, her body will need to handle cold temperatures, minimal to no food for long periods, exhaustion, little sleep and often continuous movement, and this will be excellent practice. In addition, the final part of the climb up Everest, from Camp IV at the start of the Death Zone to the summit, takes around twenty-two hours – eighteen up and between three and four back. That's truly a race against time; after twenty-four hours, a climber's oxygen will have started to run out, and altitude sickness will have set in badly.

So Alyssa feels this will be a good way to prepare for that, going twenty-four hours non-stop around Australia's highest peaks. She knows she can train all she wants in the gym and in the hills, but at some point she has to get out in the mountains and climb – and where better to test her fitness, endurance and mental toughness? Plus, there's always the excitement of being in mountains, any mountains, no matter how lofty or low. For it's among mountains that Alyssa realises she now feels her happiest, and most at home.

The plan is to go with her dad and two other men who've trained with him in the past. One, however, pulls out on the eve of their departure. The other is keen athlete and former adventure travel company director James Holden, who's previously walked the Kokoda Track seven times – including once in thirty hours and, in 2012, in just twenty-four. He hasn't done much walking in Koscuiszko before, and thought it sounded a bit of fun.

Alyssa is interviewed by ABC radio early in the morning and then falls asleep instantly in the car on their way to the park, just as soldiers are trained to do in any downtime they have – another habit she's learnt from Glenn. As soon as they arrive at 8 a.m., they get out and start walking. It's chilly but the weather's fine and there's no sign of rain or snow. It takes three hours to hit the first peak, Mount Twynam, then five of the other peaks are nearby: Carruthers Peak, Alice Rawson Peak, Mount Townsend, Abbott Peak and Byatts Camp.

Watching Alyssa, Holden is surprised how relaxed she is. Once she starts walking, he notices she goes at her own pace, and doesn't stop, with the kind of airy nonchalance others might have going for a walk in the park.

The longest part of the trek is to the top of Mount Kosciuszko, and the three have a thirty-minute break on the summit. Then they don big down jackets against the cold and, in the darkness of night, switch on their head torches, ready to ascend the last three peaks. One by one they knock them off – the unnamed peak on Etheridge Ridge, Rams Head North and Rams Head. By now Alyssa feels exhausted, but there's still the three-hour trek to the finish, which had also been the start.

For her, that's the hardest part. She feels she's done the challenge, but there's still a way to go. By the time they pass the finish line at 1 a.m., only seventeen hours have passed – seven less than their target. Holden, who was the fastest of the three, while Glenn was the slowest, is impressed. Alyssa has never once got cranky, complained or gave any indication she didn't want to be there. On the contrary – despite the freezing temperature, the killer pace and everyone's exhaustion, she always looked happy and excited. For her, he concludes, it's seemed like a normal day out, like other kids might have a day at the seaside, and she doesn't seem to have felt it at all.

Unbeknownst to him, however, Alyssa is suffering; it's just that she chooses not to show it. She has such bad blisters on her feet, from the straps keeping the boots closed against snow, she can barely walk. She just takes one step at a time, and focuses on getting to the end. 'I get into a rhythm and zone when I walk, and I just make sure I stay in that,' she says. 'I also believe you have to be comfortable with being uncomfortable, so it's an opportunity to practise that too. When I got home I was shattered, but it felt good to have achieved that. We didn't expect to be able to do it in seventeen hours, but we did have good weather.

'That's the thing I love about the mountains. They really test someone's character. You're put under pressure and who you are really becomes obvious. All pretensions are stripped away. You can't hide. All that's left are your true qualities, and they're the only things that count. It can be quite confronting. You see some big, strong guys fall apart on mountains because they can be so physically challenging and it's uncomfortable and everything's beyond your control. Then you see others you wouldn't think could cope triumphing over the odds.

'Mountains are a true test of character, and that's just one of the reasons I love them so much.'

CHAPTER 20

Everest's Most Unusual Champion: Bo Parfet

One of the most unlikely Everest climbers of all time, and one of the men Alyssa most admires as a result, is American Bo Parfet.

He was a 104-kg Wall Street corporate financier working 100-hour weeks and living on a steady diet of Coca-Cola and cheeseburgers when he first got the urge to climb a mountain. He was unhappy and dissatisfied with his life, and wanted to find excitement and adventure.

So he flew to Tanzania and started climbing Kilimanjaro. After food poisoning, exhaustion and horribly sore feet, he finally just about made it to the top, and his passion for climbing was born. Since then, he's climbed the Seven Summits, including Everest in 2007, and written the best-selling book, *Die Trying*, about his triumphs and mishaps.

Dodging avalanches, stumbling his way through the Khumbu Icefall, nearly not making it across a ladder suspended over a dizzyingly deep crevasse and burying a dead team-mate . . . He seems to have ten lives.

'I like the fact that he was in a business but wasn't enjoying it, so was determined to try something new,' says Alyssa. 'So he just caught a plane and threw himself at a mountain, without any training or preparation. That's not so wise, as he found out, but I admire him for having the courage to change his life so massively.

'I believe so much in positive thinking and chasing your dreams, it's great to read about someone who did just that, and decided to move away from their nine-to-five life to find something else, and in the process become so dedicated to climbing mountains. He just really went for what he wanted, and I like that!'

In return, Parfet has become Alyssa's newest fan. 'She's tough!' he says. 'But she'll have to be extremely tough to pull this off. Physically, a human being at seventeen hasn't yet hit their peak strength; they haven't matured physically yet, which will be a hurdle she'll have to surmount.

'Also, mentally, I don't think scientifically or biologically speaking she'll have developed the toughest mental perspective possible. That'll come later, in her twenties, thirties or forties. In addition, there's her emotional state. The hardest part of being on a long trip is being away from your support system, away from the nest, away from your parents, and away from the womb of home. There's also the loneliness that kicks in – that's off the charts. I can't tell you how many people leave Base Camp in that first fifteen days. The loneliness really starts to get to you there.

'And, lastly, there's also the spiritual side. You definitely have to believe in something bigger than yourself, whether that's a mountain god or goddess, Allah, Jesus Christ or Buddha. You have to embrace some kind of spirituality. If you don't, it's so much harder to climb.'

And Parfet knows all about how hard climbing can be. Each time he set off for a new mountain, he had no idea whether his body would allow him to make it. He was ill-prepared and ill-equipped for the series of challenges that lay in wait for him. When he made his first attempt on Everest in 2005, a member of his expedition and good friend Scotsman Rob Milne suddenly collapsed 400 metres from the summit and died of a heart attack. Then Parfet's second bottle of oxygen didn't work. Finally, bad weather closed in.

'That wasn't my time,' he says now. 'Coming back down and seeing Rob on the ground was an experience that's very hard to describe. I decided to take a break from Everest. So I went to climb Cho Oyu, the sixth highest mountain in the world. But as I was going to the summit from Camp Two, I felt terrible. At first I thought it was the altitude, but then I realised it was a panic attack. I thought, What if I can't go on? But thank goodness I had someone with me who was able to boil me some warm water and make warm chocolate and who calmed me down. But I still barely made it!

'Then I went back to Everest in 2007 and got to a quiet, humble spot on the mountain and I let go of my fears, and had the most amazing expedition. It was so smooth.'

Parfet says Alyssa's doing everything right to prepare for her own assault on Everest. He finds someone like her, who has big dreams and the courage to follow them, nothing short of inspirational. And if he can offer her any guidance, it would be to be humble when she trains, humble when she climbs, and humble when she comes home again. Humility is key, as is blocking out any negativity people try to direct towards you.

'And remember when you're up there on that mountain: the other side of fear is freedom!' says Parfet, who now divides his time between mountains and his real estate business. 'You're going to need every ounce of strength and energy to get up these big hills. It's about ignoring what other people think and blocking everything else out. Just remember who you are, and refuse to get caught up in ego and the fuss that surrounds Everest.

'Follow your dreams, and without question. If I were to stop following my dreams, a key part of me would die. It's inspirational to see what Alyssa's doing, and wonderful to have such dynamism and positivity in life.'

PART FOUR

The Final Countdown

CHAPTER 21

Icefall on Manaslu

'You won't find reasonable men on the tops of tall mountains.'
– HUNTER S. THOMPSON

At 8156 metres, Manaslu, in Nepal's northern Himalaya range, is the eighth highest mountain in the world. A series of long ridges and glacial valleys, it's been described as a jagged wall of ice and snow hanging in the sky, and was only conquered comparatively recently, in 1956, by two Japanese climbers.

The latest published statistics show that from May 1971 to May 2011, sixty-five climbers lost their lives on the mountainside, through avalanches, falls, altitude sickness, exhaustion and even lightning strikes. The following year, in 2012, in one single avalanche alone, eleven climbers were killed and dozens more seriously injured. It's considered the fourth most dangerous mountain on the planet, out of the fourteen main peaks over 8000 metres.

It's probably best known in Australia as the peak that killed our most accomplished female Himalayan climber ever, Sue Fear. In 1997, she'd led the first successful ascent by an Australian team on Makalu II, 15 km from Everest, and then reached the summits of four 8000ers, including Everest in 2003 from the Tibetan side – only the second Australian woman, after Brigitte Muir, to conquer the peak. In 2006, she climbed her fifth 8000er, Manaslu, and got to the top. But on the way back she plummeted down a crevasse to her death.

As extreme high-mountain skier Mike Marolt once said, 'After climbing and skiing on some forty of the world's major 6000-, 7000- and 8000-metre peaks, this is the only mountain I could not recommend to anyone: it is avalanche central . . . an avalanche chute.'

Sixteen-year-old Alyssa Azar wants to climb Manaslu as it's so widely regarded a good training run for an assault on Everest. Naturally, she's nervous about the climb in September–October 2013, but she feels everything is on track with her training and mental attitude. 'It's been said that fear and limits are just illusions,' she says. 'That's something I believe. Some of the most memorable and rewarding moments of my life so far are those where I was pushing my limits beyond what I once thought they were.

'We all have things that scare us, but in order to grow and become a better person we have to confront them. That makes our ability to deal with hardship even greater.'

Her training cranks up even further, and now she walks and runs with weights strapped around her ankles to simulate wearing heavy mountain boots and crampons. She's now in the gym at least three times a day, dressed in singlet and shorts, doing weights or boxing or various endurance exercises. Every so often, she goes to the whiteboard to write down her times. Above it is a huge banner: 'Strong People Are Harder To Kill.'

She and Glenn also buy a second-hand altitude machine, a portable hypoxic generator, which replaces some of the oxygen with nitrogen, simulating the drop in oxygen levels in the air high in the mountains. She often runs on the treadmill or cycles on an exercise bike with a mask over her face attached to the generator. At night, most of the space in her small bedroom is taken up by a clear plastic-walled tent erected over her bed. A similar mix of oxygen and nitrogen is pumped into it, which means she'll be able to get her lungs used to working much harder to breathe, even when she's asleep. Now, before she goes to bed each night, she decides at what altitude she'd like to sleep, and adjusts the gauge accordingly.

'Usually, I change it every night in order, as if I'm slowly ascending a mountain, then moving down, then going back up,' says Alyssa. 'I'm using the machine for exercise but also for rest and recovery, to get my body used to high altitude. The highest altitude it can simulate is 4000 metres but I'm hoping it will make a big difference to me.'

Glenn laughs. 'Worth $7500 new, I think that's now the most valuable thing in our house!' he says. 'But I thought we needed to buy it now, before Manaslu, to give her the best possible chance of succeeding – and coming back down in one piece. We can work out how to afford it later . . . The only one of us who's not so keen is Christian. It sounds like a respirator all night, and he gets a little disturbed by the sound.'

Father and daughter also decide to undertake a CrossFit challenge to raise funds for climbing equipment. The trip to Manaslu is costing a total of around $21 000 for Alyssa and someone to go with her, as well as paying the expedition company Asian Trekking for a high-altitude Sherpa guide, a cook and a camp worker. The fundraising plan involves completing twenty-four Workouts of the Day, or WODs, within twenty-four hours, with the idea of emulating, as with the Aussie 10, that tough 24-hour push to the summit of Everest from Camp IV.

It feels like such a good idea, they decide to brand it the 'Everest Challenge' and open it up to anyone else who wants to do it too. One enthusiastic backer is Jo Brooker-Clark, who owns CrossFit Toowoomba, and who first met Glenn through a mutual friend in 2010. Since then, Alyssa has done a lot of training with her.

Brooker-Clark takes it upon herself to design the WODs in line with various statistics she's unearthed about climbing Everest.

These include seventeen minutes of as many rounds as possible of six burpees, four pull-ups and fourteen box jumps – in honour of Alyssa being seventeen when she's set to climb Everest, with the first day of her climb due to happen on 6 April 2014; and four minutes for eight kettle bell swings, nine pull-downs and then fourteen minutes for six weight lifts and nine squats – since the atmospheric pressure at Everest's peak is 4.89psi and at sea-level is 14.69psi. 'It was pure genius!' says Alyssa.

With such a strong sense of community among those who practise CrossFit, they put the challenge online and soon they're inundated with over 300 eager participants from around Australia, with two more from the US and one from Malaysia.

'I was surprised how many people we got, especially over different time zones,' Alyssa says. 'But everyone seemed to love it, and even now they're keen to make it an annual event. Some people camped out or brought fold-out beds to gyms, and I went to Dad's gym and slept there in between all the workouts. We all posted what we were doing on the website and when, and it was a lot of fun, and raised a fair bit of money towards my costs. I was pretty tired by the end, but very grateful!'

Brooker-Clark is happy to help. 'The thing about Alyssa is that she is a doer,' she says. 'She gets shit done. She's a stayer and finishes what she starts. I always think how lucky she is to know what she wanted at such a young age *and* that there was a direct path to achieving that goal right in her home. Most people don't have a clue until much later in life, but with Alyssa it always seemed as if she was born to be an adventurer and she had Glenn in her corner, helping her make it happen. Most dads, if their child said they wanted to be the youngest person in Australia to climb Mount Everest, might say, We'll see, or, One day. But he actually said, Sounds great, let's make it happen. And every day from then on, he's been there, keeping her on track, helping her.

'We are all living vicariously through her. Not in a jealous or negative way, but a You-Go-Girl! way. It truly is exciting to watch her achieve things. There's no tall poppy syndrome with Alyssa – I and everyone I know is excited for her, and will be cheering her on every step of the way. It makes you realise the possibilities are endless for us all.'

Alyssa appears on the Channel 10 TV show *The Project*, and both she and the station receive a tidal wave of correspondence wishing her well afterwards. Some of it is unexpected: a boy from Western Australia writes to ask her out on a date. She declines. All her energy, she explains politely, is being taken up with her Everest quest. But most are from people saying they've been blown away by her mission, and find her incredibly inspirational.

Trying to inspire other people in that way, particularly young people, has always been high on Alyssa's list of priorities. She feels strongly that everyone has their own Everest to climb, whether it's a physical goal they want to reach or a personal challenge in their lives to overcome. It's one of her dearest ambitions after Everest to be able to use her own experiences to spur on others to achieve their dreams.

'It sounds a cliché, but it couldn't be more true,' says Alyssa. 'I'm no superhuman. I'm no more special than anyone else. I just had a dream and made a conscious decision to put in an insane level of commitment to make it come true. I've also been given support and the opportunity to help make that crazy notion inside my head come to fruition. I have failures like anyone else, critics, struggles, moments of weakness, periods of darkness, doubts, and I fear failure sometimes, but I've worked hard and have a lot more hard work to put in. I want to tell people, particularly young people: Dare to dream, be unique and different, don't be put off by fear of failure and do everything you can to make your dreams come true.

'If I can inspire even one person to do something great, then I'll have succeeded. If I can share the lessons I've learnt, empower people and convince them to aim high, then I'll be happy. Besides the actual climbing, that is easily the biggest highlight of what I do.'

* * *

Alyssa knows that Manaslu, her first peak over 8000 metres, is going to be by far the most dangerous and difficult climb she's ever attempted. The route to the top is quite short compared to most 8000ers but the temperatures on its slopes are much warmer, and parts routinely accumulate vast quantities of deep snow. Avalanches are a constant danger, as well as the seracs, or great blocks of ice, breaking off and thundering down the mountain face, while the crevasses along the glacier are deep, frequent and often totally camouflaged by snow.

As a result, Manaslu has a death rate among climbers of just over 35 per cent, relative to those who make it to the top – more than fifteen times that of the world's sixth highest mountain, Cho Oyu.

Sonia Taylor, the trekker who was on Kilimanjaro with Alyssa, is flying over with her to act as her guardian up until Manaslu Base Camp. At that point, she'll go off on a trek, while Alyssa will climb in the company of a Sherpa, Gyuliak. Taylor feels distinctly uneasy.

'I really don't know if Alyssa is ready for this,' she says. 'She has been trekking and works hard at her fitness. But climbing mountains technically is not something that she has been doing for years. Manaslu is a big mountain to do for your first hardcore climb. Climbing in New Zealand has nothing on this.'

Alyssa receives a text from Keith Fennell, wishing her luck. It reassures her. On the plane to Bangkok, where she and Taylor have a nine-hour stopover before the flight to Nepal, she reads his *Warrior*

Training for what she estimates could be the hundredth time, to keep herself buoyed.

When she and Taylor finally arrive in Kathmandu, they're phoned by Elizabeth Hawley, the ninety-year-old American former journalist who has lived in Nepal since 1960, chronicling all the records of Himalayan expeditions. Well known for her no-nonsense, blunt manner, she wants to come over to their hotel to interview Alyssa. As soon as she arrives, however, she's quick to make her opinion felt.

'Sixteen is too young,' she immediately says. 'You are too young. You're not mentally or physically ready. You're too inexperienced to take on your first 8000-metre climb.' Hawley is unimpressed by the other training climbs Alyssa has done. 'Kilimanjaro?' she says. 'That's a joke!'

Alyssa takes offence instantly, and becomes even more uncommunicative than normal. She is sullen and withdrawn and sits and reads a magazine article Taylor has given her, ignoring her interviewer. In the end, Hawley leaves, saying she'll be back to talk to Alyssa when she returns from her climb. Her parting words to Alyssa: 'Don't push yourself. Back out if you need; the mountains will always be there.'

Taylor just isn't sure what to make of Alyssa's reaction to Hawley. She knows the youngster puts great store in surrounding herself with positivity, and likes to shut out negativity. But at the same time, she thinks Alyssa should have shown the elderly woman more respect. 'Alyssa completely shut down,' she says. 'I wasn't sure if she was just trying to shut her opinion out, like she didn't care what the woman thought and didn't want her in her life, or if she was being a bit arrogant.

'But then she is still young. You forget sometimes how young she is. She didn't give anything away. I didn't know what she was thinking. Was she nervous? Would she really like to have backed out?

Or was it more: Bring it on! It's impossible to tell, sometimes, with Alyssa.'

Another day in the hotel, a male guest approaches Alyssa, saying he's heard she plans to climb Manaslu and, what's more, it will be the first 8000-metre mountain she's tried. 'You're insane!' he tells her. She smiles sweetly back. 'But believe me,' Taylor says later, 'he wasn't alone in his opinion!'

In truth, Alyssa is trying very hard to stay as positive as possible. She knows people have their doubts, but she doesn't want to let anyone or anything undermine her confidence. When she gets home, she decides, she'll take a course in Buddhist meditation to strengthen her mind still further, so others can't get in. She's grateful to Taylor for coming with her, but wishes she'd understand more her need to keep focused.

After a few nights in Kathmandu, Alyssa and Taylor are driven north-west along a rough, unsealed road towards the little market town of Arughat Bazar, the start of the six-day trek to Manaslu Base Camp. They make a couple of stops to look at the snow-slathered Manaslu towering over the horizon, as they sweat in the heat below, and finally arrive at their destination six hours later. After a night at a small tea house, with beds as hard as rocks, they meet their two Sherpa guides, Gyuliak and Buan, as well as two porters to carry their gear, and the little troupe set off along a dirt road past rice fields and waterfalls to the tiny village of Soti Khola. From there, it's up and down the narrow rocky trail to Lapubeshi, a settlement dotted over several hills.

At the guesthouse where the pair is staying, the owner expresses surprise that such a young girl is planning to climb Manaslu.

'No.' He shakes his head. 'Too young. Too young.'

Alyssa notices a rash spreading across her neck. She can't tell if it's from the heat, the bugs or the stress of so many people saying they doubt her ability.

ICEFALL ON MANASLU

* * *

The next day, Alyssa and Taylor are up early for honey on toast and hot chocolate, then they finally head for Manaslu. The trail quickly becomes slippery and waterlogged, and, in parts, there's the risk of landslides. There are yaks along the route and the trek winds upwards, downhill and then up again, through pretty villages and lonely windswept fields, over ridges and valleys and across a couple of dilapidated suspension bridges. It feels a lot more remote than the trek to Everest Base Camp, and there are fewer people. The guesthouses vary from comfortable and fairly new to old and rundown. Alyssa doesn't mind. She's intent on their destination.

For the first few days, they're walking at a low altitude, less than 1000 metres above sea level. It's sticky, humid and sweaty, which takes Alyssa by surprise. At times, she almost feels like she's back on Kokoda. She's trying not to think much about the summit. She's trying to concentrate, instead, on taking it easy, not going too hard, conserving her strength.

All the time, Alyssa's looking out for another view of Manaslu, but it remains resolutely hidden behind the rest of the giant massif. On day five, however, arriving at Samagaon, the closest village to Manaslu Base Camp, it suddenly comes dramatically back into view. Alyssa feels her excitement rising, and she gets up early the next day to watch the sunrise and see Manaslu glow in the soft pink of dawn.

The clothes she unpacks from her big bag that morning are all soaking wet. Someone must have dropped it in the water at one of the river crossings. She hopes they'll have a chance to dry before Base Camp. But while she doesn't have any dry clothes to change into, she does like not having too much gear with her. She loves the simplicity of such adventures. She's enjoying the company of nature, the mountains and the books she has with her – this time, as well as Fennell's *Warrior Training* and *Warrior Brothers*, other inspiring stories of heroic SAS members, they include Jack Kerouac's *The Dharma Bums*, the semi-fictional 1950s story looking at the relationship between the outdoors, trekking, mountaineering, Buddhism and city life, which she finds perfect for reading in this environment.

She enjoys having so much time to think as she treks, too, and ponders that this would be the kind of thing she'd love to do professionally as an adult. She thinks again about one day helping her dad run Adventure Professionals and, when the time came, taking a business course and developing it further. It'd be great to become a better rock climber as well, and incorporate some climbing expeditions into the agenda. Then maybe some public speaking about adventure travel, and motivational talks, particularly to young people. And perhaps her own brand of adventure clothing, gear, maybe even a few books . . .

Occasionally she wonders what's happening back home and in the world at large, but it all seems so remote from her, among the mountains in this other place she's come to know as her second home. She imagines what her dad must be doing, and asks herself how she can ever repay him for everything he's done for her. But coming back with a summit would be the most welcome down payment, she knows.

The group heads off straight after breakfast, with the trail climbing abruptly through a forest, then on to an exposed escarpment north of the Manaslu glacier. The scenery is spectacular: the glacier, a turquoise glacial lake below and mountains ranged all around. It's almost enough to take a trekker's mind off the steepness of the five-hour climb up the slippery trail of icy soil and rock to Base Camp at around 4400 metres. Almost.

The hill never seems to end, with false crest after false crest, until Alyssa starts thinking, There's really nothing here. Where are we going? Are we really in the right place? And then, just as she's wondering if she should talk to the guides and ask them if they really know the way, Base Camp suddenly appears. Alyssa is thrilled. But she is also so tired, and happy to have factored in a few rest days before she's set to start climbing to the peak.

Taylor spends the next days chatting to many of the other climbers staying at Base Camp over breakfast, lunch and dinner. Alyssa is quiet, and reads, listens to her iPod, organises her gear, takes some photos and scribbles in her journal. She carefully writes out the legendary three rules of mountaineering: 'It's always further than it looks, it's always taller than it looks, and it's always harder than it looks.' Then she copies out the words of famed Polish mountaineer Voytek Kurtyka: 'I like to describe Himalayan climbing as a kind of art of suffering,' he once said. 'Just pushing, pushing yourself to your limits.' She wants to prepare herself mentally for the torture that undoubtedly lies ahead.

Also safely in her pack is a copy of the Victorian poem 'Invictus', with its immortal lines: 'It matters not how strait the gate/ How charged with punishments the scroll/ I am the master of my fate/ I am the captain of my soul.' That was the poem Nelson Mandela recited to other prisoners when he was locked away on Robben Island and which he said empowered him with its message of self-mastery. Similarly, Burmese Opposition leader and Nobel Peace laureate Aung San Suu Kyi also says it has been a constant inspiration for her, her father and his fellow fighters for independence. *Invictus* – Latin for 'unconquerable soul'. For Alyssa, the meaning of the lines hit home and she felt they'd be a real motivator when times got tough. If she needed them, they'd make her feel strong.

On the third day, Alyssa's Asian Trekking expedition group assembles together with their Sherpas. There they carry out a *puja*, a little ceremony asking for a blessing from the gods for luck on their climb. They throw rice in the air three times, and the climbers put their ice axes in the middle to be blessed. Then they're finally off.

Taylor treks with Alyssa across the rocky route to Crampon Point, the area named a touch unimaginatively after the spot where the ground turns almost immediately to ice and climbers need to put their crampons on their boots to get a grip, as well as their harnesses to connect to ropes. From there, Taylor waves her farewell, struggling to hide how troubled she feels. A lot of climbers she'd been talking to at Base Camp have been climbing for years, but Alyssa is still very new to the sport. Of course, she is very fit and knowledgeable and is an experienced trekker, but she hasn't done a lot of climbing. Taylor notices how awkward the young girl looks as she stomps off in her big mountain boots, with her backpack slung across her shoulders, and secretly worries, as she herself turns back to return to camp to wait for her own, much more leisurely, trek around the mountain's base to begin.

* * *

The first part of the ascent of Manaslu is one of the most dangerous. Climbers work their way up a glacier, an almost vertical slope fretted with constant crevasses, down which a number of people have plunged to their deaths. Alyssa clips herself into the fixed lines for safety and carefully picks her way forward.

Some of the crevasses are very hard to see, but Alyssa is pumped about where she is, and full of fire. Base Camp is finally gone, and she's in a world of white, surrounded by mountains. At last, she feels like she's at home again.

She climbs for a slow, steady five hours and then inches her way up the last steep stretch into Camp I at 5700 metres. When she arrives, she's met by another climber who's also slowly acclimatising, and her Sherpa boils snow down into water and makes some pasta for their dinner. There she rests and acclimatises, and heads back down to Base Camp the next morning.

She gets down much more easily than she went up, and her

waiting tent at Base Camp by now looks pretty cosy. She goes in to take off her heavy climbing gear and put on her camp clothes: track pants, a T-shirt, ugg boots and down jacket. She looks calm, but inside she's ecstatic. All she can think is that she's just had her first experience above Base Camp on an 8000-metre peak. And that feels wonderful.

When Taylor catches up with her over dinner, she can see the teenager is glowing. She looks great, and says she feels great.

'Well done, Alyssa!' she tells the girl. 'I'm so happy and excited for you.'

Alyssa's Sherpa is reassured, too. 'She is very strong,' he tells Taylor. 'I am happy.'

Alyssa spends two more days at Base Camp, resting, waiting for her body to acclimatise, drinking as much fluid as she can, reading and listening to music. Many mountaineers find the enforced rest periods boring and frustrating as they're so keen to get out and up, but she tries to use the time productively. She welcomes the space to sit and think, work out her goals for the future and ponder what she needs to do to get there, and to try to train her mind, keeping determined and focused.

Taylor notices Alyssa isn't as withdrawn as she was the first time, though. She spends a lot more time in the mess tent, and she talks to some of the other climbers over meals. She plays cards and jokes around with the Sherpas, who say how strange it is to see a sixteen-year-old girl there. But they are terribly attentive and protective, and one tells her he has a daughter Alyssa's age. She's also smiling a lot more. Taylor is reassured. She now feels confident about leaving Alyssa at Base Camp and going off to start her own trek.

Three days later, Alyssa climbs back up to Camp I for the night, from where she plans to head up to Camp II the next day. The weather's not good, but they all hope for better in the morning.

When they wake, however, it's to a complete white-out. It's

snowing and foggy, and impossible to see even half a metre away. In some ways, Alyssa finds it a magical sight; in others, it's bitterly disappointing. The Sherpa tells them it'll be impossible to climb higher just now. The higher they are in that kind of weather, the more dangerous. They wait for a couple of hours to see if it might clear, but when it's obvious it's set in, they head back down to Base Camp to rest a few days and give the weather a chance to pick up before the next rotation.

Alyssa comes down and finds her tent at Base Camp covered in snow. She shakes it off and resigns herself to one more rotation to try for Camp II again. If she makes it this time, she'll come back down and then return back up for the last time to try to make the summit.

Eventually it's time, and Alyssa trudges off back to Camp I again. The climb feels easier this time; she knows the route a bit better now, and knows what to expect. She sleeps overnight at Camp I, but the next morning wakes up with a real feeling of dread. The path ahead is over a massive icefall from which blocks are almost constantly tearing away and crashing down below. This is going to be one of the toughest days of climbing, and she already feels drained. She tries to pull herself together; this is the kind of challenge she's spent her whole life preparing for. It makes her realise that a climber can be as physically fit as possible, but ultimately it comes down to their mind.

A six-hour climb lies ahead and she sets off up the brutally steep terrain, knowing that because it's such a technical climb she has to be careful and controlled, but also move as quickly as possible. The Sherpa explains how no one should spend any more time on the icefall than they need to, as it's just very, very dangerous. The crevasses, in the case of any false move or slip, can prove deadly, and there's the constant threat from above of falling ice blocks. Also, if it snows, the danger of avalanche increases significantly. Alyssa is soon lost in concentration as she picks her way warily across the rungs of aluminium ladders strung over deep crevasses. Occasionally she sneaks a look down and shudders. All she can see below are dark voids, and certain death.

An hour on comes the 'hourglass', a slope angled at about 40 degrees, deep in snow, from which tonnes of snow regularly fall down in a perfect avalanche. There, she also jumars for the first time, ascending with a device that slides along the rope in the path she's moving, but grips it when pulled in the opposite direction. It's the kind of technical climb she loves.

She's only another hour away from Camp II when it happens. She reaches the top of a steep snow hill and moves a little to the left. Then she stops and rests for thirty seconds while she clips her harness onto the next rope, ready to head off. A few minutes later, as she's travelling, she can hear a loud crackling sound, then the roar of what sounds like thunder close by. She can feel wind on her face and every hair on her head stands on end. The noise is deafening. With her heart in her mouth, she looks up – just in time to see a serac the size of an apartment building sheer off the mountainside and come hurtling down to her right. She clings to the rope, waiting. There's nothing else she can do. There's nowhere to go. She utters just three words: 'Oh my God!'

The pressure of the air displaced by the massive bulk of solid ice hits her full in the body as it plunges past, taking her breath away. There's a split second of the most profound silence Alyssa has ever heard and then an almighty crash, like the sound of a freight train travelling at 150 km per hour smashing into a concrete wall. The serac has fallen straight down a crevasse just 20 metres to her right. She shudders.

If she'd just decided to go that way, and moved right instead of left . . . She tries not to think about it. She doesn't want to allow her focus to slide. All climbers hear about things like that happening, but it's hard to imagine how you'll handle it until you've actually seen it for yourself. But Alyssa is fine. She mentally takes stock and, while shaken, she realises she is now pumped with adrenalin. That was an incredible sight, but it was a timely reminder that, on a mountain, anything can happen, at any time. She repeats to herself that she has to respect the mountains. They call the shots. They always will.

She continues climbing and is soon at Camp II, set in a sheltered hollow under an ice cliff, where she'll sleep in a tent at an altitude of 6400 metres – the highest she's ever spent a night. She feels good, with no headaches or dizziness, and decides, with real satisfaction, that this is the best she's ever felt at altitude. She doesn't have much of an appetite, however, but forces down fluids and some food to keep up her energy levels. She's a little lethargic too, and can't be bothered to write in her diary or read her book. At altitudes like this, that's pretty normal. One of the other climbers, however, isn't doing too well. He says he can see a black spot on one of his eyes, which seems to be growing bigger: a symptom of the start of snow blindness. His Sherpa leads him down straight away.

Alyssa feels grateful she's feeling good, but she doesn't sleep too well, tossing and turning most of the night in her sleeping bag. She's due to return to Base Camp the next day but the next time she's up here, she'll be hoping to try for the summit. From here, it's only three to four hours to Camp III at 6700 metres, and another four to five hours to the final stop, Camp IV, at 7300 metres. After a night there, it'll be straight on to the summit six to seven hours away and just 856 metres higher, at 8156 metres above sea level.

But this rotation is over for now and the next morning it's back down to Base Camp, a much quicker climb down than it was up, particularly as she gets to abseil part of the way over the icefall. Holding the rope tightly enough in her big snow gloves is tricky, so she always makes sure she is clipped on too. When she finally arrives back at base, it's busy with exhausted climbers from higher up who've been forced to turn back from their summit attempts because of the worsening weather. There are hopes, though, that it might brighten. She tells herself to be patient.

She knows climbing involves a lot of stop and go; sometimes climbing for hours on end and then stopping for days. She uses that forced downtime to think, read, write, rest and rehydrate, and eat as much as she can to build up her energy levels. Glenn stays in touch with her by satellite phone, checking she's okay. He always worries, but realises that little is controllable on a mountain such as Manaslu. He just has to have faith in Alyssa's ability to cope.

A new weather forecast comes through on the third day, indicating that there might be a few clearer days later that week. Alyssa and her Sherpa decide to try again, planning to time their ascent for that window. They prepare for the worst, but hope for the best. She climbs back up to Camp I in steady snowfall, unable to see more than a metre or two in front of her. On arrival, she's grateful to be greeted with a hot drink. But with a sinking heart she hears that other climbers are now giving up their summit attempts, as the window of clear weather just hasn't happened, and doesn't seem at all likely to happen now. The odds of being able to get to the summit are shrinking every hour. She decides to stay the night, just in case . . .

The next morning, the weather's even worse. It's almost a complete white-out, with snow and strong winds whipping at the tents. As she peers out of the opening, still in her down Gore-Tex suit from the previous day – it had been too cold to take it off before climbing into her sleeping bag – she can see the situation is deteriorating rapidly. She has to almost dig her way out to go and talk to the others at the camp. More climbers are arriving all the time from the higher slopes. A number of Sherpas haven't been able to get past Camp III because snowdrifts have buried the fixed lines and they are no longer able to work out where the crevasses are. Besides, every time they try to move forward, they sink up to their chests in snow.

One group has reached Camp IV but were unable to advance any higher. Another man has become stuck in soft snow after an avalanche and survived, but is having to call off his second attempt at the summit. Alyssa's Sherpa is adamant: it's not going to be possible. The bad weather has arrived early, and it will only worsen from this point on.

Alyssa weighs up the odds carefully. Most of the time, she knows you have to listen to your Sherpa, since they're the experienced ones who really know the mountains. If your gut instinct, though, tells you something different, then you think about it. But if everything's telling you it can't be done, then however much you want to get to a summit, you have to realise you'd be endangering not only your own life, but others' as well.

One British team insist they're going to continue up, and try to summit in two days. The others watch them disappear into the blizzard. Alyssa looks after them longingly before turning back down towards Base Camp.

When she arrives, she has another hot drink, then stays for another few days, resting, packing up her tent, gazing by day at the 360-degree view of the world's tallest mountains and, after the sun goes down, staring at the stars in the night sky, revelling in being in the middle of nowhere. Despite her disappointment, she still feels blessed to be a sixteen-year-old travelling the world. The news reaches her on the second day that the British team reached halfway between Camp II and III before they were forced to turn back round and descend. The climbing season on Manaslu, it is announced, is closing early.

Her dream of reaching the very top of Manaslu is now over. She's sad, but philosophical. Manaslu is so dangerous, she knew she really couldn't take the chance of pushing ahead when everyone else had warned her not to. On Everest, she knows she might consider pushing on in weather like that, but not on Manaslu. Yet at the same time, it served its purpose: it was a great training peak for Everest, it tested her, it allowed her to try out some technical climbing, it showed her that she was coping well with the altitude, and it allowed her to prove to herself that she was up to the challenge.

With her gear finally packed up, she takes one more glance back up the mountain towards the summit. She can see nothing at all.

CHAPTER 22

Everest's Best of the Best: Andrew Lock

Climbing Manaslu is excellent training for Everest, according to the man who's often referred to as the mountaineer's ultimate mountaineer, Andrew Lock. The first Australian to reach the summits of all fourteen of the world's highest mountains – and only the eighteenth person on earth ever to do so – believes that Alyssa Azar is well on track to achieve her dearest Everest dream.

Still, to make the top, she will face huge challenges. 'It's good that she's done Manaslu, but she still doesn't have a lot of experience,' he says. 'So she will feel a bit intimidated by Everest physically.

'She'll probably have a lot more strength than many other people, but that relative lack of experience is harder to overcome.'

His passion for Everest was first ignited back in 1985 when he heard Macartney-Snape talk about his ascent of Everest in the back room of a pub in Wagga Wagga, a country NSW city where Lock was working as a local policeman. He was swept up by the excitement and the romance of the idea of climbing big mountains. It was that which kept driving him forward up higher slopes ever since.

'It became a passion for me,' he says. 'I needed to know whether or not I could climb these peaks and the only way to find out was by climbing them. I enjoyed the environment, and I like challenging myself in an environment where the outcome isn't certain.

'I like getting away into the wilds; sometimes you have a view to enjoy if not from the summit then at some points on the way up, and it's a pretty special experience to share with a climbing partner if you have one.'

But as far as the difficulties of climbing 8000-metre mountains go, Lock knows them far more intimately than nearly any other human alive. Over his sixteen-year quest to conquer the top fourteen peaks, he's survived harrowing experiences.

In 2009, after celebrating reaching the top of his last 8000-metre Himalayan peak, Shishapangma, following three earlier failed attempts, he and his climbing partner ran into trouble. It was getting dark, and they had to try to climb down a knife-edge ridge so steep, they were forced to do it ladder-style, facing the ground, knowing there were sheer drops on either side. Even worse, a blizzard had kicked off and the falling snow and wind had covered their knee-deep tracks so completely, they couldn't work out the way back to safety. They had no option but to cut an ice ledge, sit on their packs for insulation and wait for dawn – with no cover, no food, no drink and absolutely no way of melting any of the constantly falling snow for water. As with twelve of the other peaks, he'd climbed with the minimum of possessions with him, and without supplementary oxygen.

It was the longest night of Lock's life, sitting shaking in the -20 to -30° temperatures, trying to keep his fingers and toes constantly moving to prevent frostbite. All the time, he knew the clock was ticking on their chances of staying alive at such a high altitude. No words, he says, can ever describe such misery. 'But if you're ever going to an altitude of 8000 metres and over, the outcome is never certain. It's so dangerous, and it kills people regularly.'

Eventually, the sun did rise, the weather cleared a little, and the pair managed to find their way back down to the highest camp. The mountaineering community were then able to celebrate his remarkable 'Mountaineering Grand Slam'. It was 'like winning fourteen Olympic golds, holding your breath at the same time!', as Greg Mortimer described it.

There have been plenty of other near-misses too. Lock's first summit of an 8000er was K2, at 8612 metres the world's second highest mountain, on the border of Pakistan and China. He did it in 1993, in terrible snow and wind, but on descent the team leader and another member of the small five-person expedition fell to their deaths.

In 1997, he struck more trouble on a solo climb of the 8047-metre Broad Peak in Pakistan. He'd missed on his first try and his climbing partner went home. He, however, simply pushed on and tried a different route to the top. He reached the summit successfully but was forced to spend the night on the mountain when darkness fell and he was unable to get down. That was the first time he'd been forced to stay awake all night, knowing he risked perishing from exposure if he dropped off to sleep. Only with dawn was he finally able to safely descend.

That time was, he later wrote in *Australian Geographic* magazine, 'a revelation; an insight into the inner strength we humans possess but so rarely draw upon in our regulated, sanitised, comfortable lives.'

Lock finally made the top of Everest via the South Col in 2000, after three unsuccessful tries, and climbed to the top again in 2004.

In 2012 he was forced to abandon his final attempt, solo and without oxygen, when he started suffering double vision and nausea and began hallucinating from Acute Mountain Sickness close to the top. It had been his dream to climb up one side, push through the unknown 'no man's land' and descend via the other, but he was unable to get a permit from the Chinese government. At that point, having been crowned the Australian Geographic Society Adventurer of the Year three years earlier, he announced his retirement from 8000-metre mountains.

'The more times you go up, the more chance you have of ending up dead,' says Lock who, in his non-mountain time, works as a Canberra public servant in, rather ironically, risk management. 'I'd achieved everything I wanted to, except that traverse. I'd wanted to do it because I thought it'd be fun. Once that opportunity was withdrawn, the motivation to go back was gone. I might go back one day for a charity expedition or as part of a specialist team, but not as something I'd do full-time. It's too dangerous.'

It'll be particularly dangerous for Alyssa because of her lack of climbing experience, he believes. Even though she'll have oxygen cylinders, the help of Sherpas and will be able to follow fixed ropes over the route, Everest is still the highest mountain on earth and is perilous at every stage, particularly over the Khumbu Icefall, and up the Lhotse Face.

'No one can ever guarantee success on Everest,' he says. 'Despite the volume of people going up, there are still the dangers of climbing, the altitude to cope with – even if you acclimatise well, you can still feel really bad – and the cold and the weather, and you only have a small window in which to steal the summit. Then there are the seracs, which you just can't avoid. You take the chance every time you step on Everest of getting a block of ice the size of a house falling on your head.

'For Alyssa, she'll feel significant trepidation before she sets her first step on the mountain. She'll still have lingering questions and doubts: Can she do it? Will she be good enough for it? So for her, going up and down won't be a major chore. It'll enable her to acclimatise and it'll give her more confidence each time she goes up and down between camps successfully. It's a long slog, but once she gets each stage under her belt, she'll know what's coming up, she'll be faster and she'll feel a lot more relaxed.'

Hearing that Alyssa would first climb Aconcagua, the highest mountain in South America, as her last preparation expedition before Everest, he says that will be good for adding to her experience, too. However, by the time she'll arrive in Nepal for The Big One, she'll have lost all the acclimatisation she'll have built up in Argentina.

From all his years at the top, he does want to offer Alyssa some advice. 'Generally, young people want to keep pushing themselves, but she should stop when she wants to. She should step carefully. Take her time. Don't rush.

'But most of all, believe in yourself. She does sound like a really focused young person and with the passion to do it for herself, rather than being pushed into it by parents, I'm sure she'll have the physical capability. She should just take her time and not be afraid to turn around if the weather's not good.

'The mountain will still be there a week later if she goes down and sits out the storm. If she doesn't, she might not be.'

CHAPTER 23

Aconcagua: The Last Practice Climb

'The best possess a feeling for beauty, the courage to take risks, the discipline to tell the truth, the capacity for sacrifice.'

— ERNEST HEMINGWAY

When Alyssa Azar returns from Manaslu at the start of November 2013, she only has two months until her final big climb before Everest: Aconcagua. The highest mountain in the Americas at 6960 metres, it's one of the Seven Summits, and is in the mighty Andes in Argentina, close to the border with Chile, with a number of glaciers along the ascent. She's excited, but nervous. She wonders if there's anything she's overlooked in all her training, any area in which she needs to do more work.

She asks herself who, apart from her dad, she could call on to give her an honest appraisal of where she's at. One man's name keeps coming up: *Warrior Training*'s Keith Fennell. She's never met him but emails and asks if he'd be prepared to see her, and run her through a few of his trademark challenges to give her an opinion. He comes back to say he'd be delighted to help.

'I'm thrilled,' says Alyssa. 'I know he'll give me a really honest, down-the-line answer based on my ability. He isn't going to be nice about it. He'll look at me seriously and let us know what he feels. He was in the SAS and is an expert on fitness and mental toughness.

He'll see immediately where I'm at.'

Fennell has heard a lot about Alyssa from Glenn, but dads aren't normally the best judges of their daughters' abilities. 'They're seeing their kids through love goggles,' says Fennell. 'So everything they say you expect to be tainted.' He invites her down to his home on the south coast of NSW for a day of training in mid-December, shortly after she turns seventeen.

She travels down, and the pair meet up and talk at length, mostly about her focus, her goal of reaching the top of Everest, and what she's doing to get there. The next morning, he puts her through her paces.

First off, they do a tough CrossFit session, with Fennell watching her closely to see how fit, and how strong, she is. Then the pair throw on heavy packs and start up a steep escarpment. In this thirty-minute exercise, Fennell tells her, her heart rate will go through the roof, but he wants her to keep going, no matter what. She should imagine something's happened on Everest, like an avalanche, and she's rushing to get help, or that the weather's closing in and she only has a small window of time to make camp. Every second counts. Every moment she might stop is a sign that she needs to improve her strength and endurance; it's an opportunity for self-improvement, the chance to become a stronger person.

'She understood what I was trying to do straight away,' says Fennell. 'I expected to beat her comfortably, but the difference didn't really kick in until after twenty-five minutes and closer to thirty. At the end, she said to me that she had stopped three times for a total of two minutes, so she had 120 seconds of self-improvement possible. She was almost a little bit pissed off with herself. But I know how difficult that challenge is. Your calves, even the soles of your feet burn, there's a lot of false crests, and soldiers have whinged while doing it. But I was very impressed. She was so determined, and so truthful.'

Next, he sets them both an eight and a half hour walk, with

the last 2 km up and down ravines and across waterways. Again, he doesn't expect her to be able to keep up with him. But she does. 'Every time I turned round, she would be right there,' he says. 'And there was no whingeing. I've a good friend who's a physical instructor, and while we were walking he asked me how long we had left. But Alyssa never did. It was very impressive. She's still very young, and you're not in the zone to have excellent endurance at seventeen. But her endurance was phenomenal. I thought she could go all day.'

Then he gives her a choice of activities. She can either be tied to a rope, abseil part-way down a 20-metre cliff and then be locked off and left to hang halfway down – or she can elect to be blindfolded, tie the rope herself and then step off the cliff backwards, to abseil down. Immediately Alyssa chooses the latter. Fennell smiles. He likes how she goes for the most challenging option straight away. 'Good on her!' he thinks. He then watches as she hooks herself onto the rope and steps cleanly off the edge.

'That was very impressive again,' he says. 'I'd taken her sense of control away but she was very methodical and clinical with the rope and then, with the utmost confidence, took the next step. I've seen grown men, experienced men, baulk at things like that. But a seventeen-year-old girl with very limited experience . . . It was very inspirational for me to see someone who's very driven and confident and has it together at that age.'

Alyssa chooses the blindfold option as she thinks it'll be the most difficult, and the furthest out of her comfort zone. It will also prepare her for her time on Everest when she might well be forced to abseil blindly down a cliff, either at night in the darkness, with her goggles fogged or iced up, or suffering snow blindness, like the guy on her Manaslu trip. 'Then you just have to visualise the path you've been up before, and trust you're doing it right,' she says. 'It was a little bit scary, stepping off an edge when you don't know where the edge is, but it was good to do it, and know I could adapt. You need to get over your fears. You need to be able to perform well, without being scared for your life.'

The pair also talk over a series of different scenarios on Everest. Fennell tells her how people have a plan, a performance line, but when things go wrong and the plan doesn't unfold as expected, they can panic and things go from bad to worse. But if something goes wrong on Everest, she should simply figure out what to do to get back on track, back to that point on the line where she intended to be.

Also, there'll be plenty of things thrown at her that she can't control, but she'll need to adapt quickly, reassess her position, and move on. 'At seventeen, with limited life experience, that will be hard,' he says. 'But I talked to her about challenging possibilities, like a life-threatening avalanche happening, leaving her the only person still standing. What will she do? How long might she search for other survivors before going down to save herself? She needs to think in advance what she'd do, how she'd perform. I told her she has to think: I could die, lose fingers, lose toes. But she's very aware of all that. She's under no illusion that what she's doing is very dangerous.

'I've lived through very dangerous times in Iraq and Afghanistan, and in that too, you imagine your perfect performance line. It might be impossible at times to stay on that, but when you come off it, you need to stay focused and get back to it as soon as you can. I think Alyssa could really understand what I was saying and she gave me smart and measured and mature responses. Her mental toughness, level of competence and endurance is almost unbelievable for someone of her age. I thought, Wow! At times, she reminded me of some of the much older and more experienced men in the services. It was a bit of a surprise. She's quite a special young girl, definitely a one percenter, someone who can make a big call. To say I was impressed is an understatement.'

* * *

With Aconcagua so close, and then Everest just around the corner in March 2014, Glenn and Alyssa sign up with a sponsorship company to try to raise more money. But it's tough going.

Many companies don't believe a seventeen-year-old girl could possibly climb Everest. The kind of people who'd usually sponsor such a venture also have at the forefront of their minds the attempt made in 2006 by fifteen-year-old Australian Christopher Harris to become the youngest kid ever to reach the summit. Climbing from the Tibetan side, as the Nepalese authorities don't grant anyone under the age of sixteen a permit, he was sponsored by, among others, *Australian Geographic*, Dick Smith Foods and an investment company. Unfortunately, however, he was forced to turn back after suffering extreme breathlessness on the way to the top. He'd been accompanied by his mountaineer father Richard Harris, as well as filmmaker Mike Dillon to record his trip and . . . Lincoln Hall, who was there to write a piece on the youngster's summit. It was on that fateful expedition that Hall was left for dead by his team, and later rescued by Dan Mazur.

Four years later, in May 2010, a thirteen-year-old American boy, Jordan Romero, successfully climbed with his paramedic father and stepmother, again from the Tibetan side. But everyone seemed to consider him an exception . . . and a boy.

As a result, there are few sponsors around for Alyssa's attempt to become the youngest non-Sherpa female in the world to summit – the record is currently with American Samantha Larson, who climbed aged eighteen in 2007. Nima Chemji Sherpa is the youngest Sherpa female to have ascended, aged sixteen in 2012, and the youngest Australian is still Rex Pemberton at age twenty-one.

With Aconcagua costing $30 000 and Everest an extra $70 000, Glenn starts to feel nervous about the urgency of raising the necessary cash. His business has been going well, to the point where he now has nine full-time employees. His adventure treks have also expanded to include the Overland Track in Tasmania, the Black Cat Trail in PNG, Mount Kinabalu in Borneo, treks in the Kimberley and dog-sledding in the Yukon in Canada. So when a good offer comes in to sell part of his business, the Fighting Fit gym, he accepts it.

'It was a wrench, but I'd made a commitment to get Alyssa ready for Everest, so I had to get the money together,' he says. 'She was uncomfortable with it, but I said I was happy to do it. It's been expensive to get to this point, but hopefully interest in her will grow. You never know.'

Alyssa is taken aback by her dad's resolve. 'I guess in a way I felt selfish and a bit bad but in some ways I think he was also glad and it was just time to sell,' she says. 'I've always had it in my mind that I'll pay back all the money he's spent on my trips one day. That's from the first Kokoda trek, all the way to Everest. I'm determined to do that in the next few years. He's shown so much loyalty to me, and I want to repay that loyalty.'

* * *

For Alyssa's expedition up Aconcagua, Alyssa and Glenn choose a South African company. Another participant on the trip is Australian adventurer Stephen Bock who's climbed in the Andes over many years, and also reached the summit of Everest in 2010 as part of an international climbing team.

Alyssa contacted him on social media twelve months ago, to ask him for advice about Everest. He was coached for his attempt by mountaineer trainer and expedition leader Joe Bonington, who grew up with climbing in his blood. As the son of British mountaineering legend Sir Chris Bonington, the man who led the 1975 Everest expedition that conquered the immensely difficult southwest face of Everest – a feat that has only been attempted three times since – he's an acknowledged world expert.

Bock has seen Alyssa speak before, and knows she is an exceptional girl. He is happy to share some of the lessons he learnt from Bonington to help her on her quest. 'It wasn't my intention to scare the shit out of her, but I talked to her about how the mental aspect is more important than the physical one,' he says. 'Nothing on Everest goes without dramas, or according to plan, so you have to plan all the time for contingencies.

'You hit the wall on Everest the first day, so mentally conditioning yourself to be able to cope is very important. As part of our training, we'd train hard, vomit, then start training again, which is very intense. But it's about conditioning. When you have nothing left in your tank on the mountain it'll be second nature to keep going. And the higher you go, the less you have in your tank. So you have to become increasingly focused and move into a place of amazing grace, a place that's so far beyond any reference point you have, or ever thought yourself capable of having.'

He was last on Aconcagua eight years ago, so has decided to take part in the same expedition Alyssa is on. It's being led by the South African who will also lead the expedition Alyssa has booked to Everest.

A week before they leave, Alyssa has a tattoo etched onto her left wrist, a Taoist yin-yang black-and-white circle with the dots inside, symbolising how completely opposite forces are interconnected. Above it is the script signifying 'Om', the Buddhist chant heard everywhere in Nepal. 'I'd wanted to have those two done for a while,' she says. 'I like the meaning behind them. I like the idea of opposites being balanced, darkness and light, good and bad. It hurt at the time, but I love them.'

A few days later, she returns to the tattooist to have a third: the word INVICTUS stencilled on her right bicep. 'Looking at it makes me feel even stronger, and I'll use it for strength during tough times,' she says. 'I'm nervous but I think I really am prepared for the year.

Everest will be about suffering. It will hurt, but I'm ready.'

Alyssa leaves Australia for Santiago, Chile, on 4 January 2014. That day a timer appears for the first time on her website, the Everest Countdown. At the moment her connecting flight to Mendoza in Argentina, the closest town to Aconcagua, lands, the timer reads: 84 days, 10 hours, 3 minutes and 45 seconds . . .

* * *

Aconcagua starts disastrously. On the day Alyssa arrives, two American climbers who've gone missing on New Year's Eve are found dead, their bodies at the bottom of a crevasse. Park rangers report they'd both been trying to ascend the peak when they fell. Local newspapers confirm that Aconcagua has the highest death rate of any mountain in South America primarily because of its accessibility; its lack of glacier or sheer rock-face climbing lures many totally unqualified and unprepared climbers.

Alyssa, however, remains upbeat. She knows this will be an important training climb for Everest, but the double tragedy serves to remind her that this mountain deserves plenty of respect of its own. To underestimate it could prove similarly catastrophic. There have always been fatalities. At least two climbers died in the 2012/3 season, five died in January 2009 when two were caught in a storm, two more died in falls, and another had a heart attack, while in 2000 four climbers died in the same accident when one fell and took the other three with him. There are also numerous rescues and injuries every year.

While Aconcagua's been described as the highest non-technical mountain in the world, since climbing the northern route – nicknamed 'the normal route' – doesn't always involve ropes and axes, still only around 30 per cent of climbers who attempt the mountain make it to the top. Alyssa's group, however, will be ascending via a much quieter and more demanding combination of the so-called

'Polish route', named after the Polish climbers who pioneered it, the Ameghino Traverse, the Upper Guanacos and the normal route, up to the base of the glacier.

Yet even before Alyssa leaves Mendoza, she hits her first problem: when the officers issuing permits for the climb hear she's only seventeen, they insist her paperwork isn't in order. She has a letter from Glenn giving his permission for her to climb Aconcagua, but because she's under the age of eighteen they also want the written consent of her mother, and to have both signatures authenticated by an Australian notary. The officials are adamant. If they don't receive the documents within twenty-four hours, she won't be able to climb Aconcagua, and she'll be put on a plane back home. Alyssa phones Glenn.

It's 11.30 p.m. in Brisbane when he receives her call. He then phones Therese in Toowoomba, and races over to see her. She signs and he then tracks down one of the only four people in the city who are qualified to notarise the document, someone he once took over to Kokoda, lawyer Paul Emerson. Unfortunately, Emerson happens to be in Gatton, 50 km away, but Glenn and Therese drive there to have the papers signed.

Over in Argentina, Alyssa is determined to remain calm. At first, she thought, Oh my God! I've only just arrived, and now I might have to go straight home without being allowed to climb! But then she took herself in hand. She didn't want to panic. Things are always going wrong on expeditions and that becomes a measure of how well climbers cope with the stress. She doesn't want to worry and get out of her focused mindset, in case she's still able to climb.

In the meantime, Glenn is speeding back to Brisbane to the local Department of Foreign Affairs and Trade, to have the papers sent over officially to Mendoza. It takes hours of battling the bureaucracy, racing from office to office and phoning and turning up at people's office doors to finally have the papers sent over. They trundle off on the fax.

By then, the expedition leader, together with most of its members, has already left for the mountain, but the Australian man and their Argentinean guide, Angel, another veteran of Everest, have agreed to wait with Alyssa. As soon as the papers appear on the fax and she receives the go-ahead, they work out how they'll be able to catch up with the others. They're a day behind, but Alyssa asks them if they're prepared to walk all day, from early in the morning into the night, to make the others' camp. They agree, and they set out at a blistering pace. By 9 p.m. they've joined the others, who are plainly astonished that they've travelled so fast. For the first time, Alyssa allows herself to relax.

They're a total of twelve on this trip, including one other Australian, Jake Davison, who'd previously done an Aussie 10 trip with Adventure Professionals, a few Canadians and the rest South Africans. The expedition leader believes in creating a friendly atmosphere between them all, and has them talk about the high point of each day and the lowest moment. Alyssa's not so interested in the social aspect as she's more concentrated on the climb, but she understands that aspect might be important for the others, and joins in with as much enthusiasm as she can muster – which isn't really much at all. It's noticed, and noted.

The first morning, the group sets off trekking through the Vacas Valley along dusty grey scree – broken shards of stone from centuries of rock falls. Alyssa looks around and soaks up the feeling of being among the mighty Andes. They're nowhere near as high as the Himalayan peaks, but they have the same imposing grandeur. The atmosphere is different, though: the culture of the people they glimpse, the clothing, even having mules carrying their tents and equipment instead of yaks. Alyssa looks up and sees the snow-capped Aconcagua for the first time. 'It's HUGE!' she gasps. The guide Angel laughs and tells her, 'No, keep walking.' A few minutes later, on her left, an even bigger monolith looms up. '*That's* Aconcagua!' he says.

Nothing is quite as it appears. When they come across a raging torrent of a river, Alyssa assumes they'll wade across. But the trek leader shakes his head, and three mules are roped together to ferry the climbers across on their backs in a series of crossings. It's then that Alyssa realises why they didn't simply paddle across. The water comes up to the mules' haunches – a sure sign of plenty of snow up above, melting down below to feed the river.

On 11 January, the group treks up the steep Relicho slope into Base Camp at Plaza Argentina, at an altitude of 4200 metres. Alyssa's having no altitude issues, although she's had a stomach ache for a couple of days, but she's still feeling strong. Every day, she's been walking briskly and is usually at the front, and among the first to reach their destination. When they have to leave the mules on the lower slopes, she carries her tent and equipment, as well as a share of the communal supplies, on her back with ease. All that pack walking seems to be really coming into its own. The group has a rest day, undergoing official medical checks to make sure they're holding up well enough to go on.

That evening, they have their first 'group chat'. When it starts, Alyssa stands up and leaves the mess tent, saying she needs to collect her head torch. Again, it creates a stir. The expedition leader likes to hear from people, how they're going, how they're feeling, any issues they're having, their highlights and lowlights. He feels irritated that she left, and while he realises that sharing with others isn't necessarily comfortable for her, he feels it's important for her to learn that. Her single-mindedness might in some ways be a strength, but in others it could be a weakness. He'd like to see her become more of a team-player.

The following morning, everyone sets out for Camp I. It's a solid climb up to 5000 metres and Angel points out all the peaks on the way that have yet to be conquered. Alyssa looks at them each curiously; that's something that's very different from the Himalaya, too. The approach to the camp is a very steep hill and everyone is relieved to reach the top with all their gear, ready to sleep over to acclimatise before going back down to Base Camp. That afternoon, it begins snowing, and Alyssa overhears a snatch of conversation between the leaders. The snow seems to be settling into a pattern of arriving a little earlier each afternoon on the mountain, which is a worry, especially with strong winds predicted to arrive later that week.

The next day, they all return to Base Camp, and the trek leader announces that they're going to have to shuffle their plans and bring forward the summit attempt in the hope of outpacing the weather. Alyssa feels her first tinge of anxiety about reaching the top. She hopes desperately that the weather won't defeat this climb, but knows they'll just have to wait and see.

They move back up to Camp I the following day, skipping a planned rest day at Base Camp, and trek straight into more snow. That night, it snows heavily again and Alyssa shakes the tent walls regularly to stop it settling and leaking through onto her and her tent mate, South African Lisa. They have a rest day at the camp and Alyssa watches everything becoming blanketed in white. It's beautiful, but at the same time it makes her feel even more anxious.

Next comes the climb up to Camp II, at 5500 metres. With the snow covering the scree, it becomes harder to walk in the heavy mountain boots, as the scree tends to move but the boots are so firm that they don't allow the foot to flex with it. Still, Alyssa's feeling good. Some of the others have paid for personal porters to carry their gear, but she wanted to see how she'd manage on her own. As a result, she ends up the only woman on the trip carrying her own pack and is now carrying as much as most of the men – around 15 kg, which feels pretty light – and she's still up at the front of the group. She's feeling like a strong member of the expedition and is excited to be climbing higher and higher.

That afternoon, it starts snowing heavily again and soon they're in a fresh white wonderland. It's also getting colder. Originally, they'd planned to have a rest day at Camp II but instead they'll just spend one night there and go up to Camp III, at 6000 metres, the following day to strike out for the summit from there. With a bit of luck, there'll be time to beat the snow and winds to make the top.

The next morning, the sun is out and it's surprisingly warm. They all swelter in their down clothes, but Alyssa smiles to herself. This is just like it was when she was rock climbing in New Zealand and exactly how it might be on Everest. She'll just grin and bear it. Very soon, the temperature plunges back down. It's a tough walk. She can often see Camp III in the distance, but it never seems to be getting any closer. It feels like one long, never-ending climb. She tries to concentrate on taking one step at a time. Just before she finally arrives at the camp, she can feel the beginning of an altitude headache, and it starts snowing again.

There's another discussion that evening about their chances of reaching the summit, and it's decided they should try to leave early the next morning, at 3 or 4 a.m., to make that final push, to stand any chance of reaching it. Alyssa takes half a Diamox tablet and tries to sleep, to give her brain time to get used to the altitude.

In the pitch black of 3 a.m., Alyssa's among the first up, and quickly dresses by the light of her head torch, clipping and strapping crampons onto her boots. This will be hours of walking on snow and ice, so everyone will need the extra grip they'll afford. It snowed during the night so the leaders of the handful of other expeditions also at Camp III have gone ahead to 'break trail' – wading out through the half-metre of freshly fallen snow to show other climbers where the route should be. Alyssa's feeling nervous.

There's something amazing but nerve-racking about being in the pitch black and cold ready to hit a summit that's so special to her. She just hopes against hope the weather will hold off for long enough so she'll be able to get there.

The group sets off at 4 a.m., crunching through the snow and ice, and following the little line of flickering head torches. Alyssa makes sure she's near the front. She catches up to the leader and is excited when he says this all reminds him of his time on Everest. She feels good, but an hour out of camp the wind-chill hits, and she notices her fingers are so cold they're starting to sting. She knows that's a sign they might be getting frostbite, so hastily puts on her down gloves, wriggling her fingers all the time to make sure enough blood is getting through to them. After about half an hour, they feel normal again, and she relaxes. She makes a mental note to put gloves on earlier when she's on Everest. Her hair ties are broken too, and with a buff and balaclava over her face, she keeps having to tuck her long blonde hair back into her jacket, something that's tricky with the down mittens now on. She curses herself for not bringing more spares. That's a mistake she'll be sure not to make on Everest.

Others are having more serious problems, however. One member of the expedition turns back at 6200 metres, and Lisa is having trouble breathing and starts coughing at 6300 metres. She's advised to turn around and head back to Camp III too. Looking totally forlorn, she does so.

Alyssa and the forward pack reach the last plateau, 400 metres away from the summit, just 160 metres below the peak. She can't wait to get on, but everyone has to stop here for a quick drink to make sure they're hydrated enough for the final push. They're now at an altitude of 6800 metres, and this is the point where they're supposed to see the sun rise. But no one can see anything. It's a pure white-out. There are only occasional glimpses of the sky, but they're not heartening. There seems to be a huge bank of clouds moving in, signalling the start of the strong winds that were forecast. The expedition leaders gather for a quick confab. They're all in agreement: the falling snow, the existing soft snow from the previous few days and the wind make the risk of avalanche extremely high. It will be far too dangerous for anyone to try to summit.

Alyssa is devastated. So close, and yet so far. She looks towards the summit longingly. Never has she felt so strong. Her headache has gone and her body is coping well with the altitude. She feels fit and ready and full of energy. She knows she could have summitted comfortably if it hadn't been for the weather.

Everyone turns back; no one is allowed to carry on. For two people in their group, it's the second time they've not been able to make the summit. Aconcagua is now closed for business. It's exactly the same situation as it was for Alyssa on Manaslu. Two of the stronger guys commiserate with her on having to turn back. 'You would have had that summit, no stress,' one of them says. 'You were going so well.' The date is 19 January 2014 – the same day her parents' divorce is finalised.

The group starts to head down and now fellow Australian Davison begins to suffer from altitude sickness and has a splitting headache. He looks pale, is plainly exhausted and has trouble speaking. At one point, he trips and tumbles over a few rocks before coming to a halt on the ground. The others divide the contents of his pack between them to help, and Alyssa carries his heavy water bottle. Davison is amazed that she's managing so well. He finds her phenomenal. 'She's so quiet and calm and collected but put her in the mountains, and she's in her element,' he says. 'I'm blown away by how fit and strong she is. And her determination is second to none.'

Stephen Bock says it was just unlucky that the mountain was closed down because of the avalanche risk, especially since they'd been at the front of the pack, within striking distance. Up to that point, he knew Alyssa would make the summit comfortably.

'Alyssa was incredibly strong,' he says. 'She was by far the strongest of the ten we took up there; she was just solid with no whingeing or complaining; she just put her head down and bum up and got on with the job. I had a chat with the expedition leader after the climb, and we both said we think she's where she needs to be for Everest in terms of her fitness and her mental perspective. She's got the cone of focus on, is in a single-minded headspace and there are no chinks in her armour that I can see.'

That expedition chief certainly agrees on Alyssa's strength. 'Aconcagua is a tough mountain, a real heart-breaker, but Alyssa was strong,' he says. 'She's an amazing young woman. She had a minor issue with her hands but sometimes the training climbs teach you valuable lessons; that's what they're there to do. On Everest, everything you can control, you really need to control because you need to be able to concentrate on dealing with the elements you can't control.

'Alyssa is very, very single-minded and focused and committed. But while that's a strength, it can also be an Achilles heel. She can be so focused, she's almost unaware of what's going on around her; the others are almost not in view, and you start losing a little bit of your humanity. I say that in the kindest way. She was always pleasant and nice and smiled but she was never proactive in terms of communication. She never came out of herself and offered herself. On Everest, we are going to spend two months with each other, so it would have been good to have got to know her a bit better on this trip. But hopefully I understand her a little more and will have the wisdom and age to work with her in a very positive way about who she is, and maybe encourage some things that may not be so natural or easy for her.'

On the way down Aconcagua, Alyssa is again silent, wrapped up in her own thoughts. 'I took not being able to summit pretty badly at first, but if anything, it's making me even more determined for my next climb on Everest,' she says.

'There, you have more chances in a way, as you can keep going up and back down, and then trying again. But I'm determined that on Everest, the weather won't hold me back. I will summit Everest. I won't accept failure.'

CHAPTER 24

Everest's First Australians: Greg Mortimer

Greg Mortimer has stared death in the face many times on mountains both in the Andes and in the Himalaya. While he and Tim Macartney-Snape share the line honours of being the first Australians on Everest's summit – which they reached without oxygen and up the hitherto unconquered North face in 1984 – his climbing career has never been short on drama.

'Everest is really hard,' he says. 'It's being at such an extreme altitude, and at the mercy of the cold and winds and extraordinary events of natural phenomena that are both ghastly and wondrous at the same time.'

Mortimer, who originally trained as a geologist and geochemist, has a number of firsts to his name. He was the first Australian to climb the dreaded K2, the second highest mountain on earth at 8611 metres with the second highest fatality rate among the 8000ers, the first Australian to climb Annapurna II (7937 metres) by its precarious south face, and the first Australian to reach the top of Antarctica's highest peak, Mount Vinson (4892 metres), another of the Seven Summits.

There were many times when he thought he mightn't make it up those mountains; and many more when he didn't think he'd make it down again. One of his worst experiences happened close to where Alyssa climbed Aconcagua. He had just made it to the summit of Chakrarahu in the neighbouring Peruvian section of the Andes and was standing admiring the view, when the ground shook under his feet, and the whole of the top of the mountain avalanched beneath him.

'I went off with it,' he says now. 'It was very steep and I was ripped off and flung from the side through the air, and fell a very long way. I can still remember falling through the air and if I close my eyes, even today, I can still feel it.

'That would be categorised very much as a "meet your Maker" moment. I thought I was going to die. But I fell probably 75 metres and bounced along the way and got knocked out. I woke up with a broken collarbone and my head banged in. It was amazing I survived.'

On the descent of Annapurna II, he had to struggle through blizzards, wade through snow that was thigh-deep and just hope for the best as avalanches thundered down both in front of him and behind. The storm continued through that night, so the next morning he had to help dig through three metres of snow to free another climber and then push on through chest-deep snow, with a constant wary eye on avalanches on the higher slopes. It took him two and a half hours to travel 200 metres. He slept again in the snow that night before he reached Advanced Base Camp to find all his ropes swept away by icefall down the glacier.

Everest, later, was no less perilous. First there was the avalanche that wiped out their group's camp and buried much of their equipment forever. Then there was the afternoon he climbed without sunglasses, and ended up snow blind – with the glare from the snow having burnt his eyes – unable to see a thing and in immense pain. His companions helped him to climb on, and dug a snow cave on an ice ledge to sleep on. It was then that an avalanche crashed down right where they were digging, while Mortimer, who was tied to a fixed rope below, was swept off the slope amid a torrent of snow. The rope stretched under the force of the landslide but, thankfully, held. He said, miraculously, it took his mind off the agony of his eyes.

'Tim and I were both caught in that huge avalanche,' he says. 'We were very lucky to survive that. When you think about it now from the comfort of your home, it's a very different thing from at the time. Then, it's a little more cut and dried! It's less emotionally loaded.'

These days, he believes, there's a lot more known about Everest, the weather can be more accurately predicted and the routes up are more certain. It's still, however, immensely dangerous. 'There are a lot more people climbing but it's still as windy and as cold and as high. Those things haven't diminished.

'Like Alyssa's already found on Aconcagua and Manaslu, the weather can change everything, which engenders that sense of humility you always have on high mountains. Whenever you're over 8000 metres, you get an overwhelming sense of extraordinary forces at work that make our human efforts seem almost puny and pathetic.'

At that height, it's a race against time to get up and then back down, yet it takes around two hours to melt enough snow for a small drink of water, to slowly get into four layers of clothing, to put on foot liners, warm expedition socks and boots, and to tie the laces and affix crampons. Then you might only be capable of walking slowly for five minutes at a time before you have to stop for a rest, with your blood dangerously thick with red blood cells and your brain operating as if in a fog without enough oxygen. And if you're unlucky enough to want to defecate, then that can be the closest any man gets to the pain of giving birth. 'That's a really serious, major event!' says Mortimer.

'You can physically prepare your body by training, but to have the mental fortitude for it is another thing altogether. That's a huge part of climbing Everest. I find it pretty bloody amazing that Alyssa is so ready. I certainly wouldn't have had that in me at all at the age of seventeen. It's impressive.'

Alyssa herself is humbled that someone who looms so large in Australian mountaineering folklore is so encouraging. 'Greg Mortimer has had so many near-death experiences and he knows how serious the mountains can be, yet he's still so positive about me trying. It shows the great spirit of Australian mountaineers, and really helps give me the confidence to go for Everest!'

These days Mortimer is well known as one of our greatest adventurers, now spending a great deal of time in the Antarctic, firstly as a scientific affairs advisor for the New Zealand Antarctic Division, and then leading more than eighty expeditions there, many through his company Aurora Expeditions and Adventure Associates. He spent Christmas 2013 stuck in ice off the coast of Antarctica aboard the Russian ship *Akademik Shokalskiy* after strong blizzards pushed pack ice against the ship, wedging it tight. It was halfway through its month-long expedition following in the footsteps of the great Antarctic explorer and scientist Douglas Mawson, repeating his wildlife, ocean and weather observations to build a picture of changes over the past 100 years. A Chinese icebreaker, the *Xue Long*, had to abandon its rescue effort when it too became stuck in the ice and the passengers were finally rescued by its helicopter, which transferred them to the Australian icebreaker, *Aurora Australis*, for the voyage home.

'I really believe there are no boundaries to where people should go,' he says. 'Everest offers a mind-expanding set of experiences that are valuable for anyone to have. And, hopefully, you're lucky, and things don't go wrong and cut you down to size. With Everest, it's simply the dominant force and you go there on its terms rather than your own.'

CHAPTER 25

Ready to Risk Everything

'You've got what it takes, but it will take everything you've got.'
— ANON

Alyssa Azar returns from Aconcagua buoyed by how well she's done, and eager for the final test that lies ahead: Everest.

She knows it's going to be the hardest thing she's ever done, and probably the most life-changing, but she feels as ready as she'll ever be. 'Of course I do get nervous,' she says. 'Part of it is the danger, and part is that I want so much to do well. I'd be lying if I didn't admit I get scared at times. A goal like that is exhilarating, but it can also be daunting. I know it's going to be painful. We all have our psychological demons. But pain is just a factor of the mind, and I'm learning to control my mind and body, so I'll have more and more tolerance to pain.

'The hardest thing for me is having some people say there's no way I'll be able to climb Everest. I find that very difficult but it makes me even more determined never to quit.'

As well as the journals she keeps, she takes a small hardback notebook and writes out once again all the quotations she likes to keep her motivated, as well as poems and fragments of speeches. Any time she feels self-doubt, she goes straight back to the words she's written to keep her feeling strong. She also writes lists of things she needs to do for the future, her professional ambitions and her personal goals. She wants to learn to drive, buy her own car, get her own place, earn her own income, be independent. She wants to climb the rest of the Seven Summits and all the other 8000ers. But first, above everything else, she wants to get to the top of Everest.

She's well aware of the dangers lying in wait with every step. The first major difficulty of the South Col route will come on the very first day after Base Camp, with the Khumbu Icefall at the head of the glacier. Here, crevasses open without warning, and seracs can thunder down.

'That's probably the most dangerous part of the whole climb,' says one of Australia's most experienced and skilled mountaineers, Andrew Lock, 'because it's a moving glacier and massive blocks of ice as big as home units will just collapse without warning. There's no way of avoiding them. The first step onto the icefall could be your last.' Camp I lies just above the icefall.

Between Camp II and III, there's the Lhotse Face, a steep wall of ice, which can also prove perilous, he says. 'It's exposed pre-monsoon season and it's very hard ice. There are lots of places where you can slip and where your crampons don't bite. It's scary when you slip and fall down for a few metres and are then stuck there, hanging on to the rope. Then between Camps III and IV there's the Yellow Band, which can be a real scramble over rocks, and the Geneva Spur over loose steps is tricky, although you're roped all the way. Then there are the challenges of the Death Zone . . .'

Altitude is always difficult and all climbers fear a negative reaction to it. For Alyssa, though, it might be more difficult than for older people. She's still very young to be doing all this, believes Professor Chris Gore, who's in charge of physiology and altitude training at the Australian Institute of Sport in Canberra.

'Marathon runners are considered to be at their best in their early to late thirties because of the mental attitude to the sport, and physiologically you don't get close to your peak until the late teens, early twenties,' he says. 'Women also have lower haemoglobin concentrations than men, which is a lesser ability to transport total amounts of oxygen through the body.'

Professor Gore lost a good friend on Everest and knows exactly the kind of risks Alyssa will be facing. 'If she succeeds, I think it would be extraordinary, a remarkable feat. The Death Zone is very dangerous. Those who've climbed without oxygen often sustain long-term cognitive effects as a result. Some of the ones I've spoken to say their memory and cognitive functioning has never been the same since. But for those who dare to dream and want to inspire us, all power to them!'

Happily, many of the experts Alyssa's been learning from are confident she's up to the challenge. Stephen Bock, who's reached the summit of Everest before, and climbed with her on Aconcagua, says she's not like a normal girl of seventeen. She's wise beyond her years, very capable physically and mentally, and she's paid her dues in terms of experience.

'I'm very impressed with her,' he says. 'But the most important thing you can ever have with Everest is ownership of the summit. You have to absolutely see yourself there and picture yourself at peace on the summit. You have to put it as a foregone conclusion into your mind. On Everest you just can't doubt yourself. The moment the slightest doubt filters in, it will kill the climb. If you think, I *might* make it, I *hope* I make it, then that's the end.

'Instead, Alyssa will just have to focus on that day, then the next, and break it down into bite-sized chunks. She won't be able to afford to think about two days' time; just the next day, the next hour, the next minute. That's the way you get through. As they always say, Don't stare at the mountain as she'll always stare you down. That's good advice, too.'

Keith Fennell also feels confident. He says she's learnt the lessons of *Warrior Training* well, and is a marvellous candidate for such a climb. 'She's fit, has good endurance and is confident,' he says. 'She's smart, driven and hardworking. That's a great start. But she will need every bit of all that if she's going to do something that could claim her life. A lot of people die every year doing what she wants to achieve, and many of them are far more experienced and physically capable. If the conditions are right, and she has the luck everyone needs, there's little doubt she'll be successful. There's so much up there, though, that you can't control.

'But she's wired a certain way and has the temperament to pull it off, and I don't think she's capable of giving up. If someone can succeed at seventeen, it will be her.'

* * *

Alyssa's mum, Therese, shudders every time she thinks of her daughter going into such harsh terrain. She's read books and watched documentaries about Everest, and has a fair idea of the kind of torture Alyssa will be putting herself through. Being a nurse, Therese knows she tends to dwell, perhaps too much, on what can go wrong.

'But I know she has all the right things in place, and she has some experience now, so it might even be enjoyable at points,' she says. 'One of the benefits of being young, too, is that your body does repair itself. She looks great after a trek where some people might feel rotten; she doesn't seem to skip a beat.

'I don't think people *shouldn't* do things. Of course, there are risks. But she is prepared and does have good support. And in life, none of us knows how long we are here for . . .'

Glenn too has mixed feelings. In some ways, he'll be relieved when Everest is over. It's been a long, hard slog, physically, mentally and financially. He's always been keen to give his kids plenty of time and love, and that's been easy with Alyssa since they're together so much of the time, but he's very conscious of the others' needs too.

'Of course, if any of the other kids said they wanted to climb Everest, or wanted to do something else, I'd do my very best, in exactly the same way, to make sure that happened. But it would always be a bit easier if one decided she just loved hairdressing and that's what she wanted to do!'

From these years of helping Alyssa live her dream, though, he loves the fact they've been able to become so close. Naturally, they do fight, now and again. Just as they can be honest and open with each other when things are going well, they can be just as blunt when things go badly. One of their favourite sayings to each other is 'Pull Your Head Out of Your Arse', or 'PYHOYA' for short.

'We can be blunt and honest, but once she's made up her mind about something, you can't get her to change it,' Glenn says. 'She's always been very stubborn. Even as a small kid, if she didn't get her way, she'd come out with lines like that one from the movie *Tommy Boy*: 'Why say No when it feels so good to say Yes?' Then you couldn't help laughing, and she'd often end up getting what she wanted. So she's a normal teenager in a lot of ways – I guess people don't get that. I don't see her as being any different to a kid who loves footy who's out there in the backyard playing every day and you're trying to get them in to do homework. It's just that her pursuits are a little bit different.'

Others looking on simply hope for the best. Alyssa's aunt Tanya, a performance coach in the superannuation industry, says it's amazing what Glenn has done for Alyssa, and what, in turn, Alyssa is doing herself. She's always got on well with Alyssa and reads her blog when she's away, but with a racing heart, even though she often doesn't quite understand what she's doing.

'When she said on her blog from Manaslu that she'd seen a serac, I thought, How cute! That must be a nice floppy animal!' Tanya says. 'Only later did I understand what it really was. It was a huge chunk of ice that could have killed her. I try not to think too much about the dangers.'

Alyssa's grandparents similarly try not to dwell too much on the risks. Glenn's mother Carmel Clark says there are so many things that can go wrong, but so far, so good. She still thinks of her as a little girl, but then has to remind herself that Alyssa's been doing these kinds of adventures now for years.

'Glenn has got her as prepared as she can be, and is constantly checking what she's doing, and how she's coping, but it will be a very long three months for him with a lot of sleepless nights,' she says. 'We'll all be waiting for the message that she's down safely. He's told her if she can't or doesn't feel like it on the way, she shouldn't summit. But even if she can't do it, and comes down, it's nothing against her – it'll still be a huge achievement.'

Her grandfather Richard says he admires her sense of adventure. 'I'm very proud of Alyssa, but I do have a little bit of trepidation at the same time. I've always been a challenger myself and played a hell of a lot of sport, but I've never done anything of that magnitude. It's a little scary. She seems a bit of a loner, but adventurous and a challenger.'

Others watching on wish her well. The then Queensland premier Campbell Newman says he's incredibly impressed by what Alyssa has already achieved, and in awe at what she plans to do next. 'Young Australians like Alyssa Azar give us tremendous hope for our future,' he says. 'She embodies everything our nation could possibly wish for in the next generation of leaders, dreamers, pioneers and adventure-seekers. I'm blown away by her courage to tackle, at the still tender age of seventeen, one of the hardest challenges known to mankind – the gruelling ascent of Mount Everest.

'I'm only too happy to concede that her "can do" attitude in this regard outstrips mine.

'It is obvious that this very determined and capable young

woman has put in the hard yards, mentally and physically, to make her dream a reality. It is also obvious that Alyssa's strong self-belief and high sense of adventure have been fanned by the love and support of her family, especially her father, Glenn.

'As she sets out on this exhilarating yet undeniably dangerous quest, I join the people of Queensland in wishing her a safe and successful expedition. Whatever the outcome, we are proud to claim her as one of our own.'

In her hometown of Toowoomba there's also lots of interest. Mayor Paul Antonio says it's great to see someone so young aim so high, and achieve so much. 'Those kinds of feats take a lot of willpower – and not many people have that much!' he says. 'I see Alyssa as setting a great example to others about what can be achieved when you're so determined, and have such a great aim in life.'

For Alyssa is also one hell of a hard worker. Occasionally, she might feel like staying in bed instead of getting up at 4 or 5 a.m. to train, but never gives in to the temptation. She's too aware that, if she's tested on Everest, she might need that one tiny extra iota of strength she managed to build that morning. Now she's mostly pack-walking outdoors, tyre-dragging and hill-running, as well as doing strength workouts in the garden of their home. Now his gym has been sold, Glenn has installed all the equipment Alyssa will need in the backyard instead: a rowing machine, a treadmill, an iron edge matrix – a metal cage for chin-ups and other exercises – 300 kg of Olympic weights, a set of kettle bells from 14 kg to 32 kg, and heavy ropes for an intense upper body workout. He's even had welded in an 8-metre tower from which a rope dangles down for her to practise rope climbing. A ladder is yet to arrive for her to practise walking across with heavy mountaineering boots and crampons, for when she has to inch her way over similar ladders flung across deep crevasses on Everest. Even in any downtime, watching TV or on the computer, she squeezes a little ball specially designed to strengthen fingers for rock climbing.

Alyssa's also started eating to gain weight. The hardship of the Everest climb, and all the time spent at altitude, strips kilograms off climbers like nothing else – many of them, on their return, can look like walking skeletons. So she knows she'll have to put on at least 5 kg now to withstand the punishment in store for her. 'It's difficult as you can really eat a lot when you train, and you don't want to train too much as then you'll risk losing the additional weight as soon as you put it on,' says Alyssa. 'So I'm having to taper my training and my eating just a few weeks prior to going. Then it'll be a case of eating as many carbs as I can manage . . .' And, of course, there's still the schoolwork to fit in; she hopes to take her HSC late in 2014, with Everest behind her.

But she really doesn't mind all the hard work and concentration. Her mindset is all about giving it everything she has; there's no point, she reckons, in going in for anything half-heartedly. Even some of the teachers who had so many doubts about her path now seem to agree. One of the schools asks her back in to talk to their pupils about motivation.

Many successful Everest mountaineers talk about how climbers need to believe in something bigger than themselves to make it, whether it's Jesus Christ or Buddha, a mountain god or Allah. They simply need that spiritual side to attempt something so massive. Alyssa agrees completely.

'I never really thought I was that religious because my family's not, but I'm glad I could find my own beliefs,' she says. 'Over time I've realised you can't climb the highest mountains without having a belief in something, particularly when you see the scale of the world. I guess my personal beliefs are along the lines of Buddhism. I've studied a little bit and I do believe in a higher force. It sounds silly, but a lot of climbers believe in the mountain goddess and I'm very much part of that. I'll go to the stupa and temple in Kathmandu and walk all the way around and touch the prayer wheels before the climb. Travelling to these other countries and seeing the cultures opens your mind to the way others live – how they don't need possessions to be happy; they have a minimalist way of living rather than the drive to accumulate, and they're very spiritual.'

Yet there are things Alyssa will never be able to get completely used to, or come to terms with. On her Facebook page and website, trolls routinely post vicious messages, calling her nasty names and questioning why she has to do something so extreme. She insists she doesn't let it affect her. Glenn says, 'We are just big believers in living your dream. You get out of bed every day with a choice to make, no matter how bad your life is. You can choose how you react to it, you can choose whether or not to pursue your dreams. With Alyssa's dream of Everest, I'm not saying whether or not she's capable of it, but if she's willing to put in all the preparation, year after year, then who am I to stop her? I don't want to get to the end of my life and regret firstly, not having a go or secondly, stopping someone else from having a go. So I'm not going to be that person who tells Alyssa, No, you can't!

'Most people don't fail to achieve things because they are not capable; they're just not willing to make the sacrifices, to put the work in. In my professional life, I love to help people realise their dreams and, in my personal life, I'm there to do exactly the same for all my kids.'

For Alyssa, it's all about that dream. It's not for fame or dubious fortune or for the records she might smash. It's just her drive to see if she can achieve something she's put her mind to for so long. 'When you step on a mountain, there's no fame or records. There's just a big mountain you attempt to climb, one step at a time. No one else can possibly do it for you. You can be given lots of support in the years before, but the amount of preparation you do, all the training, the mind stuff – that's all about how hard you alone are prepared to work. For when it comes down to it, it's just you and the mountain. It's all you up there, either making it to the top or falling short. It's you, and you alone. And making the summit of Everest has been my dream for over ten years now.'

Not even the risk of dying in the attempt can put her off. 'You know, I would prefer to die on the side of a mountain at twenty than to limp through my life until I'm eighty hating what I do,' she says. 'You see people on Facebook, writing about how much they hate every day. To me, another day is always another chance to take a step towards my goal.

'People may think I have a death wish or I don't see the risks or don't think it'll ever happen. Maybe I do sometimes have a more casual attitude to danger, but I am aware of my mortality. It's just that to me, the risk is something you have to accept if you're going to do things like climb Everest. And I'm ready to face that.'

CHAPTER 26

Everest at Last

'The price of discipline is always less than the pain of regret.'
– NIDO QUBEIN, PRESIDENT OF HIGH POINT UNIVERSITY,
NORTH CAROLINA, US

It's 4 a.m. on 2 April 2014 and still pitch black when seventeen-year-old Alyssa Azar leaps out of bed in her small Kathmandu hotel, ready to catch one of the first planes of the Everest season to Lukla to start the trek to Base Camp. This is the day she's been waiting for and working towards for three solid years. She can barely contain her excitement.

Yet even as she takes her seat in that tiny plane to start the first leg of her historic assault on Everest, the mountain is already claiming its first victims of the year.

One of the icefall doctors – the group of Sherpas who go up before the climbers to fix the ropes up to Camp II and the ice ladders over the most treacherous crevasses and up the cliffs – has fallen down a ravine on the Khumbu Icefall, and has been carried back to Base Camp and helicoptered down to Kathmandu for treatment. Meanwhile, in a separate incident, another Sherpa, Mingma Tenzing, complains of feeling unwell while helping organise Base Camp. He is taken down to Lobuche where he is treated by doctors who realise that, despite being just twenty-six years old, strong and used to altitude, he is suffering signs of acute mountain sickness and pulmonary oedema, with dangerously high levels of fluid in his lungs. At first light, he is also choppered down to Kathmandu. He dies that same morning in hospital.

'It's very sad,' says Alyssa. 'It's terrible for those men and their families who give so much to Everest every year. It's also a reminder of how perilous Everest can be, how unpredictable and how even the most experienced, tough and courageous Sherpas can still suffer so much.'

As soon as the plane lurches and bumps onto the runway at Lukla, Alyssa scrambles off, collects her gear and, together with the four other members of her expedition, sets off immediately on the trek to Base Camp. She's back with the same expedition leader, this time with his wife and two South Africans, Mark and Donna. Neither of them are particularly experienced climbers, neither seem terribly confident about what lies ahead and, even more worryingly, Mark has never been higher than 2000 metres. Alyssa feels her first stirrings of doubt. Lukla itself is 2800 metres, and from there they'll be trekking steadily upwards. If her team members aren't up to it, she knows they might slow the whole expedition down. But she tells herself to take it day by day and just focus on her own efforts.

This year looks likely to be a big one in any case. Alyssa is going up in the hope of reaching the summit and, in so doing, will become the youngest non-Sherpa female in the world to make the top, as well as the youngest Australian. At the same time, another young Australian is also climbing, twenty-year-old Will Sayer from NSW. The media make much of what it assumes must be rivalry between the pair. Also on his way up this year is American adventurer Joby Ogwyn who plans to jump from the top of Everest in a wingsuit, a feat that will be filmed live by a Discovery Channel team. Theirs aren't the only cameras, either. An Australian–UK documentary team are already in Nepal, making a film about the veteran Sherpa

Phurba Tashi, who is preparing for a world-record twenty-second ascent of Everest. Australian director-writer Jennifer Peedom and producer John Smithson, who previously made the hit *Touching the Void*, plan to accompany him most of the way from Base Camp.

It's going to be a little crowded at Base Camp, but Alyssa's team are in high spirits and make good progress. They hit Namche Bazaar in beautiful weather but as they continue to Tengboche, Everest remains shrouded in clouds and snowfalls. That just serves to make the surroundings even more beautiful, however.

Alyssa feels she's back home among the mountains and with everyone trekking well, her anxiety gradually subsides. At Upper Pangboche, they drop in on Everest legend Lama Geshe, who is visited every season by overseas climbers and local Sherpas alike to receive blessings, then they move on to Pheriche. By now, Mark is clearly feeling the altitude. Pheriche lies at a height of 4720 metres and Mark is coughing and complaining of headaches and not feeling well. They all decide to take a rest day while Mark visits the doctor. He's given some medication and told to try to take it easy. But the next morning he feels worse. Mark and Donna decide to take a second rest day, while Alyssa heads off with the leader and his wife. The plan is for the other two to meet up with them later down the track.

This year, there are a few new rules to observe around the climb. Because of an altercation the previous year between a few western climbers and some Sherpas, guards from the Nepalese Army and armed police have been posted at Base Camp to stop any more trouble breaking out. In addition, a checkpoint has been set up at the entrance to make sure everyone has their climbing permit. And finally, all climbers are being instructed to collect and carry down 8 kg of rubbish each to try to keep the route pristine. 'That's a great idea,' says Alyssa. 'We're going up there anyway, so why shouldn't we bring down rubbish? It's much better than asking Sherpas to risk their lives to collect other people's debris.'

Alyssa's finding the trekking very comfortable, and she's loving the excitement of approaching Everest. The next stop is Lobuche and it's there she hears that Mark has been evacuated back to Kathmandu. She's sad for him but surprised that he's fallen so sick so early, without even reaching Base Camp. Donna, however, seems to be doing better and is on her way up.

The four catch up along the way, and at Gorak Shep, the last stop before Base Camp, there's a major surprise in store. Mark has been choppered back up and has trekked there, ready to continue to Base Camp.

'Seeing him was a shock,' says Alyssa. 'I wondered why he'd come back since he'd been so sick at a lower altitude, and you'd imagine he'd remember how that felt, but he said he was determined. But he looked ten years older than when we'd last seen him. He looked terrible. And by the time we reached Base Camp on 10 April, he could barely move. He was trying to eat but he couldn't, and he fainted a few times on the way to his tent, so we helped him there. He was on oxygen that night, and then said he didn't want to climb Everest. He was evacuated out again the next day.'

Alyssa goes about making herself back at home at Base Camp. This is her third time there, but the first time she's planning to move on up to the summit of Everest. She's feeling strong and confident and can't wait to get going. She talks to some of the Sherpas she knows from previous years and generally gets ready for the adventure of her life. She does some training climbs to get used to the altitude, ascending the southern flank of Pumori, with its spectacular views of Everest, and the dreaded Khumbu glacier. 'You're waiting for your opening to start climbing Everest, so you use the time to train for it,' she says. 'You have to keep moving and keep climbing to higher altitudes to acclimatise yourself. You're just waiting for the green light for your rotation. Every day you hope it might be that day.'

Then, in the early morning of 18 April, Alyssa wakes with a start, crawls out of her tent and makes her way to the mess tent. The atmosphere feels strange, but she can't quite work out why. There are a few people running around and she can hear a man shouting. As she gets closer to him, she can make out the words. 'Avalanche!' he's yelling. 'Avalanche!' She instantly knows that something is terribly wrong. At Base Camp and on the lower slopes of Everest, you're constantly hearing the crash of distant avalanches; the noise becomes almost the background track to your life up there. But this must be different. To be sending out the alarm in that way, it must be something serious, very serious.

Alyssa doesn't know it yet, but an immense tragedy is playing itself out on the Khumbu Icefall. On that first part of the route up Everest, the most perilous part of the climb, a block of ice the size of a ten-storey apartment building and weighing an estimated 64 000 tonnes – heavier than the *Titanic* – has sheared off and plunged 400 metres down towards around 100 Sherpas toiling below. Most of the Sherpas, who are on the mountain fixing ladders or carrying gear up for the foreign climbers, hear the falling serac and have just seconds to either get out of its way or take shelter. It smashes into the slope with a deafening crash, sending great fragments of ice and clouds of snow in all directions. One Sherpa later describes it as being like a thunderbolt, striking and scattering its victims.

Down at Base Camp, people quickly realise what must be happening and teams of rescuers are sent up to help. On arrival, they find the bodies of the dead, either crushed or suffocated by the debris, and many stunned and partly buried injured survivors. A huge operation is launched to bring the survivors back down.

Alyssa sits and waits down at Base Camp, knowing there's nothing she can do to help. As if in a trance, she watches the helicopters flying up and bringing the injured back on stretchers to be flown straight down to Pheriche, Lukla and then Kathmandu. Later, the operation switches to body retrieval. The choppers go up and then return, dangling the bodies on ropes below them, and then unloading their terrible cargo in full view of everyone at Base Camp. The climbers can only look on in stunned horror.

The final toll is another shock. Sixteen Sherpas have been killed in the avalanche, and many more badly injured. Only thirteen bodies, however, have been recovered; the other three either are not found or have to stay in their icy graves since it's been judged too dangerous to try to bring them home.

'As the day unfolded, the toll went up and up and up,' says Alyssa. 'At first, we thought there were five dead. By the end, we knew it was sixteen. Everything went very, very quiet. It felt very surreal. There's such an air of invincibility around Sherpas and you know them as the best climbers in the world. So when something like this goes wrong, you keep asking yourself, How and why? A lot of Sherpas are related to each other, so everyone knew everyone. It was just so terribly, terribly sad.'

At first, the Sherpas ask the climbers to join them in a few days of mourning and suggest no one goes through the icefall as a mark of respect. All the foreign climbers agree. They're still in shock, and feel it's the very least they can do to show their sympathy with the bereaved. After all, the Sherpas were only up there to help them. But after three days, an air of impatience starts to seep into Base Camp. No one seems to be in charge, no one knows what's happening and rumour and counter-rumour spreads through the ranks. Some people say the Sherpas now want to resume their climb; others say they want to abandon Everest for the season. The Sherpas themselves are in a bind. Local custom means they don't like to upset the climbers, financial imperatives make some want to continue the season, but others, deeply shocked and saddened, would rather call the whole thing off, preferably without losing face.

Back home, the *Today Show* contacts Alyssa and she gives them a live interview at 3.30 a.m. her time when the temperature's -20° C. She talks about what's happened but says she just doesn't know what might happen next. Other media try to get comment. 'But all we're doing is sitting staring at the mountain, waiting to climb and wondering whether we'll be able to,' she says. 'We all feel so desperately sad for the Sherpas, but would it be better for them for us to climb, so at least they'll have an income from this season? No one knows. It is a very difficult and frustrating time.'

News of the tragedy echoes around the world and starts a fierce debate about whether the Sherpas are paid enough to risk their lives for rich overseas mountaineers. The Sherpas themselves are angered by what they see as the low levels of compensation offered to bereaved families. One foreign climbing expedition leader reports that their Sherpas have been threatened if they insist on climbing. The truth gets lost somewhere in the cracks between anger, sorrow and confusion.

Meetings are held at Base Camp between Sherpas and a government minister, between Sherpas and the commercial expedition companies, and between Sherpas keen to continue and those eager to call off the season. Two more Sherpas perish on their way home from Base Camp; one in an accident and the other after being struck by lightning. The government finally lifts the life insurance for Sherpas to $15 000 and more money is raised by climbers and companies to help the families of the victims.

Eventually, with the situation still in stalemate, the government offers all the climbers a permit that will be valid the next time they come to Nepal to climb Everest. With many of the icefall doctors' ropes and ladders destroyed by the avalanche, and the Sherpas mostly reluctant to return up the glacier where so many of their colleagues have just perished, it gradually becomes evident that no one will be continuing their climb this year.

There are a few who don't want to accept defeat. Ogwyn, the

would-be wingsuit jumper, says he still wants to complete his stunt until finally he's persuaded to back down. A Chinese woman, Jing Wang, flies part of the way up by helicopter to skip the Khumbu Icefall and makes it to the summit, an effort not officially recognised as a real climb from bottom to top. An American climber hires a helicopter to take her to Camp II but then abandons her attempt shortly after Camp III. The documentary film team change the focus of their film to record the arguments and politics among Sherpas and foreign climbers over whether to continue the climbing season. They emerge with the award-winning film *Sherpa*, eventually released in 2016. Australian Will Sayer goes home.

* * *

Alyssa was among the last people left on the mountain. She didn't leave until it became clear that her team had no other choice. The long trek back to Lukla then gave her plenty of time to think about what had happened.

'I felt very sad for those Sherpas who had lost their lives and their families,' Alyssa says. 'Of course, it was devastating that I couldn't climb, but you have to keep things in perspective. The mountain will be there next year. I think my main feeling was one of disbelief. Nothing like that, on that scale, had ever happened on Everest before. Everest had never been shut down. It took me a while to process everything that had happened.

'It was a tragic accident that hit everyone hard. The whole trip almost felt like it didn't happen, as I think everyone was in a state of shock at the magnitude of the accident and just general disbelief of all that went on. Unfortunately it also turned very political and everything that unfolded was out of our control. I hung in with high hopes, but this year I now know just wasn't the year. Once it was clear no one could climb on I was ready to leave and reset myself for another year.

'I've had other attempts on mountains where I got turned around by outside circumstances and so I dealt with it. I have a lot of respect for the Sherpas and climbing with the Sherpas is always an honour. They're incredible people and this accident has proven that no matter who you are, anything can happen.'

Alyssa's supporters tried to buoy her with the news that, if she were to climb in 2015, she still stood a chance of becoming the youngest non-Sherpa female in the world to summit Everest. The current eighteen-year-old record-holder's birthday was after Alyssa's. But that wasn't to be either. On 25 May 2014, thirteen-year-old Indian schoolgirl Malavath Purna scaled Everest from the northern, Tibetan, side. That record was now unassailable.

'But, honestly, I didn't really mind about that at all,' Alyssa says. 'That didn't affect me. I think it's great that she did it. Any time anyone achieves something like that it is wonderful. It encourages other people to follow their dreams, and realise that anything is possible. I was happy that she'd been successful. Good on her!'

What was much more important to Alyssa was whether she'd be able to try again the next year. Her dad's agreement to help back her next trip, in 2015, came as a huge relief. He'd been enormously thankful she was safe, but felt for her after all the effort she'd put in. 'It had been such a massive build-up to this,' he says. 'To see it snatched away from her like that was heartbreaking. I could tell she had so many mixed emotions, from the hurt and respect for the Sherpas to her own personal disappointment. But I've always been happy to support her. I know Everest is risky, but it's what she's always wanted to do since she was very little. I also know it's going to be hard to raise the money again, but we'll do the very best we can.'

For Alyssa, the decision to try again was an easy one. From the moment she walked off Base Camp, she was already planning how to make it happen. 'I immediately decided to reset myself and go again next year,' she says. 'It's going to be hard to raise the funds again for another try, but I'm not willing to give up on Everest. R.I.P. to the Sherpas who lost their lives on Everest this year. You will never be forgotten. And I'm not going to forget my dream of climbing to the summit of Everest either. There may be hurdles in life at every stage, but I want people to realise that they only make you stronger, and your goals somehow so much more worth achieving.'

CHAPTER 27

In the Event of My Death

*'You don't overcome challenges by making them smaller,
but by making yourself bigger.'*

– JOHN C. MAXWELL, AUTHOR

If you're reading this, it means I have died on Mt Everest, Alyssa wrote.

But I don't want people to feel sad for me, or to criticise my decision to make another push on Everest. I'd rather they feel happy that I died as I wanted to live – challenging myself to reach the roof of the world.

I'd like to be remembered that way too, as someone determined to follow my dream, wherever it ended up taking me, and whatever the final price. And, of course, that decision to climb was mine, and mine alone.

Alyssa was determined to return to Everest to try to climb in 2015, a year after the deadly avalanche down the Khumbu Icefall. But she was now under no illusion at all about how dangerous her dream could be. She'd already seen too many people die on the mountain for that, and this time she was even more prepared than before.

She even wrote out a letter to be published in the event of her death, to make it absolutely clear that she would have died doing what she most wanted to do in the world and that no one, particularly not her parents, was responsible. It was a morbid, desperately sad task, but she decided it was also one that was absolutely necessary.

The past twelve months had been extremely tough for Alyssa. She'd been through the whole gamut of emotions – from feeling so low following her aborted 2014 climb to the thrill of finally being able to raise enough money to support another attempt in 2015 – and she'd worked as hard as she ever thought possible in the interim to make sure she was ready, in mind, body and spirit.

'When I got home last time, I was a bit depressed and I felt really flat, without any motivation,' she says. 'That wasn't like me at all. I felt completely mentally drained. It was a hard lesson for me as I'm always so determined to follow my goals. But I managed to get myself out of it by focusing on the possibility of climbing Everest again this year. I had no idea whether we'd be able to raise the money or not, nor even whether the mountain would be open again, but I just had to tell myself I was going, concentrate on that and know that if the opportunity came up, I'd be completely prepared. That's the way I ended up getting out of the mood I was in. I know that sometimes facing hurdles and difficulties just makes you stronger in the long run.'

Glenn was keen to see exactly how mentally tough his daughter was, and was pleased when she suggested she go on a three-week program at theMill, an elite training facility in Fremantle, Western Australia, run by ex-SAS soldiers. Applicants for their courses are required to go through a tough 'initiation' process to see if they're fit and disciplined enough to take part in the strength, power and endurance regime, with two-thirds routinely rejected. Gruelling workouts at theMill include circuit training, dragging tyres, clambering up rope ladders, swinging on Olympic rings and battling a variety of punitive exercise machines. The physical demands are only part of the story, however. They usually come with a series of ruthless mind games, where participants are exercised to exhaustion and then told to do more. It was similar to the kind of training she'd done with that other ex-SAS soldier Keith Fennell in November 2013, but it was even more gruelling and for a much longer period.

'They want to see how determined you are, and how you'd never give up,' says Alyssa, who attended in June 2014, a month and a half after her return home from Nepal. 'It was pretty tough. I worked with an ex-Marine Commando from the UK who was 6 foot 7 and as intense as hell. He pushed me so hard, but I quite enjoyed it! It's great to see how hard you can push yourself. Sometimes you think you're finished but you can still keep going. That was a valuable lesson for me. If I'm on Everest and I think I have nothing left, I'll know in my heart that yes, I can keep going. So many of us don't realise how much we can achieve when we put our mind to it . . .'

While Alyssa learnt a lot from her theMill experience, they were so impressed by her, they even featured her on their website. *The youngest Australian to complete the Kokoda track at age 8, Alyssa (now 17) shows what passion, hard work and dedication can achieve*, they wrote under a photo of her.

Three months later, Alyssa took part in her third Kokoda Track trek, this time helping Glenn run a Mates4Mates adventure challenge, devised to assist in the physical and psychological rehabilitation of current or former members of the defence forces. Alyssa was there to help a participant who'd lost a leg in Afghanistan and was tackling the trip with a prosthetic leg. 'But he didn't miss a beat!' she laughs. 'He didn't need anything!'

While Alyssa was still growing in confidence about her ability to summit Everest, she and Glenn just weren't sure about their ability to raise the necessary funds for the next trip. To make up the money needed for the 2014 attempt, Glenn had borrowed a sizeable sum of money from a friend who was setting up a branch of his Fighting Fit fitness business in the UK, and who'd said he'd be happy to give him a loan towards his daughter's climb. He still had to pay that back. 'But I told Alyssa to concentrate on her training, and somehow we'd find a way,' says Glenn. 'I didn't want her to get sidetracked thinking about the money. I felt sure we'd manage, somehow.'

Gradually, little by little, the money mounted up. Glenn decided to combine one of his expeditions with Alyssa's 2015 trek to Base Camp, to kill two birds with one stone, so to speak. Alyssa was interviewed for a few ambassadorships for various companies. And the pair made a fresh bid to win new sponsors. In that, they found a valuable ally.

The general manager of talent brand agency Ensemble was watching TV one night when he saw Alyssa appear as a panel guest on Channel Ten's *The Project*. He contacted the company's brand-partnership account director, Olivia Santilli, and suggested they approach Alyssa and Glenn for a meeting. 'We support rising stars and we felt Alyssa fitted the bill perfectly,' says Olivia. 'For me, it wasn't a hard sell. Once we met her, saw her personality, her dedication, her determination and her confidence, she won us over immediately. She's an amazing young woman. She doesn't even seem to fear death; she just wants to follow her dream. She's a girl who's really gone for it. As a brand, that really has value.'

With the help of Ensemble, a major sponsorship from Acquire Learning – an online education-to-employment business with offices in both Australia and the UK – quickly followed. They saw Alyssa as an inspirational figure, keen to improve her life and aim for her goals, whatever the price. That seemed a perfect fit with an organisation intent on improving other people's lives – particularly those of young Australians – through access to education and online training.

'She'd achieved so much already and her message is all about challenging yourself and achieving your aims and getting everything you want if only you're dedicated enough, and want it enough,' says Acquire spokesman Simon Mossman. 'For us, it's brilliant brand alignment. Alyssa's drive, her tenacity and her approachability and friendliness and the fact that she loves doing work for charity . . . They're all the qualities of our organisation as well. She comes across as wise and experienced beyond her years, and she has the kind of charisma and magnetism of a real star in the making.' Acquire's marketing project manager, Matthew Boyd, was similarly won over. 'When I met Alyssa, I couldn't believe that this seventeen-year-old girl was tackling such a huge feat as Everest,' he says. 'Alyssa joined a very small and elite list. She knows exactly what she wants, and takes all the steps to get there, and she really inspires others.'

Alyssa and Glenn were always extremely careful with the sponsorships they took on, however. A mining company approached her, offering $150 000 if she'd be the face of their firm. She refused. 'At the time, we were really struggling,' says Glenn. 'But we just couldn't accept their money. We didn't like what they were doing, and we felt we had to be true to our own values.'

Previous sponsors like Di Bella Coffee and psyborg were still on board and some other newcomers were also welcomed. Alyssa was still giving talks wherever she could, and entrepreneur Dick Smith came forward to say how impressed with her he was and donate $10 000 to her cause.

Finally, in October 2014, Alyssa returned to Nepal, this time to climb Ama Dablam, the soaring snow-capped Himalayan peak that dominates the eastern skyline during the trek to Everest Base Camp. Alyssa had often gazed at it and hoped she might one day tackle it after she'd successfully climbed Everest. She never dreamt that she'd be trying it before she'd had the chance to summit Everest. At 6812 metres, the mountain nicknamed the 'Matterhorn' of the Himalayas is just over 2000 metres lower than Everest, but its high ridges and steep faces make it a challenge, with a demanding combination of rock-climbing and scaling inclines deep in ice and snow, with plenty of jumaring on ropes. Sir Edmund Hillary once called it 'unclimbable'.

'I really enjoyed being back in the area,' Alyssa says. 'On the trek there, I passed through a lot of the places, like Namche Bazaar, that have so much history for me, since I've been going from a young age. And it was wonderful to see Everest again, and think, yes, one day I'll be back!'

It's a steep climb from Ama Dablam's Base Camp to Camp I, trudging mostly upwards for seven hours. Once there, Alyssa didn't feel too good, and realised she wasn't at all hungry, recognising the first signs of altitude sickness. She didn't panic, however. She tried to sleep and the next morning climbed higher for about an hour to acclimatise herself a little more before turning around and heading back down for the next two nights. By the time she returned to Camp I, she felt good, and ready to tackle the steep climb, using crampons and ropes on rock and ice, up to Camp II. She made steady progress until a Sherpa alerted her that she'd have to edge her way past a dead climber whose body had been left on a narrow rock ledge until he could be taken down.

The dead man was forty-two-year-old Russian climber Murad Ashurly, who'd successfully summitted the mountain, but had died when his fixed rope broke while he was descending from Camp II to Camp I. No one had been able to take him down by helicopter because of the bad weather. 'It's the first time I'd seen a dead body that close up,' Alyssa says. 'You feel very sad, but at the same time you know it's a normal part of climbing and it happens on every mountain. The Sherpas had hidden his face but because we were on a ridgeline, there was no space to avoid him so you had to kind of step over him. I know people criticise climbers as being cold-hearted but sometimes there's no other option. It was upsetting, but it's a risk we all face every day. Every climber up there knows that could be any one of us one day.'

On reaching Camp II, the Sherpa guiding her trip suggested they skip the avalanche-prone Camp III and head straight to the summit in one day instead. The glacier that hangs over Camp III is considered extremely dangerous and in 2006 six climbers were killed there after a large serac collapsed from the overhang, sweeping away the tents of Europeans and Sherpas alike.

'So we got up at 2 a.m. the next day and set off in the pitch black, just focusing on what's in front of you that you can see by torchlight,' she says. 'The snow and ice were pretty deep and we were just digging in our crampons and jumaring up the ropes. After a few hours, you get into a rhythm and eventually the sun came up and we could see the clear blue sky, but then you'd go back into the shade and then back into the bright sunlight as you curve your way up. We could see Camp III in the distance, but we carried on, up and up. Finally, the summit of the mountain appeared, which is so cool! It looks just like a picture.

'We hit the second plateau and then started walking again. It's fairly steep and, again, it's one foot in front of the other. The last little section, you can't see the peak until you're right on it. And then you get there. It felt incredible, especially after the disappointments of Manaslu and Aconcagua. I had a photo of me taken, and put an Australian flag and a sponsor flag there and I just stood there, marvelling. To actually be able to stand on a summit was a very good feeling. From there, I was looking right at Everest in the background. It was magnificent. I vowed that soon I'd be standing on that summit too.'

But even as Alyssa was celebrating her own personal triumph, disaster wasn't far away. On the slopes below, on the popular hiking route the Annapurna trail, thirty-nine trekkers were killed in snowstorms and avalanches, and 384 others had to be rescued in

Nepal's worst-ever trekking disaster. 'I had no idea about it until I was back down in Kathmandu,' Alyssa says. 'Then I heard people talking about it. When you're in among mountains, you just never know what will happen. You're at their mercy. It makes you realise, yet again, how dangerous they can be. But that will never put me off. Never!'

And just to show how seriously she takes the whole thing, she continued to put pen to paper to write her own final words – if the worst should happen. If she didn't survive her attempt, she planned for her letter to be published posthumously as part of this book.

I want my family to know that regardless of what anyone else says, the right decision was made and there is no reason to be sad about my passing. I died on the mountain I have wholeheartedly dedicated myself to for most of my life and I have no regrets. I don't fear Death and I am prepared for anything on Everest.

Climbing Everest is something I've thought about constantly, trained for since I was a little girl, and prepared for in every single way I knew how. Plenty of people tried to talk me out of it; they all failed. I'd done everything I could to ensure it would be a safe climb, but there are some things you can never control on Everest. As this book says so often, the great dangers of Everest are exactly those things that are impossible to foresee – avalanches, the weather, accidents.

I knew all the risks and made my decision to climb in 2015 with my eyes wide open, hoping for the best, but preparing for the worst. If the worst does happen while I'm up there, and I don't make it back, I also still really want this book about my life to be published. I'd like what I have to say and how I've led my life to live on beyond me.

I have always believed there is no such thing as a victim on Everest. Any climber who chooses to set foot on the mountain accepts the risks, and I was one of them. The truth is, if there were no risks, no pain and no possibility of my Death then I wouldn't have been that interested. All of these things make up the challenge that is Everest and I wouldn't have wanted, nor accepted, any less.

I've also been proud to be called a role model for young people from a very early age, right from when I first walked Kokoda at the age of eight, to show them that anything is possible if you want it enough. I'd love it if people could still learn from what I've experienced.

If I had my time all over again, I'd live it exactly the same way: pursuing my dream to the end, to climb Everest.

CHAPTER 28

The Deadliest Year

'If you're going through hell, keep going.'
— ANON

It's been a cold, crisp night in Everest Base Camp and at 2 a.m., in the pitch black, Alyssa is gathering together her gear in her tent by torchlight, ready for her first climb up Everest. It's Saturday, 25 April 2015 and Alyssa, now eighteen, can't wait to get going on the Khumbu Icefall. This is the moment she's been waiting for her whole life.

'I felt huge excitement that here it was,' she says. 'I was about to start climbing on the mountain. My first day climbing on Everest was about to begin. This marked the true beginning of the expedition. Finally I was about to get my chance.'

Her group are set to leave at 4 a.m. but, it seems, not today. The team's head Sherpa, Ang Kami, calls softly outside the tent that the conditions aren't great and that they should delay their departure for a day. Alyssa instantly feels the weight of crushing disappointment, but the Sherpas know this mountain, and know its moods too well to be argued with. She knows she'll be just as ready tomorrow for the trip of her life.

She pushes her gear to one side, climbs back into her sleeping bag and waits for daybreak. Tomorrow morning isn't so far off. She can wait one more day. She'll have to.

That morning, everything is as normal. She goes over to the mess tent for breakfast, stays there to write a few lines in her diary and reads. Then, at 11.40 a.m., she leaves the mess tent and walks back to her own tent, where she sits and reads quietly. She's half-dozing inside when she feels the earth suddenly shudder.

She's confused. Maybe she was dreaming. It doesn't feel real. Then she hears a distant crash. That's nothing unusual; she's used to the sound of the small avalanches that occur all the time around Everest. But there's something different about this one. She can hear everything shaking in her tent and in the tents nearby and outside around her. For a split second, she wonders if she's suffering from altitude sickness. That can change your perception of everything. But then she realises. No, this is something real, and far more serious.

Alyssa scrambles to the front of her tent, facing Everest, and opens it up. She can see her team members outside standing still and looking up at the side of the mountain. Donna, who did the trek to Base Camp with her last year, is among them. Then she hears a deafening rushing noise from behind. Almost by instinct, she crawls back inside the tent and clambers to the back. Whatever's happening, she knows her tent will offer her some protection, however minor. Then, she swiftly unzips it to see what's actually going on behind. The rumbling is getting louder and, as she looks, the peak of Pumori, a mountain popularly known as Everest's Daughter, shivers before her eyes and then a wall of white heads straight towards her. With trembling fingers, she rips the zip back up and dives now to the front of the tent, curling up in a crash position and covering her face with her arms to try to create an air pocket in case she gets buried by what she now realises is an oncoming avalanche, and the biggest she's ever seen.

Exactly three seconds later, it smashes into her tent. 'I didn't really even have time to be scared,' she says. 'It all happened so quickly. I knew I just had to react quickly if I was going to survive. I couldn't get out of the way. As the avalanche hit, I could feel the weight getting heavier and heavier on my tent. I just had to crouch there and wait it out. It felt like an eternity. I didn't even know if it was going to stop.'

Every serious mountaineer faces the possibility of one day being buried alive. Alyssa just hopes that, this time, she'll be lucky. After a few minutes, the pounding on her tent stops and there's a terrible silence. Realising that whatever is going on has just stopped – if only for a short time – she reaches for the front zipper of her tent. This is the moment of truth. She may open it to find a wall of ice, rocks and snow that she might not be able to dig her way out of. But there's light at the top of the tent, and she's able to scramble out to safety.

Once clear of the tent, she looks around for the others. She sees Donna, completely covered in snow and ice, and races over. She helps dig her out and Donna tells her she's fine, except her hands are stinging from the cold. Alyssa grabs her own down mittens and puts them on Donna's hands to try to warm her up. All the other members of the team seem fine; around them, the camp is gradually coming back to life, with the injured being treated and people running to collect others with stretches. There has been an earthquake – the deadliest one in Nepal's history.

* * *

The earthquake had hit at 11.56 a.m., and was later measured to be of a magnitude of 7.8 – the biggest quake to hit Nepal since 1934. Its epicentre was in Lamjung, just over 100 km north-west of Kathmandu, and 220 km west of the Everest Base Camp. The ground at Base Camp had shaken, and surviving climbers later talked about how the mighty Everest had also shuddered. But while everyone had been staring up at Everest, the quake had triggered a massive avalanche too on the nearby Pumori – used by Alyssa several times for her acclimatisation treks – which had sent down a mass of snow, ice and rocks that engulfed most of Base Camp from the other direction. The force of that avalanche had also swept up the Khumbu Icefall and killed and injured some of the climbers already there. Around 100 others higher up at Camp I and Camp II were trapped, with all routes down sealed off by the tide of debris.

If Alyssa had gone up that morning as planned, she would have been in the direct line of fire of the falling boulders, crags, rocks, ice and snow. Her letter about death might have fulfilled its grim purpose.

* * *

Early that afternoon, as Alyssa rushes around the camp, doing her best to help others caught in the avalanche, she has no idea that twenty-one people have already been killed on the mountain and in the camp. That toll makes it the deadliest day on Everest in history, surpassing the Sherpas' deaths in 2014. Later, three more Sherpas are to die in an aftershock while they're on the Khumbu Icefall trying to repair the damaged route. At least sixty-one people have been injured.

'It had all happened so quickly,' Alyssa says. 'There was a complete air of disbelief. The adrenalin had hit by then, but still it was hard to believe something like this had happened. As we stood there, people were being rescued or their bodies being brought out and put on stretchers. We did what we could but then were told we should try to get out as aftershocks were quite likely.

'So I packed a few things I might need and we trekked down to the nearest tea house at Gorak Shep, and met up with two other women who had been planning to be on our expedition for the season. That tea house felt quite safe as there aren't any mountains either side. I then texted Dad to tell him I was safe. I'd just assumed something had happened in this area. But then I found out from him that it'd been an earthquake further away, and it had caused massive devastation. It was huge.'

The news is slow to come in, but gradually Alyssa starts realising the extent of the casualties and damage. In total, the earthquake has killed over 8000 people and injured more than 21 000. Hundreds of thousands of Nepalese have lost their homes, entire villages have been destroyed and ancient national monuments and buildings left shattered. The country will never be the same again. Alyssa and her other expedition members stay in their tea house, feeling the constant aftershocks. She goes to bed that night wearing her shoes in case she has to make a quick exit.

The next day, 26 April, Alyssa and three of her teammates decide to trek back to Base Camp to see if they can help any more of the injured or salvage any of their gear. The others stay at Gorak Shep, too nervous to move and far too frightened of what might happen at Base Camp. The four set off but halfway into the two-hour trek, just before 1 p.m., suddenly the ground moves, and this time much more violently than the other aftershocks. Alyssa dives for a big rock nearby and takes cover behind it, in case there's another avalanche or landslide. The shaking continues for a good sixty seconds and she later finds out that the shock reached a magnitude of 6.7.

'The ground shook so hard I almost fell over,' she says. 'I grabbed on to the rock to steady myself and waited. Eventually it stopped. We got back together, but none of us wanted to turn back. We all wanted to get to Base Camp. But we didn't know what to expect.'

When they finally arrive, the sight takes their breath away. 'The camp had been completely wiped out,' she says. 'That big mess tent had been pretty much crushed. It was shocking to see something that massive just torn away like that. Then I went to where my tent was, and that was even worse. It had been flattened and ripped and was pretty mangled. The force of the avalanche had even broken the tent poles. Most of it was buried under the weight of the snow.

'Only a little part of the front section seemed to be okay – that part where I'd gone – and if the snow was a little higher, or I'd have camped a bit higher, I wouldn't have been able to get out. I could also see that if I'd stayed at the back of the tent, I wouldn't have survived. I was so lucky that I'd been partly awake when it happened. If I'd been asleep, it would have been too late to do anything.'

To the background noise of helicopters still rescuing the stranded from the mountain, and airlifting the dead and injured from Base Camp, Alyssa starts to dig around her tent to retrieve some of her gear. It's then that fatigue starts to hit. She realises she feels more tired than she ever has in her life. It's probably delayed shock. The camp feels strangely deserted but a Sherpa she knows, Lhakpa Rangdu, sees her and invites her to what's left of his camp. Luckily, he and his party had been off trekking when the earthquake happened. Only one tent is left standing, which Alyssa shares with another female climber. They'd been planning to sleep in their own, but they now know that's impossible. Once Alyssa drifts off, she sleeps quite soundly. Her tent-mate doesn't seem to sleep at all, too nervous about what might happen.

The next day, they trek back down to the lower lodges, seeing how many of the homes and tea houses have been damaged in the earthquake and subsequent landslides and aftershocks. Some climbers, it seemed, had been planning to continue up the mountain after the first quake and some icefall doctors had gone back up to fix ropes and ladders. When the aftershock hit them, the climbing season was again closed for the year – now just the second time in history that had happened.

'I had no idea what was going to happen,' says Alyssa. 'Some of my teammates just wanted to go home, but there were rumours continually on the trek about what might be happening. Then we heard it was finished. So we carried on trekking down to Namche Bazaar.'

By now, some members of the expedition are feeling ill, and whether that is also shock or the effects of altitude, no one can tell. Some are also dead tired. They have a few rest days in the town.

Afterwards, most decide they want to catch a helicopter back to Lukla, but Alyssa volunteers to walk, as the choppers are in such high demand from the rescue services. They, she feels, have priority. In the end, she walks all the way from Phakding alone, seeing firsthand the toll the earthquake has taken on the remote valleys. By the time she finally arrives in Lukla, she is exhausted and struggling with a bad cold.

'But I got a flight the next morning to Kathmandu,' she says. 'I thought I'd have to wait a time before I'd get a flight but I was lucky. I knew it was all over for the year. I felt terrible for Nepal. I'd been going there since I was ten years old, and come to love it, so to see it hurting so much was awful. So much was devastated and so many people had their lives changed forever. It was such a shock. Just a few days before, I'd been looking forward to living my dream: climbing to the top of Everest. Now I was on my way home again, knowing I was leaving so much desperation behind. It was a really unsettling time. But I really felt this time that I wanted to go home.'

Alyssa takes an early flight out of Kathmandu and is met at the airport by her dad and a gaggle of media. She does a few interviews, hoping it will bring more attention to the plight of the Nepalese and help the fundraising efforts. She also donates the money she's been given towards her Everest expedition by Dick Smith to the charities helping Nepal, checking first that he's okay with that.

Then she goes home. 'I suppose I was very lucky, but I just didn't feel so lucky!' she says. 'The past two years had been very difficult. Not since Everest was first climbed had there been so much tragedy in the mountains. I didn't admit it to anyone, but I felt almost kind of angry. I'd put so much into this, and I'd been powerless to change things in the end. I felt incredibly sad for the people of Nepal and the Sherpas and other climbers who'd lost their lives or been injured, it was all just so terrible.

'But as much as I knew I still wanted to go back and climb Everest, I didn't think I'd be able to get there again. It was starting to look more and more impossible.'

CHAPTER 29

Touch and Go

'If you'll not settle for anything less than your best, you will be amazed at what you can accomplish in your lives.'
– VINCE LOMBARDI, AMERICAN FOOTBALL
PLAYER AND COACH

When Alyssa returns home in May 2015, she sinks into a profound depression. For once, all her determination is sapped from her and even those inspirational sayings she's been treasuring for years don't help. She shuts herself away in her bedroom, and whiles away the hours reading and sleeping. She doesn't want to talk to anyone. She doesn't even want to see her family.

'I know it might be hard for people to understand, but when you put so much into something, it can be hard to come to terms with not achieving it,' she says. 'I felt so sad for the people of Nepal, the earthquake was so tragic and so senseless, and that should have put my goals into perspective, really. But I couldn't seem to shake myself out of the mood. I didn't want to do anything. Mum and Dad tried to talk me out of it, but I wouldn't listen.'

That world-weariness lasts three weeks until, at last, she realises she just can't continue this way. Either she keeps sliding down – or she makes a concerted effort to pull herself together and drag herself back up. She decides on the latter and one day grabs her training gear and heads off to the gym. As soon as she arrives, she feels marginally better. After a good long run on the treadmill, her head has started to clear. She then makes an effort to start thinking about the future, and allows herself even to imagine a return to Everest the next year.

Over the following days, she trains each morning, and then goes for coffee or lunch with Glenn. Gradually, she feels herself returning to the world. At one point, she goes to stay with her mum, sisters and brother, and for almost the first time, finds herself talking to Therese about Everest. Up until now, it has been a subject the pair have avoided; Alyssa knows her mum isn't keen on her going. But this time, mother and daughter open up to each other. Alyssa talks about her passion and her dream of summitting the mountain, and Therese says she understands.

'We talked about what happened on Base Camp, with the earthquake, and she talked about how single-minded we both are,' Alyssa says. 'We both have goals that we're determined to achieve, and she said sometimes that makes life difficult. She said she knew I'd be thinking of going back, and that it was good to be so passionate about life. That was great, talking like that. It really helped, and all over again, I knew I needed to get back to Everest.'

At the same time, she knows an eagerness to return, a readiness to train physically hard for it and being mentally and emotionally prepared for another assault, is only a fraction of what's needed. The biggest barrier, as ever, is financial.

Her biggest sponsor of her 2015 trip, Acquire Learning, is not able to help fund another climb in 2016, and Alyssa knows others of her past sponsors might blanch at the thought of forking out again after the failure of two previous attempts. They might even rethink how dangerous it is, especially for a teenager coming up to her nineteenth birthday, and not want to be seen to be encouraging such a potentially treacherous venture. She'd already cheated death twice in the foothills of Everest. To be helping send her up further a third time could be considered almost reckless.

Her old sponsor, Mountain Designs, comes forward, however, and invites her to help promote their new range of clothing, ominously named White Limbo after one of the most dangerous routes up Everest along the north-west ridge, which has a 50 per cent fatality rate. They'd like her to do the first testing of their gear on Everest – although obviously not on that approach. She happily agrees and, as well as providing so much of the gear she'll need, they also throw in $5000 for expenses.

Every little bit helps and Alyssa works hard at pushing former sponsors and possible future sponsors to come on board. With the help of her agents, Ensemble, she and Glenn set up a new Summit Club, asking twenty companies each to contribute a modest sum and become part of the venture. In return, Alyssa will speak at functions for them and offer free tickets for any other functions at which she's presenting. It sparks fresh interest, and a number, including Steve Keil from Laser Plumbing and Electrical, make a commitment to come on board.

'I think the hardest thing was that there was a lot of doubt now about whether I could actually make it a third time,' Alyssa says. 'The last two years had shown everyone that anything can happen up there. You never know, and you can't control circumstances. The mountain's in charge. But I had faith in myself, I knew I could do it. And the whole of Nepal wanted climbers to succeed in 2016, too. They needed the season to work out.

'Of course it was at the back of my mind that there was a chance something could go wrong, but I couldn't afford to have any doubts. I could only imagine how tough it would be if I didn't go and I was forced to sit at home hearing about other people summitting and reading all about it on the internet. I knew I had to put everything I'd got on the line. And in the meantime I had to work at keeping my fitness up so I'd be ready to go if we could pull it off. I wouldn't be able to afford to climb any more mountains in the interim, so I vowed instead to be the fittest and strongest I'd ever been to make up for it.'

She also takes a job as a waitress in a local Chinese restaurant to help contribute money towards the trip. She'd never actually got around to finishing her schooling at home and is now starting to regret not working to pursue her HSC as, without it, she doesn't have too many choices of work. She hates waitressing, but tries to view it simply as another challenge. She's awkward with customers, impatient with their orders and finds it strange to be spending time with the other restaurant staff, young people her own age, which is something she hasn't experienced since leaving school so many years ago.

In addition, some of the customers recognise her and want to ask her about Everest, which she finds hard. There's fresh interest in the mountain after the release of the hit British–American movie *Everest* in Australia in September 2015, starring Jake Gyllenhaal, Keira Knightley and Elizabeth Debicki. The film is about the 1996 disaster on Everest, when a blizzard struck climbers both ascending to the summit and trying to get down, killing eight people. Alyssa steadfastly avoids it. She's seen enough death on Everest for real; she doesn't want to see a Hollywood version, however accurate it might be. Besides, she is totally focused on experiencing the summit herself, rather than watching it in a movie. So every time a customer brings up the subject, she fixes a smile on her face, answers politely and reminds herself that every cent she can earn will get her closer to her goal. Glenn, watching on, silently applauds his daughter.

'I think it was very, very hard for her, on so many levels,' he says. 'It wasn't playing to her skillset at all! She'd just come back from a huge adventure and seen life and death in its rawest form on Everest, and here she was getting hell from people when the kitchen muddled up orders or brought dishes out at different times, or they felt their coffee wasn't hot enough. I'm sure at times she found it was hard to take too seriously, but she tried hard at it, and I was proud of her for giving it a go. I thought it was good for her, and I know she found it quite humbling.'

Glenn works out how much he can afford to pay from his Adventure Professionals trekking business, and starts thinking about approaching banks for a loan to cover any shortfall.

Towards the end of 2015, he also makes the decision to move from Toowoomba to Brisbane. His company is going so well, but he's having to commute to Brisbane two to three days every week for meetings. It would be easier, really, to set himself up there and just travel back to Toowoomba to see the family instead. Alyssa stays at her mum's during the move and prepares to join him in Brisbane once he's settled. Accordingly, she quits her restaurant job with a sigh of relief, but then finds another job in a cafe at a shopping centre in Brisbane.

Life in Brisbane gradually assumes its own routine. Work takes up a lot of Alyssa's time, learning to drive and fitness training even more. She also spends time looking after her brother Christian or youngest sister Samantha, who come to stay with her and Glenn for weekends. Christian, now twelve, still doesn't really understand the concept of Everest, but seems to realise his sister loves climbing mountains and asks her when she'll be off again. Samantha, eight, is fascinated by Everest and really excited by the prospect of Alyssa one day reaching the top. She does a project on it at school and often talks proudly about her big sister to her teachers and classmates.

By the end of February 2016, things are starting to look up. Glenn's business is going great guns now he's at the heart of the action in Brisbane, and he finds he can afford to contribute more to another Everest expedition. Another movie comes out about Everest that month, the British–Australian documentary *Sherpa*, about the 2014 deaths on the Khumbu Icefall, and he goes to see it without

Alyssa. He talks to her about it, though. He finds that watching the horror as it unfolded on Everest and the disputes between the Sherpas and foreign-owned expedition companies who wanted to continue their climbs regardless, brings his daughter's experience that year into stark relief. It's good for her to have someone so close who understands, but she still resists going to see it herself.

Glenn also talks to the banks, in earnest, about loans, showing them his business plans and projections of future earnings as equity. In the back of his mind, he formulates a Plan B, too. If he's turned down, he knows a few friends who'd be willing to help him out. He also suggests Alyssa give up her job and get back to training harder and for longer hours every day to make sure she's ready if all the pieces of the puzzle do suddenly fall into place.

She does two big sessions of training a day, with running, endurance sessions in the gym, kettle bells and weights, squat training, tyre-dragging, push-ups, rope climbing, everything, and mostly with a pack on her back and wearing her elevation training mask to strengthen her lungs. Her oxygen tent is by now worn out, so she just steps up use of the mask. She becomes a familiar figure in Brisbane, wearing it to run laps around Taylor Range and up and down its highest peak, Mount Coot-tha.

Alyssa then embarks on a special nutrition program written for her by Scott Evennett, a former special-ops soldier turned fitness trainer and life coach. It consists of lots of lean protein and vegetables, bringing in more good carbs as it heads towards the time when she'd depart for the Himalaya, if she does end up going. It also introduces more lentils, rice and the other kinds of food she'll eat on the mountain, so her body will be ready for the change in diet when she gets there. She then travels down to Sydney for some sessions of mind and body training with him.

'Alyssa's ability to know her own physical strength and emotional intelligence became very apparent to me early on,' says

Evennett. 'She has the ability to see anything that comes to her as a problem or an issue instead as a challenge, and then take it on. That's her real strength. She doesn't waste any energy on emotions.'

His training involves both hard physical work, and playing with the mindset. He gives Alyssa one of his favourites: running 10 km, but stopping every five minutes for seventy-five squats. The slower she runs, the more squats she has to do. The faster she can cover the course, the fewer. Knowing how much that kind of work is going to hurt before you actually start tests someone's strength of purpose like little else.

'It's about creating a mountain in her mind and testing that she'll be able to get over it, just like the real mountain she hopes to face next time,' he says. 'But by the end of our two sessions, I was definitely very impressed by her. Her mind and her determination are her greatest assets. They're unwavering, and that's very rare for someone her age. I think she's grown up in a certain environment with both her mother and father ex-military, and that can sort of set you up. She's been sharpening those early tools all her life.'

Still, everything continues to be very much up in the air when she declares on her Facebook page that she's definitely returning to Everest and receives a slew of publicity as a result. In truth, she knows it's more wishful thinking than anything else, it's still touch and go. But no one gets anywhere without taking a punt here and there.

'But it was extremely stressful,' she says. 'I didn't know if I was going, but all the time I was trying to pretend that I was. Things changed every day. And I knew that even if it did come off, it was going to be a pretty last-minute thing. But I was training to be ready, and telling myself that I was ready, too.'

Finally, in the second week of March, Glenn has a rush of bookings for a couple of his trips, and is contacted by one of the banks he's approached to say his application for a substantial loan has been successful. Suddenly, the trip has become a reality. Alyssa is thrilled – and very, very grateful to her dad. Always her biggest supporter, he's managed to come through yet again.

'Learning I was going to be able to go back to Everest was incredible,' she says. 'When it actually happened, I could hardly believe it. I've always really appreciated everything Dad's done for me. He told me I'd have to pay back the loan, but that's fine. I'm very happy to do that. It just felt incredible to think I'd have another chance at my dream.'

CHAPTER 30

Cyclone Alert

'Life isn't about finding yourself. Life is about creating yourself.'
– GEORGE BERNARD SHAW, IRISH PLAYWRIGHT AND CRITIC

Walking along the gangway to the plane at Brisbane Airport on 3 April 2016, Glenn's last words ring in Alyssa's ears. With a schedule to reach the summit of Everest on 19 May, he hugged her hard and said, 'Now, I don't want to see you until June!' She smiles to herself. The last two times, with her climbs cut short, she'd been back home by the end of April. This time, she is even more determined than ever to make it through.

'You just can't afford to have any doubts,' she says. 'If you do, it's easy for them to take over. You have to have absolute belief and faith in yourself. I really wanted this, and I knew Nepal really wanted a successful climbing season too. After two years of disasters, everyone was going onto the mountain very, very keen to summit.'

Glenn, who's off to lead five consecutive expeditions walking the Kokoda Track during the time his daughter is on the mountain, feels wary. In 2015, he was absolutely convinced she'd make it to the top, and while he's just as confident about her abilities and training this time, he knows that anything could happen to stop her. He consciously scales his expectations down to 'cautiously optimistic'.

Therese warned Alyssa to be careful but wished her well, while Christian hugged her goodbye. He still doesn't understand the idea of Everest, but he knows she's going away on another climb. Samantha, meanwhile, can barely contain her excitement. She'll be plotting her big sister's progress every day, she told Alyssa proudly, just before she left for the airport.

Alyssa's signed up this time with a different expedition company from her previous two attempts. This one is the Sherpa-owned Asian Trekking, started in 1982 by Ang Tshering Sherpa, one of the first graduates of the school started in the Nepalese Himalaya by Sir Edmund Hillary. It's a company that's been twice in the news over the past ten years, and both for the wrong reasons.

In 2006, one of their clients, experienced British mountaineer David Sharp, froze to death on the north-east slope of Everest as around forty trekkers passed him on their way to the top. His death proved enormously controversial but, say observers, he had elected to be on an 'unguided' climb, where the company's services end at Base Camp, and the client chooses to continue on with no support, no radio and no Sherpa. He died crouched under an overhang beside the corpse of a climber who'd died six years earlier, and just days before Dan Mazur's dramatic rescue of Lincoln Hall. Six years later, in 2012, four more climbers with Asian Trekking also perished on their descent from Everest while taking part in an 'eco expedition' to help with a clean-up on the slopes, collecting some of the debris littering the site from several decades of climbers. They were four of the eleven Everest deaths that year. Back then, it had been the worst disaster on Everest since 2004.

But Alyssa has climbed with Asian Trekking before, on her attempt on Manaslu in 2013, and has found them to be a company very well organised, logistically. She's set to meet up with everyone on her expedition the next day, in Kathmandu. The leader is also the expedition doctor, Dr Nima Namgyal Sherpa, and the main guide organiser is an experienced guide himself, Nanga Dorje Sherpa. The other expedition members are from all corners of the earth, and most of them have tried to climb Everest before in either 2014 or 2015. A couple had, like Alyssa, been driven back both years.

When she arrives, Alyssa notices Kathmandu looks battered as a result of the earthquake, with many of the buildings cracked, and others flattened or just starting to be rebuilt. But the warmth of the Sherpas' welcome is unmistakeable. Climbers returning to Nepal means a much-needed injection of funds into both the local economy and Sherpas' lives.

The group flies into Lukla on 6 April and start the now-familiar trek to Base Camp. All along the way, Alyssa's sobered by the sight of many of the beloved monuments that have been damaged, and the locals' houses in some spots that have been completely destroyed. 'But we were greeted everywhere as fresh hope for the country,' she says. 'You could feel the pain of suffering, but people were very glad we were there.'

By the time Base Camp heaves into view, Alyssa feels at home again, among the mountains, but she won't allow herself to think about summitting. That will be for later, when the time comes. For now, she just wants to enjoy being in the foothills and the hiking they do as part of the long acclimatisation process.

On their second day there, she's surprised to discover they're going to start climbing the Khumbu Icefall as their first rotation. The doctor wants them to get a feel as early as possible for the 2.6-km climb 610 metres upwards across the moving glacier, and sees it as a great way to acclimatise early. The Sherpas set up ropes and everyone's woken at 3 a.m. to eat as much as they can for breakfast and be ready to put their crampons on their boots and start climbing by 4 a.m. – to avoid being on the slope after the sun rises and starts melting the ice. They trudge an hour up the sleep rise and then encounter their first gaping crevasse, where they step carefully over the rungs of aluminium ladders slung across.

Alyssa knows this is usually the most treacherous part of the climb, with more people falling to their deaths here than any other section on the south side. Above them, she can see the massive seracs hanging down, glittering threateningly. Any one of those could shear off at any moment and come crashing down. But everyone makes it safely to the top inside the allotted six hours, and then they part scramble, part abseil back down. Alyssa's thrilled. She has sat at Base Camp and gazed up at the icefall so many times now, it feels almost unreal to have been finally setting foot on it, and climbing up.

The group spend a couple of days back at Base Camp, resting. Then it's time for the second rotation, climbing up to Camp I at 5943 metres high, staying the night there, then moving the two to three hours on to Camp II before returning to Base Camp. That morning, they start climbing at 3 a.m., back up through the icefall and along ever steeper stretches of ice and across more ladders before finally hitting the flat snow bank that marks the way to the first camp.

'It was all just so amazing,' says Alyssa. 'To get to the top of the icefall felt so incredible. From there I could see the Western Cwm – the glacial valley basin they've also nicknamed the Valley of Silence – and the route I'd be following up Everest. It just felt fantastic!'

That night, Alyssa shares her tent with a young woman from India, and is too excited to sleep much. Besides, the wind builds up during the night and the tent walls bang constantly. She doesn't mind a bit.

The next morning, the team's preparing to walk to Camp II at 6400 metres when someone shouts, and they look up to see a massive avalanche thundering down ahead of them. Happily, it's far enough away not to be a threat, but it's yet another reminder of what a treacherous environment they're in. By 8 a.m., the avalanche is finished and they're ready to take off. With Everest to the left, the Lhotse Face directly ahead, and great views of Pumori – which Alyssa saw shiver with an avalanche the year before during the earthquake – they start climbing.

The main difficulty on this part of the mountain is that it's simply so hot. The snow and ice of the valley reflect the sun's rays and it heats up quickly after sunrise. It has been known to reach 38° C. On the other hand, if the cloud comes down or it starts to snow, it can be mind-searingly cold. Alyssa gradually peels off layers of clothing to cope.

'It's quite a long trek and a bit of a grind,' says Alyssa. 'You see tents and you think you're there, but you actually have another hour to your camp. That's the killer, but at the same time it is great. It feels like another milestone. I guess it's about halfway up to the summit!'

The little group finally arrive and spend a couple of hours at camp to help with acclimatisation. They wander around in the mess tent, chatting to other climbers and taking photos. Alyssa longs to continue upwards, but knows she can't. She has to be patient. Instead, she gazes over to the Lhotse Face, a steep, rock-hard wall of ice and snow that's the fourth highest peak in the world, at 8510 metres, which she'll hopefully one day soon be climbing to reach Camp III. She can't see the top of Lhotse from here, but suddenly she hears something: the wild roar of the jet stream, that ferocious westerly wind that can gust around the summit of Everest at up to 281 km an hour. All climbers try to time their final ascent for that narrow window of time when the jet stream isn't raging at the peak, making climbing safely absolutely impossible.

'It was then that, for the first time in my life, I actually heard the jet stream,' she says. 'It sounds like an incredible wind. I found it quite exciting to listen to, but at the same time, you're desperately hoping that you'll be able to find that window to summit when it won't be there . . .'

On that thought, she starts to descend to Camp I for the night, then back to Base Camp.

Over the next three days, Alyssa eats, sleeps and relaxes. It's important to give her body recovery time, she knows, and she tries to just think about the next rotation. On the third day, the aim is to make it to Camp II in a single push, stay the night, then up the Lhotse Face part-way to Camp III, at 7162 metres.

But the day they're meant to be starting the ascent, they arrive at the base of the icefall just as a section on the right suddenly peels away and comes crashing down. Luckily, no one is in its path, and no one gets hurt. While everyone's still keen to continue, the Sherpas say it's too dangerous and put the climb off for a day. No one argues.

The next day, they start again and Alyssa watches the little trail of head torches in front of her gradually rise up the icefall. She crunches her way up, feeling more and more confident now with every step. Her acclimatisation seems to be going well, and she feels strong and fit and ready. It's still a long day to Camp II, however, with that last stretch to the camp extremely tiring, both physically and mentally. By the time she dives into her tent, she has a slight headache. But she's happy at how well she's coping; all the mind-training and hours in the gym are standing her in excellent stead. She sleeps soundly and by the morning her body has adapted and her headache is gone.

She sets out up Lhotse, clipping onto the ropes going up the face, and digging her crampon points into the ice to gain firm purchase. It's enormously tiring, but she feels exhilarated. This is everything she imagined climbing on Everest would be. Almost up at Camp III, she then turns back down. The next time she's back at this height will be during her fourth – and last – rotation when, conditions and

God willing, she'll be able finally to make that push to the summit. She feels a stir of excitement at the thought. She climbs down the Lhotse Face with a grin, ready to return to Camp II for the night, and then back to Base Camp for the last few days.

Five days later, it's finally time. This is going to be the last climb up, with an overnight at Camp II, another night at Camp III, a quick rest at Camp VI and then on to the summit itself.

'I was so excited,' Alyssa says. 'I was also a bit nervous. I felt I knew the section from Base Camp up to Camp III pretty well now, and knew I was capable of it, but there's always that little bit of fear of the unknown. As well, the season's getting warmer and warmer and it brings with it the danger of more avalanches as the snow and ice start to melt, especially on the Khumbu Icefall.'

The start of the climb up the icefall goes well but she freezes as she hears the telltale rumble of an avalanche somewhere near. It's still pitch black, however, and there's no real way of telling whether it's directly above or off to one side. She simply has to stay still, try to cover her head against falling rocks and wait it out.

'We're just starting out when we hear the noise of one, maybe two, going off,' she says. 'It sounds really close but we have no idea where it is. Nobody is hurt though, so it can't be that close. But it's near enough for three of our climbers. They decide to turn back. Maybe it's the avalanche that freaked them, but I know some of them are homesick too. I never get the chance to ask them why they don't continue, but if they don't want to be there, then it's not the right place for them. But for me, there's never any question of not going on.'

Alyssa reaches Camp II comfortably, but it's there that things suddenly start looking ominous. The weather's taken a turn for the worse, the wind's picking up and there are even warnings of a cyclone approaching from India. Alyssa's summit had been planned for 19 May, but now that date seems impossible. It's put back to 20 May, then 21 May.

Alyssa tries to stay calm. Everything has been going so well, it's almost inconceivable that she could be robbed so close to her goal. 'I definitely start to fear it might not happen,' she says. 'We're concerned.' She tries to banish the possibility from her mind. The weather may well improve just as quickly as it deteriorated. She can't afford to spend precious energy worrying.

In the end, she spends just two nights at Camp II, and then her guide, Nanga Dorje Sherpa, says it's safe to press on. Her hopes rise. Three other climbers from Asian Trekking turn up at camp, having just summitted in their allocated window. She's cheered even more. If some people are getting to the top, then there's hope for the rest. She sets out one last time up the Lhotse Face towards Camp III. Some of the other expedition climbers ask to use oxygen from Camp II, but she says she doesn't need it. She's feeling stronger than she ever has in her life.

It's only at Camp III that Alyssa agrees to start on oxygen overnight and for the rest of the climb. She's still feeling good when they set out the next morning at sunrise to Camp VI, sitting at an altitude of 7950 metres, just on the lip of the start of the Death Zone.

The route is steep at first, and is usually bitterly cold from the beginning before very quickly becoming uncomfortably hot. After two hours, Alyssa reaches the Yellow Band, a strip of limestone that's around 50 metres of smooth rock, angled sharply upwards. She clips onto the ropes for help. When that band ends, the terrain becomes flatter snow and ice until the next landmark, the Geneva Spur, with its 80 metres of uneven rock, snow and ice at a 40-degree angle upwards. Alyssa chooses her footholds carefully, willing herself to move steadily through despite wanting to hurry.

'I feel really strong,' she says. 'You do all this training but you still never know how you'll do; you don't know how your body is going to react. But being up there is such a beautiful feeling. It's just how I'd imagined for so many years. I'd created a little picture in my head of what it would be like, and it's just like that. I'm thrilled.'

After about six hours of climbing, Alyssa finally steps onto the South Col, which serves as the platform for Camp VI's tents. She catches sight of Everest's summit close up for the first time. It's so beautiful, it takes her breath away. It looks so near, too – but she knows that, at that height and in the midst of all that blindingly white scenery, distances are deceptive. She wills herself to stay focused as she huddles into a tent with two other climbers for a quick two-hour sleep. She closes her eyes, but sleep fails to come. She simply has too much running through her mind.

At 8 p.m., she rises in the darkness of evening, quickly packs her gear and sets off by the light of her head torch once more. It's only 1.72 km to the summit, but it's a climb that could take up to nine hours. First is a steep slope up directly out of the camp along the south side of Everest, and it takes three hours before she's on the next defined stage, the Balcony. There, in the pale moonlight, she changes oxygen bottles and has a quick drink and snack before continuing. Now she can see down into Nepal on one side and Tibet on the other.

She soon hits the ridge that leads towards the summit. She and Nanga Dorje Sherpa are the first people to be there that morning, breaking ground between them. The snow here is knee-deep and their progress is painfully slow as they trudge through, having to lift their feet high with every step. Finally, they hit more rock and while it's steeper still, the climbing feels much easier.

Three hours on, they reach the South Summit, the point of the climb where you can see the path to the real summit and the so-called Hillary Step, a narrow piece of jutting rock. Alyssa can hardly believe her eyes.

'I'm surprised how quickly we reach the South Summit and there I put on a fresh oxygen bottle,' she says. 'Then we start climbing the ridge. I'm, "Oh my God! I'm almost there!"

'Then you see some prayer flags fluttering in the wind and . . . you're there. I step on the summit and feel overcome with emotion. It's a moment I've imagined so many times, over so many years. I feel disbelief.

'I take some photos, take out the photo of my brother Christian and show him. I just like having him there with me. That's so cool. It's all just as wonderful as I thought it would be.'

Standing on top of the world at 8850 metres, at 3.45 a.m. on 21 May 2016, Alyssa feels a maelstrom of emotions. The nineteen-year-old is immensely proud to be Australia's youngest Everest summitter, but she knows that was never her real motivation. It was always about setting her goal early in life and then throwing everything she possibly could at it to achieve it.

'I take a moment to reflect on my whole journey, on how hard I've worked to get there, on all the hopes and disappointments and sacrifices that have gone before,' Alyssa says. 'It's just so special. It's maybe the best moment of my life. It's everything I've ever imagined.'

CHAPTER 31

Triumph and Tragedy

'I'll always wonder, Could I have done anything?'
— ALYSSA AZAR, MOUNTAINEER AND EVEREST SUMMITTER

As Alyssa makes her way carefully down the mountain, she passes two other Australian climbers. The couple, a man and a woman, engage one of her fellow climbers in conversation. They were on their way up to Camp VI when they started feeling ill, they say. They eventually decided to abandon their climb and are now heading back.

They seem disappointed but resigned, and even cheerful at the prospect of being back down at Base Camp in a couple of days. They continue chatting with the person on Alyssa's expedition until they all say farewell. They seem bright and healthy and don't ask for any help at all.

It's only the next day, after one night at Camp II, and then finally arriving back in Base Camp, that Alyssa hears an Australian woman has died on the mountain. She realises that must have been the woman they passed.

It was Monash University finance lecturer Dr Maria Strydom, aged thirty-four, who fell ill with altitude sickness after turning back from the summit, and died with her partner holding her hand. Her husband, vet Dr Rob Gropel was also sick, suffering from fluid in the lungs and swelling of the brain, and had to be helicoptered off the mountain. Another man in the same expedition, Dutch climber Eric Arnold, also died during the descent, while three other deaths occurred in another team of Indian climbers, Subhash Pal, Paresh Chandra Nath and Goutam Ghosh. One Nepalese, Ang Furba Sherpa, fell to his death while fixing ropes for climbers on Lhotse.

'The Australian woman's death is something I've thought about a lot since,' Alyssa says. 'We had no way of knowing how serious her altitude sickness was. If we'd known, maybe I could have put my oxygen mask on her and helped her get down to Camp II, at a much lower altitude. Maybe it would have made a difference? We'll never know, and have no way of ever knowing. But it does make you realise how dangerous Everest can be. Even when things look all right, they're not necessarily anything like they seem. I think I'll always wonder, Could I have done anything?'

It's a sobering thought, but it's also hard not to feel elation at what she's personally achieved. Stepping off the summit, Alyssa tried to phone her dad on the satellite phone and, although it went through all the way to Glenn's remote location on the Kokoda Track in Papua New Guinea, he missed the call. She tried again, and couldn't get through. Finally, on her third attempt, they connected.

'That was the one call in your life you never want to miss!' says Glenn. 'When I realised I missed a call, I didn't know whether it would be good news or bad. Of course, I always worry about her, and I wondered if anything had gone wrong. But I had no way of finding out until I got to the next camp – four hours away – so I just kept on hoping it was good news. It seemed a bit early to me for her to have summitted, but I just didn't know. Then on the third try, I got the message that she'd done it. I was so pumped. I was so excited. I couldn't sleep that night for thinking about it. It was so hard to fully comprehend.'

Back in Toowoomba, there are some excited people too. Samantha has been interrupted in class by her principal coming in to break the news that her sister has made it to the top of Everest. The whole class celebrate. Therese is also thrilled. 'Despite her young age, I knew no one was better prepared or as fiercely determined to summit Mount Everest,' she says. 'I was also certain that Alyssa would stay on the mountain until she did.'

Everest experts are also generous in their praise. Renowned Everest chronicler and 2011 summitter Alan Arnette is quick to congratulate her. 'To summit Everest requires skills, confidence, luck and unbridled determination,' he says. 'Alyssa had all of these, rarely found in a nineteen-year-old. Climbers twice her age gave up after the tragic events of 2014 and 2015, but Alyssa showed unusual perseverance and resilience to become the youngest Australian to stand on top of the world in 2016.'

The keeper of the official records, Billi Bierling, is also very happy for her. 'Amazing feat that she did it!!' she says.

But Alyssa has to wait another ten days to celebrate herself. She has the long trek from Base Camp back to Lukla to think about it, then has to wait for a flight back to Kathmandu. She spends a few days there before flying out to Singapore to rendezvous with her dad on his way back from his fifty-fifth Kokoda, stop overnight, and then fly on to Brisbane. Glenn and Alyssa are picked up by helicopter from Brisbane airport and taken to Toowoomba for a reunion with the rest of the family. They receive a hero's welcome. In addition, Alyssa visits Samantha's school and is the star guest at an impromptu Q&A for the eight- and nine-year-olds, with her little sister proudly presiding over the whole event. Christian, not sure what all the fuss is about, is just happy to have her back home again.

'I think the hardest thing over the past few years was that no one was really sure this would ever happen,' says Alyssa. 'But happily, it has. I always said I was never motivated by the idea of being the youngest Australian to climb Everest but I now definitely feel very proud of that title. I'm just very happy and grateful to everyone who's helped on the long, long journey.'

* * *

If anyone thought that Alyssa's success on Everest would cure her of her ambition to climb mountains, they were wrong. Her next goal is to climb the rest of the Seven Summits – the highest peaks of the seven continents. With Everest, Mount Kosciuszko and Kilimanjaro already summitted, that leaves just Aconcagua, Mount Elbrus, Mount Vinson and Mount McKinley, and she has until the age of twenty-three to break another record as the youngest Australian to do that. She'd also like to reach the top of all the fourteen mountains on earth that are over 8000 metres, particularly Manaslu, which beat her back in 2013.

In the meantime, she plans to work with her dad in his Adventure Professionals business, helping lead his expeditions in between taking off on her own. She's also considering going back to distance learning and maybe taking a degree in business administration in order to become even better equipped for helping grow the family firm.

'But first, I want to take some time out to reflect on the fact that this Everest dream is now over,' she says. 'All my life I've had that one goal and now I've achieved it, I need to take some time out to come to terms with that.'

Yet Glenn sees his daughter as unlikely to take much time off. After all the years of people doubting her ability and saying she shouldn't – or couldn't – get to the top of Everest, he sees her as being on the verge of much greater things.

'To think she's done something like this when she's just nineteen, and plenty of others far older and more experienced have failed, is pretty amazing,' says Glenn, who's now developing an adventure fitness app with Alyssa that will help users prepare physically and mentally for expeditions as varied as Kokoda, Kilimanjaro, the Kimberley and Everest itself. 'She's remained so positive throughout all the negatives and I think she's now in a position to really inspire lots of young Australians. They see her and learn from her example that they too can achieve anything, if they're determined enough and ready to work hard and put everything into it.

'I think that's definitely Alyssa's brand, and what she wants to do. She realises how inspiring it can be to see someone achieve something they've worked their whole life for. I saw how she lit up all those little kids at her sister's school. She has that ability, and she's determined to help other people achieve things they want to, too. She just happens to have found her path in life early, and I'm very happy for her.'

As for Alyssa, she can't wait to get started. 'I've always had goals and always will have goals. Now it's great to be in a position to talk to others about goal-setting and how to get there. It's a wonderful thing to reach your goals, and it can be life-changing along the way. I want others to experience the excitement, sense of fulfilment and confidence to make the most of what life can bring.'

ACKNOWLEDGEMENTS

Climbing can, at times, be a very lonely endeavour but in no way has my journey been solo. I have received an incredible amount of support from some wonderful people along the way who made my journey possible.

Thanks to my dad, for his relentless and ongoing support. His desire to help make my dreams a reality, his work ethic and his strength have amazed me time and time again. I will be forever grateful.

Thanks also to my mum, one of the strongest people I've ever met. Even without knowing it, she helped me get through a lot of tough times in the mountains. It's been such a great gift to grow up with the influence of someone who taught me what true strength is and how to value myself.

My beautiful siblings Brooklyn, Christian and Samantha have all seen the work and effort that go into every climb, and it often wasn't easy for them dealing with me while I prepared. Yet throughout the years they constantly supported me and kept me grounded and honest. For that I am truly grateful.

Another treasured supporter has been Keith Fennell. His books, *Warrior Brothers* and *Warrior Training*, have served as a great inspiration to me and a source of extra strength when in the mountains. To have had the opportunity to meet and train with someone

I respect so much was awesome. Thanks for your humility and honesty, and for allowing me to learn from you and your experiences.

A special mention to Scott Evennett, too. It was a huge step in my preparation to have someone of his calibre helping me and sharing his knowledge and experience. It was extremely valuable, thank you for your belief and support.

My sponsors have been invaluable, too. I have used Mountain Design products for as long as I can remember and the team there has been a huge support in my last few climbs, as well as the Everest adventure, supporting me with all the gear necessary to have the best experiences possible. Thanks, guys!

Phil Di Bella of Di Bella Coffee amazed me with his generosity and how willing he was to mentor me and help me to learn how to make this happen. Without him, there wouldn't have been the training climbs necessary to get to Everest. I owe him and his team so much.

Daniel Borg and psyborg were my first-ever sponsors and really kicked the Everest campaign into action several years ago. I won't ever forget that. To have had their belief in this dream so early on was a huge bonus. As their slogan says: Part Mind, Part Machine!

Thanks also to the team at OBT Financial. Speaking to them was a great boost for me and their positivity, as well as their sponsorship, really helped me along.

John Harrison, Chris Thompson and everyone at Infinity Solar came on board early and showed a great deal of faith in me, and passion for what I was trying to achieve. It's always been greatly appreciated.

Bella Magazine also donated and gave me support, living the message and helping empower young girls and women. I'm so proud to be associated with them.

Olivia Santilli and the team at Ensemble came on board later and worked hard to support me, so I could be more free to focus on the climb.

And a special mention to Michael McNab of construction company McNab, Danny Clifford and Ben Gouldson of Clifford Gouldson Lawyers, and Tom McVeigh from Murdoch Lawyers for their great help, as well as the support given to me by Brisbane's hit radio station Nova 106.9 featuring Ash, Kip & Luttsy, and its general manager Jay Walkerden.

And a huge thank you to everyone who donated money towards all my training climbs to help make Everest happen. Some of them I know, like Steve Keil, CEO of Laser Systems Ltd, and managing director of Laser Group Management, Grant and Bec Statton who personally donated $2000 in 2015, and some I don't. Many simply gave because they wanted to help. None of that has gone unnoticed and I am, and always will be, extremely grateful.

Finally, for this book, I want to thank agent Selwa Anthony, who showed huge enthusiasm early on for my endeavours, and faith that I'd continue. Without her, this would never have happened. Also, thanks to my publisher, Penguin, and all the team that have worked together to make this book something I'm immensely proud of.

And, of course, Sue Williams. It was great to work with you on this book throughout the journey – in fact, it has been an honour. Your work ethic and dedication to the book has been amazing. Thank you!

Alyssa Azar